McDonaldization
Revisited

McDonaldization Revisited

Critical Essays on Consumer Culture

Edited by
Mark Alfino, John S. Caputo, and Robin Wynyard

Foreword by Douglas Kellner

Westport, Connecticut
London

Library of Congress Cataloging-in-Publication Data

McDonaldization revisited : critical essays on consumer culture /
   edited by Mark Alfino, John S. Caputo, and Robin Wynyard ; with
   foreword by Douglas Kellner.
      p. cm.
   Includes bibliographical references and index.
    ISBN 0–275–95819–1 (alk. paper).—ISBN 0–275–96104–4 (pbk. :
alk. paper)
    1. Consumer behavior. 2. Consumption (Economics). 3. Fast food
restaurants—Social aspects. 4. Social structure. I. Alfino,
Mark, 1959– . II. Caputo, John S., 1946– . III. Wynyard,
Robin.
HF5415.32.M395   1998
306′.0973—dc21   97–21852

British Library Cataloguing in Publication Data is available.

Copyright © 1998 by Mark Alfino, John S. Caputo, and Robin Wynyard

Library of Congress Catalog Card Number: 97–21852
ISBN: 0–275–95819–1
     0–275–96104–4 (pbk.)

First published in 1998

Praeger Publishers, 88 Post Road West, Westport, CT 06881
An imprint of Greenwood Publishing Group, Inc.

Printed in the United States of America

The paper used in this book complies with the
Permanent Paper Standard issued by the National
Information Standards Organization (Z39.48–1984).

10 9 8 7 6 5 4 3 2 1

Copyright Acknowledgments

The author and publisher gratefully acknowledge permission to use the following material: Excerpts from *The Theory of Communicative Action: Reason and the Rationalization of Society* (Vols. 1–2) by Jürgen Habermas, translated by T. McCarthy. Copyright 1984–1987. Reprinted with the permission
of Beacon Press.

Contents

Foreword: McDonaldization and Its Discontents—Ritzer and His Critics

Douglas Kellner

George Ritzer's *McDonaldization of Society* has generated an unprecedented number of sales and critical interest—as attested by the present volume and the expanding literature devoted to the book. Ritzer's popularization of Max Weber's theory of rationalization and its application to a study of the processes of McDonaldization presents a concrete example of sociology in action, of applied social analysis which clarifies important developments in the contemporary era, calling attention to their costs and benefits, their positive and negative sides. Its many-sided reception—and the controversy it has evoked— suggests that Ritzer has touched some vital nerve centers of the contemporary era which I will suggest has to do with discontents over modernity and the rapid transformation of the present for which the term "postmodernity" has been coined.

The choice of McDonald's restaurants as an example of defining some problematical aspects of our contemporary world is a felicitous one. The phenomenon of McDonaldization which Ritzer elicits from his analysis of McDonald's fast food restaurants encompasses both production and consumption and applies to a wide range of economic, political, social, and cultural artifacts and processes. Ritzer is able to apply his concepts to phenomena ranging from work to leisure, from food to media, from education to politics. Encompassing such a diverse field of topics and artifacts exemplifies the sociological moment of illuminating abstraction, of generating a concept so broad as to conceptually grasp and interpret a wealth of data in a way that both preserves the concretion of the particular and allows a more general societal optic, which helps us critically view key social processes, institutions and problems.

McDonald's certainly provides a useful example of a familiar sociological datum that can be analyzed to generate a more universal level of conceptualization. Few artifacts and institutions of the contemporary world are as well known and ubiquitous as McDonald's with its Big Macs, golden arches, Ronald McDonalds, promotions with tie-ins with popular films and toys, and saturation advertising. Both the rationalization of production and consumption in McDonald's is unparalleled in the contemporary era, and serves as a model for what Ritzer calls the "McDonaldization of society" defined by increased efficiency, calculability, predictability, and control through substitution of human labor power with technology and instrumental rationalization.

Yet it is precisely the generality, abstraction, and critical optic of Ritzer's analysis of McDonaldization that has been the target of his critics. Ritzer is accused of offering a reductive analysis and expressing "cultural elitism" (Parker) that is insensitive to the variety and diversity of consumer practices and local inflections of McDonaldization (Miles; Wood; Taylor, Smith and Lyon; and Wynyard). He is accused of neglecting gender analysis and the meanings that McDonaldization has for women (Rinehart), or one could add, for people of different classes, races, regions, and countries. Ritzer is also accused of neglecting the cultural dimension of McDonaldization and in particular of the way the semiotic construction of McDonald's functions to make the McDonald's experience as much a social and cultural experience as a culinary one (Caputo; Wynyard; and Alfino), or as "missing the cultural basis of irrationality" (wa Mwachofi).

There is no doubt that Ritzer does neglect the cultural side of McDonald's and in particular the ways that the corporation mobilizes television advertising to create an experience of fun, of family togetherness, of Americanization itself which is associated with the McDonald's experience. Thus when one bites into a Big Mac they are consuming the sign values of good times, communal experience, consumer value and efficiency, as well as the (dubious) pleasures of the product. As wa Mwachofi points out, McDonaldization is an ideology as well as a set of social practices, a cultural construct with its myths, semiotic codes, and discourses. Many of the articles collected in this volume, however, compensate for Ritzer's underplaying of the cultural aspects of McDonaldization and thus supplement and fill out his analysis.

Ritzer's critics often complain that his analysis is too pessimistic and fails to articulate an adequate response to McDonaldization (Rinehart), or that he over generalizes his analysis, neglecting the side of consumer practice and the various uses to which consumers can put McDonaldization, using its products to serve their own needs (Parker; Taylor, Smith and Lyon). But his critics themselves often fail to offer adequate responses or to articulate in more detail how one resists McDonaldization. Or, Ritzer's critics sometimes offer apologetics and celebration of the mass culture he criticizes thereby uncritically replicating a position increasingly widespread in cultural studies that puts all the weight of praxis and production of meaning on the side of the subject, thus effectively erasing the problematics of domination, manipulation, and oppression from critical social theory (see the critique of this position in Kellner 1995). Such positions put a positive gloss on McDonaldization, mass culture, or consumerism in which moments of resistance and the construction of meaning are suggested, as if these phenomena merely provided resources to empower individuals and resist dominant meanings or practices.

In general, it seems to me a mistake to be overly positive or negative in relation to a complex phenomenon like McDonaldization, or, for that matter, such things as mass culture, consumerism, or the consumer society itself. Contemporary positions often are skewed into one-sided optics that primarily celebrate or denigrate the phenomenon under scrutiny. Perhaps Ritzer does not adequately appreciate or valorize the positive features of McDonaldization, but often his critics do not acknowledge the negative side and are all too eager to defend mass culture, consumption, or McDonaldization against Ritzer's often scathing criticisms.

In my own view, Ritzer's book is valuable for provoking a theoretical and practical debate concerning key novel and defining features of our contemporary world and forcing us to define our response to crucial aspects of our everyday life. Although Ritzer's critics chide him for being too pessimistic and negative, precisely this dose of critical negativity is salutary in an age of positive thinking only too eager to embrace and celebrate the joys of consumer capitalism. Ritzer's analysis of McDonaldization is thus valuable for articulating discontents of critical individuals with the process of relentless rationalization and accordant standardization, homogenization, and massification of experience.

Indeed, in response to his many critics who argue that Ritzer is too hard on McDonald's and rationalized consumer practices, I would argue that at least his sharp critique of McDonald's itself is perfectly justified and that there is little good which one can say of this particularly noxious institution. Yet neither Ritzer himself nor many of his critics always adequately distinguish between McDonald's and the broader phenomenon of McDonaldization. Failure to make this differentiation often skews normative judgements and evaluations of the respective phenomena. For instance, I would not hesitate to develop the most sharp negative critique of McDonald's itself as a corporation and junk food emporium, whereas I would offer a more nuanced evaluation of McDonaldization as a social phenomenon. From a nutritional point of view, I think it is fair to say that McDonald's food is simply junk—as indeed the popular term "junk food" denotes. As Ritzer himself notes (1996, p. 127, p. 130, p. 164), McDonald's food is overly saturated with salt, sugar, and fats, producing high cholestrol and dubious nutrients. It is standardized and homogenized fare, providing predictably bland and unexciting taste. The McDonald's experience in eating is an example of assembly-line consumption that is hardly conducive to conversation and social interaction. Its products are environmentally degrading and contribute to depreciation of the soil, rain forests, and nutrients that are used to make its beef and dairy products.

As a corporation, McDonald's ads are highly misleading and as Ritzer points out its practices often contradict the imperatives of value, efficiency, and wholesomeness that its ads and corporate propaganda proclaim (1993, p. 121ff). Its production process is an extremely blatant and degrading form of low-paid and alienated labor which is a career dead-end. The McDonald's environment is a sterile and dehumanizing site of standardized and banal architecture signifying sameness, corporate homogeneity, and artificial massified space.

The phenomenon of McDonaldization, however, interpreted as a set of processes geared at increasing efficiency, calculability, predictability, and control is more complex and ambiguous. There are times when one wants what Ritzer calls McDonaldization, when efficiency and various modes of instrumental rationality are particularly beneficial and when one wants to avoid their opposite. Rationalization/McDonaldization of the labor process might serve to de-skill labor and oppress the work force as Braverman (1974) and Ritzer remind us (see Wood), but this same process might free workers from dehumanizing and alienating labor that is better done by machines, and assembly lines. Likewise, there are some products and services that one wants to be as rationalized, predictable, and instrumental as possible, such as habitable hotels and hospitality services (as Wood argues). Ritzer's celebration of such things as bed and breakfast establishments or the older forms of non-franchised and unchained motels could be the site of unpleasant surprises as well as quirky novelty and more customized service. When travelling, seeking food or shelter, or caring for machines and products, one often wants rationalized and predictable forms of service and product.

The same can be said of Weber's analysis of bureaucracy and rationalization as Gouldner (1976) and others remind us. Whereas bureaucracies can be insensitive to individual differences and oppressive of particularity, precisely rational and legally articulated rules and regulations can protect individuals against the excessive power of potentially oppressive institutions and individuals. Thus rationalization can promote the forces of domination and hierarchy, but they can also empower individuals against institutions via standardized practices and regulations.

Rationalization is itself equated with modernization in standard interpretations of Weber, and many of the studies contained in this volume raise the question of whether McDonaldization is properly interpreted as an expression of modernity, as Ritzer argues, or of postmodernity. My own answer is that we are currently between the modern and the postmodern, in a borderline space between two cultural and social paradigms, and that therefore there are identifiable features of both the modern and the postmodern involved in McDonaldization. In particular, McDonald's production process and McDonaldization as a form of production is clearly modern in inspiration and form, whereas the production of sign value in the McDonald's experience through advertising and publicity stunts has postmodern ramifications, as Caputo, Wynyard, and Alfino argue in the articles that follow.

Ritzer is thus probably mistaken to distance his analysis of McDonaldization from postmodern theory (1993, p. 152ff), though he is certainly correct to see and emphasize the links with modernity and modernization. Ritzer's downgrading of the postmodern elements of McDonaldization are related to his failure to adequately theorize the cultural dimension of McDonaldization. And yet Ritzer does see how there is something like a McDonaldization of culture in the culture industry's rapacious lust for audiences and profits. Likewise, it is clear that McDonaldization can be linked with globalization, including its postmodern elements. Part of a postmodern globalized culture is the way that transnational cultural forms help produce a global culture, but one that is inflected by local conditions and practices (see the studies in Cvetovitch and Kellner 1996 for examples).

For instance, Ritzer notes how McDonald's varies its product, architecture, and atmosphere to local conditions. I experienced its varied dynamics myself one night in Taichung, Taiwan, as I sought a restroom in the midst of the city. While wandering through the space of the local site—a three-story building within a densely populated urban region—in search of a men's room, I noticed that the place was packed with students studying, young people talking, and couples coupling. My host said that in a crowded city, McDonald's was a good site for studying and socializing and obviously the locals were taking advantage of this. Obviously, the social purposes and functions were quite different there than in the U.S. McDonald's that I had seen which neither encouraged, nor in some cases did they even allow hanging out and using the site as a study den or make-out pit.

My Taiwanese host told me that it was especially young children who sought the McDonald's eating experience, demanding that their parents take them to McDonald's for special treats or celebrations. For people in non-Western societies, McDonald's seems to signify Western modernity and to offer genuine alternatives to local cuisine and social experience. Yet no doubt it is also advertising and promotion that helps produce these meanings, providing a postmodern, hyperreal, and hybrid consumer experience for denizens of the many corners and crevices of the globe.

Thus, it seems to me a mistake to either insist that McDonaldization is primarily an expression of modernity or postmodernity for it is arguably both. Indeed, McDonaldization relates to both Weber's analysis of rationalization and Marx's analysis of commodification, but also Baudrillard's analysis of implosion, hyperreality, and simulation, as well as the hybridization of identity and practices that some see as central to the postmodern condition (see Kellner 1989 and Best and Kellner 1991). As Wood argues, the weight of Ritzer's argument is on the side of consumption and he does not focus as intently on the rationalization of production and its effects on the workers as, say, Harry Braverman (1974). Yet it is a merit of Ritzer's analysis that he does focus on both production and consumption, grasping the two sides of the process of McDonaldization. Some of his critics focus too exclusively on the side of consumption, which often leads them to defend McDonaldization on the grounds that Ritzer overlooks the variety and diversity of consumer practices and the varied meanings and effects McDonaldization can have on different types of consumer. While there is some validity in this criticism, it overlooks the extent to which McDonaldization constitutes a standardization and homogenization of production that is often highly dehumanizing and degrading to workers.[1]

Clearly, McDonaldization is linked to the problematic of global capitalism and the project of rationalization of the labor process, markets, and consumption to increase capitalist profitability and power—as well as the forces of instrumental rationality and efficiency. While Ritzer primarily focuses on the phenomenon from the optic of Weber's theory of rationalization—and it is perhaps the intensity and the relentlessness of the Weberian optic that lends Ritzer's analysis both its power and limitations—he is not oblivious to the role of profit in constituting the phenomenon of McDonaldization, although one could argue that Ritzer could better situate McDonaldization within the context of the problematics of capitalist rationalization.

I would indeed argue for what I call a multi-perspectival social theory (Best and Kellner 1991; Kellner 1995) to engage the phenomenon of McDonaldization. This requires mobilizing the resources of both modern and postmodern theory, using both Marx and Weber, Baudrillard, and postmodern feminism, as well as the resources of cultural studies and a critical multiculturalism. Indeed, many of the articles in this volume deploy culturalist, Marxist, feminist, ethnographic, and other methods to supplement Ritzer's own analysis and add illuminating perspectives to Ritzer's primarily Weberian optic. Jeannot proposes using a Marx/Weber synthesis to theorize McDonaldization and both he and Wood privilege Marxian perspectives, whereas many of the contributors propose using postmodern perspectives to theorize contemporary culture and society. McDonaldization is a many-sided phenomenon and the more perspectives that one can bring to its analysis and critique, the better grasp of the phenomenon one will have and the better one will be at developing alternative readings and oppositional practices.

In sum and to conclude, Ritzer's study is valuable for helping us better understand important changes in the contemporary world that enable us to practically intervene and shape the social conditions that circumscribe our everyday experience and to empower us against oppressive forces. Ritzer's critical analysis calls attention the dehumanizing and irrational sides of McDonaldization and forces us to think of forms of resistance and alternatives. The criticism that Ritzer doesn't adequately articulate alternatives to McDonaldization or spell out a program of resistance is partly beside the point for each individual has to choose her or his own alternatives and produces practices that are empowering and life-enhancing for one's own singular situation. Perhaps Rinehart is right that Ritzer's approach is too individualistic and fails to articulate collective responses to McDonaldization, but other than designing collectively social alternatives and producing oppositional practices and subcultures it is not clear what form a collective practice would take.

Yet Ritzer challenges us to consider precisely what form of society, values, and practices we desire. There is no question but that McDonaldization is here to stay and we need to decide how social rationalization can serve individual and social needs and what sorts of alternatives we need to McDonaldization. I have suggested that we should simply refuse McDonald's (and other junk food sites) as a form of culinary practice, that we should exercise Herbert Marcuse's "great refusal" (1964) and simply refuse to have anything to do with this terrible form of assembly-line junk food. The social processes of McDonaldization are more complicated to evaluate, however, and Ritzer leaves us with the challenge to determine which forms of McDonaldization are positive and beneficial and which are harmful and destructive. It is the merit of Ritzer's book to force us to think through these issues and the articles collected here help articulate some of the vital issues that Ritzer's study confronts us with and the varied responses of a group of readers and critics who have seriously engaged Ritzer's work.

NOTES

1.   As I write this in May 1997, I have just received an internet message from the University of Texas Progressive Faculty Group:

From: IN%"clr2@igc.apc.org" "Mike Rhodes" 3-MAY-1997 07:19:40.99
To: IN%JIMSENTER@delphi.com URGENT ACTION ALERT!
            Disney & McDonald's Linked to $0.06/Hour Sweatshop in Vietnam

Summary: Seventeen year old women are forced to work 9 to 10 hours a day, seven days a week, earning as little as six cents an hour in the Keyhinge factory in Vietnam making the popular giveaway promotional toys, many of which are Disney characters, for McDonald's Happy Meals. After working a 70 hour week, some of the teenage women take home a salary of only $4.20! In February, 200 workers fell ill, 25 collapsed and three were hospitalized as a result of chemical exposure.

Background: Included in the Happy Meals sold at McDonald's are small toys based on characters from Disney films. According to McDonald's senior vice president Brad Ball, the Happy Meals characters from the "101 Dalmatians" movie were the most successful in McDonald's history. Ball adds, "As we embark on our new global alliance, we anticipate ten great years of unbeatable family fun as customers enjoy 'the magic of Disney' only at McDonald's" (PR Newswire Associates, March 19, 1997).

Located in Da Nang City, Vietnam, the Keyhinge Toys Co. Factory employs approximately 1,000 people, 90 percent of whom are young women 17 to 20 years old. Overtime is mandatory: shifts of 9 to 10 hours a day, seven days a week. Wage rates average between six cents and eight cents an hour—well below subsistence levels. Overcome by fatigue and poor ventilation in late February, 200 women fell ill, 25 collapsed and three were hospitalized as a result of exposure to acetone. Acute or prolonged exposure to acetone, a chemical solvent, can cause dizziness, unconsciousness, damage to the liver and kidneys, and chronic eye, nose, throat and skin irritation.

All appeals from local human and labor rights groups continue to be rejected by Keyhinge management which refuses to improve the ventilation system in the factory or remedy other unsafe working conditions. Along with demanding forced overtime,

Keyhinge management has not made legally mandated payments for health insurance coverage for its employees, who now receive no compensation for injury or sickness.

Many of the young women at the Keyhinge factory making McDonald's/Disney toys earn just 60 cents after a 10 hour shift. The most basic meal in Vietnam—rice, vegetables, and tofu—costs 70 cents. Three meals would cost $2.10. Wages do not even cover 20 percent of the daily food and travel costs for a single worker, let alone her family.

REFERENCES

Best, S., & Kellner, D. (1991). *Postmodern theory: Critical interrogations*. London and New York: Macmillan and Guilford Press.

Braverman, H. (1974). *Labor and monopoly capital*. New York: Monthly Review Press.

Cvetovich, A., & Kellner, D. (Eds.). (1997). *Articulating the global and the local: Globalization and cultural studies*. Boulder, CO: Westview.

Gouldner, A. (1976). *The dialectic of ideology and technology*. New York: Seabury Books.

Kellner, D. (1989). *Jean Baudrillard: From marxism to postmodernism and beyond*. Cambridge, MA and Palo Alto, CA: Polity Press and Stanford University Press.

Kellner, D. (1995). *Media culture*. London and New York: Routledge.

Marcuse, H. (1964). *One-dimensional man*. Boston, MA: Beacon Press.

Ritzer, G. (1996). *The McDonaldization of society*. Thousand Oaks, CA: Pine Forge Press.

Preface

This book is the outcome of a joint venture, a collaboration with scholars on two continents and from six different disciplines. It began with a suggestion from Robin Wynyard that the time was right to bring more theoretical reflection to bear on George Ritzer's original thesis in *The McDonaldization of Society*. The prescience of his suggestion was demonstrated to us by the strong response to our initial call for proposals. Approximately eighteen months later, after fielding inquiries, proposals, and papers from many scholars on several continents, we are pleased to present these for your consideration.

We wish to express our appreciation to the contributors to this volume. The authors whose work appears here not only wrote original essays for the book, but also read each other's work, commented on each other's papers, and reflected on each other's comments in making revisions. Many of us were new to the use of a web site and electronic file transfers in effecting this level of international collaboration so quickly. Thanks are owed to various technicians who helped us overcome glitches along the way.

In addition to the contributors, we would like to thank Nancy Masingale and Sandy Hank of Gonzaga's Faculty Services for help in preparing the manuscript, as well as the material support of Gonzaga University in absorbing various costs of transatlantic collaboration. Thanks to Beacon Press for permission to quote material from the work of Jürgen Habermas.

We wish the reader an enjoyable and insightful journey into McDonaldization and consumer culture.

Introduction

Mark Alfino, John S. Caputo, and Robin Wynyard

As stated in the title, this book is a revisitation. It is a return visit to George Ritzer's successful book, *The McDonaldization of Society*. There is no doubting the importance of Ritzer's book, which has "roused a sleeping dragon." Along with the contributors to this volume, many others have engaged with Ritzer on the subject of McDonald's. Hopefully, the reader will find the references to follow the story through from beginning to end.

The success of Ritzer's book is all the more creditable in raising discussion and interest on both sides of the Atlantic. This volume reflects such international opinion, with five contributions from America and six from the United Kingdom. All the contributors feel revisitation is necessary. Some are highly critical of Ritzer's original book, others much less so. All, however, feel that something new needs to be said about McDonaldization as posited by Ritzer in his 1993 book, revised in a new edition 1996. In order to accommodate a wide range of thought and discussion, the editors prefer to see this volume as a critique rather than an out and out criticism of the Ritzer book. Consequently, we have selected materials that are broadly based and comprehensive. Therefore the book can be read on its own merit or as companion volume to Ritzer's work in the area.

There are many admirable aspects of Ritzer's book, but it is rather like the curate's egg, that is, in the early Punch cartoon, where a timid curate breakfasting with his bishop is served a bad egg. When the bishop enquires about the meal, the curate informs his superior, "that parts of the egg are excellent." This, of course, does not answer the question, whether the egg should have been presented at all.

The three editors come from different disciplines (philosophy, communication, and sociology) and the contributors include those disciplines as well as a variety of other fields and areas of applied knowledge so we hope that there will be something in this volume for students from a wide range of disciplines. We feel that the argument in Ritzer's book can only benefit from wide-ranging critique.

Concerning the tone of, and audience for, the contributions in this volume, our aim was to pitch the work at advanced undergraduates and graduate students in America and undergraduates as well as postgraduates in the United Kingdom. This is not to say that the book, as a whole, is an easy read. While the contributors had this audience in mind as they wrote, they also expect the reader to do his or her part to get the maximum benefit from the collection. All of the contributions do, however, give a brief sketch of any theory or theoretical concept made use of in their argument. In doing this, we hope the collection works for students with different degrees of exposure to theory, especially social theory, allowing the McDonaldization thesis to be further explored.

But this collection is also intended for scholars and teachers working in universities and other institutions of higher education who share our desire to make the good even better and who will turn to this collection in order to view McDonaldization through new eyes. As a concept, McDonaldization has been used extensively in both the countries represented here. We feel that many students are prepared to go further in following a theoretical discussion than Ritzer takes them. We also feel that teachers and researchers who have used Ritzer's original work for some time may be looking for new ways to complicate the discussions and thoughts the book engenders, both in the classroom and at conferences.

The sole theorist used by Ritzer is the German sociologist Max Weber who died in 1920. Whether this was a good choice or not by Ritzer is dealt with by some of the contributors to this volume. There is no doubting Weber's stature as one of the founding fathers of sociology, and although there is no substitute for a detailed reading of his work, a very brief summary of the main direction of his thought might well help the uninitiated reader. It may provide a context for some of Ritzer's thought and argument and motivate the reader to go on to further study.

On the face of it, Weber seems a good choice for the line of argument pursued by Ritzer in his book *The McDonaldization of Society.* Max Weber, in a short but very productive life (1864–1920), attempted to deal in the main with how individuals made choices, how they justified these choices, and how they developed them to form the basis of further action. In order to provide a framework for his study, Weber wrote *Economy and Society* (1968)—a massive study largely published after his death—which attempts to formulate a set of concepts that will enable the social scientist to move on from pure speculation into the more predictable realms of theory. Two main planks of such developmental work lay in the formulation of what he called ideal types and how such types might lead to different kinds of social action. Weber was not merely concerned to describe human behavior or action. He was also attempting a probabilistic study of it (i.e., What is the likelihood of predictable human behavior given certain identifiable variables?). Weber also wondered what can we say about human behavior when there is uncertainty on the part of the individual, particularly when the variables in the proposed action are not easily verifiable.

Often transactions in society are obvious. For example, if I go into a florist's shop to buy a bouquet of red roses on Valentine's Day, I would not expect the shopkeeper either to give me a bag of flour or to tell me that "flowers are not sold here." This much is obvious. But social contexts are not as determined and predictable. Suppose, though, I am hungry and in a country a long way spiritually and physically from my own, for example, Pakistan. I stop at a stall where nothing is on show, and I do not speak Urdu and am suddenly surrounded by an interested and curious crowd. What happens next? What would you do in such a situation? How would you make sense of it? What mental framework would you locate it in to take action?

We do not have to go that far afield in order to encounter situations where our knowledge of situations is scarce and frightening. Weber came from a middle-class family in the small town of Erfurt in what is now Germany. Then it was part of the Prussian dominion; the nation of Germany had yet to emerge in its modern form. It was a time of uncertainty for the emerging middle classes throughout Europe. It was also a time of revolution, where middle-class wealth was located in their role as industrial entrepreneurs and as the providers of services for the new industrialists. Hence the growing importance of legal study. Max Weber himself taught law at university.

The middle classes there, as in the rest of Europe, were caught between a declining land-owning aristocracy and a rising, unifying working class. For any new group, being caught in the middle of uncertainty is not a good position to be in: who do you ally yourself with? Those up above you, who are in decline, or those below you, who are inferior but potentially very powerful. This position for the middle classes in the emerging Germany of the time is well summed up by the theorist Siegfried Kracauer, who labeled them as being in a situation of ideational homelessness. He went on to say about this:

The middle classes thus refuse, out of a vital interest in their own survival, to declare their solidarity with the proletariat. This raises the question of what means remain available to them for escaping their ideational homelessness—a homelessness stemming from the fact that they feel unable to find refuge in the liberal system so shaken by economic crisis but are also unwilling to take shelter within Marxism. They are standing in a void and have no choice but to try to develop a new consciousness that will provide the ideational framework for their social survival. (Kracauer, 1995, p. 123)

The German state at the time was a total mess, and although Weber wrote with an emerging German nationalism in mind, his actual thought was rooted in Prussia where he lived. Also, the dominance of Prussia could not be excluded from a burgeoning German nationalism. Amidst all the turmoil and political upheaval going on around him, Weber the sociologist wanted to understand, to impose some societal framework, in order to make sense of what he saw.

Understanding any emerging state like Germany is going to involve, in some degree, an argument about rationalization. A similar argument is required to understand the emerging modern European union. All of the arguments concern common currency, common foreign policy, common tax laws, and a common customs union. Likewise the argument surrounding an emerging Germany in the nineteenth century concerned rationalization as a process. For theorists like Weber, also at issue was the exact nature of a rational individual in that society.

Weber saw the growing industrial might of Germany as something requiring explanation. How is it that a nation like Germany, in spite of major set backs, can industrialize so rapidly, and sustain and develop this over a period of time? Of course, Germany had natural advantages, but so had a lot of other nations. Yet, these nations either do not industrialize, or if they do, eventually pall into insignificance alongside more rapid German expansion.

Weber's initial efforts to explain this seemed, on the face of it, to counter Marx's proposals regarding societal development: that the material base of any society determined the ideological superstructure. Weber, in his study of world religion, seemed to conclude the opposite, that is, that the way people thought determined the kind of material society in which they lived. His work on the Protestant ethic, *The Protestant Ethic and the Spirit of Capitalism* (Weber, 1930) is perhaps his best known work. In this book his argument is that strong German Protestant religious belief was the major, if not the sole, cause for German material success. Hard work was the order of the day, not because, you wanted riches as such, but because the "devil found work for idle hands." How else, apart from being successful in what you did, were you able to gauge if the Lord smiled favourably on your endeavor?

Needless to say, Protestant economic endeavor did not include any underhand activity; it was all above board. Totally rational, in terms of the thought processes of individual merchants and industrialists, was gaining resources and selling the finished products made from them. Rational seems to require that if two competing industrial nations like Germany and Britain are selling an identical product on a world market, then purchasing nations will buy the cheaper of the two products. If your competitor manages to sell it at a cheaper price, then you must improve on something else, for example, supply dates or technical support and backup. Weber used this argument concerning rationality in an ideal typical way to form the basis for a comparative study of nations. As the sociologist McRae succinctly put it:

An act to Weber is rational when it can be described as being in accord with the canons of logic, the procedures of science, or of successful economic behaviour; that is to say, when it is end attaining in its intentions and in full accord with factual knowledge and theoretical understanding in its means. Where the choice of an end from among other ends and the choice of means satisfied these criteria an act is fully rational. (1974, p. 68)

All things being equal, rational behavior in humans was the outcome of a development starting with the charismatic individual and the wonder that is accorded to inexplicable behavior, and the attribution of such behavior to magic. Later, economic rationality, through the impartial logic of the market, gave the two other aspects of human behavior—charisma and magic—the systematic formulation they needed for the modern-age. Even with modern age rationality, we do not lose the charismatic, for example, there are plenty of management gurus like Tom Peters around, who speak with individual wit and authority, and charisma still attaches to entrepreneurial success. The big difference is that now, as opposed to the strictures of a Jesus or Buddha, we have an existing system in which to locate our gurus—in this case, management science developed from the modern social science of economics, which in turn developed from earlier political economy.

That Weber was aware of the burgeoning industrial and technological hegemony must be taken for granted. He served (albeit in an administrative capacity) in the First World War, which was the first to use the full panoply of modern technological devices. In order to gain high degrees of efficiency and the quite detailed organization of labor needed to maintain production for a mass market, a special type of administrative organization was needed. For Weber, who had seen Prussian bureaucracy in action, via the law, civil service, and the army, the bureaucratic type of administrative action was essential. To quote Weber from *The Theory of Social and Economic Organization*:

Experience tends purely to show that the purely bureaucratic type of administrative organization—that is, the monocratic variety—is, from a purely technical point of view, capable of attaining the highest degree of efficiency and is in this sense formally the most rational known means of carrying out imperative control over human beings. It is superior to any other form in precision, in stability, in the stringency of its discipline and in its reliability. It thus makes possible a particularly high degree of calculability of results for the heads of the organization and for those acting in relation to it. (quoted in Merton, 1952, p. 24)

In such bureaucratic organization, order is based on knowledge. Those with more of it are located in a higher strata of the pyramid, while those without it are located in the strata below. Likewise, orders go from the point of the pyramid in an unbroken chain to those merely carrying out, in a totally prescribed and often unthinking way, mechanical tasks. Take the following example of a bureaucratic instruction for cooking food:

To cook one you plonk a frozen slab of breadcrumbed cod in its steel receptacle and lower it into a vat of fat, boiling at precisely 330 degrees Fahrenheit. A timer alerts you to when the 2 minutes 25 seconds recovery time is up. By then you will have broken an oblong of processed cheese in two and steamed a pre-cut bun for 90 seconds. Assembly of bun, cheese and fish in its foam container is completed by a shot from the Tartar Sauce Gun. (*The Sunday Observer*, 1993, pp. 49–50)

The above exhibits an extreme form of division of labor which, although it still exists, cannot be applied to big business organizations with uncritical rigor. For the counter staff of a fast-food chain, it cannot be assumed that they are all identical, that is, young, lower class, lower intelligence, intending to make a career out of it, and so forth. Rationality, or rationalization as part of a process, is one thing, but rationality as a form of individual behavior is something else again. In the crude application of Weber's theory the subtlety of his thought is ignored. A large business organization does indeed have to assume rationality on the part of thousands of workers. To assume that the ends of such workers are the same as organizational ends is to commit a grave category mistake. Young people, including plenty of graduates, can and do work in organizations like McDonald's for a variety of reasons. They may also enjoy working there; for example, there was plenty of evidence for this when McDonald's extended its empire into Russia.

For Weber such argument was the limiting case for inexorable rationalization, and formed the basis for a conflict between formal and substantive aspects of sociology. Formal rationality can be seen in terms of efficiency, calculability, and predictability. This, taken to its logical conclusion, entails considerable loss of freedom on the part of workers in large organizations. However, why people work in such organizations and what they bring with them in terms of identifying with the work that they do is not easy to predict. Workers attach meaning to their behavior and, in terms of individual logic, will only engage in behavior while it is advantageous for them to do so. The undergraduate will leave when she obtains her degree. The single parent on welfare will leave it if he can obtain enough benefits to go to college full time. Big organizations know and accept this from their staff working at the cutting edge of receiving orders. They have to accept that there will be a large turnover of such staff in businesses like McDonald's. High turnover, in fact, has become accepted as a good thing (rational), because the employer incurs less cost with part timers than with full timers. The phrase "flexible hours" serves to encourage this phenomenon. In order to maintain the organization's structure in terms of efficiency, calculability, and predictability, a system of training new staff rapidly has to be put into place. Both aspects of behavior, formal and substantive, have to be brought into concert in more ways than one, if the organization and the individuals making it up are going to survive. It is a complicated process, one which Weber was trying to understand and explain. We might all work on a rational basis, defined by what is best for us, as individuals, but this often conflicts with what appears as the rationality of a large individual organization. This is not to suggest that any organization like McDonald's exhibits free will in the way an individual does. To say that the individual's ends are often in conflict with organizational ends is to say something quite different from this:

Rationality transcends values in that its formal qualities (e.g., its clarity, consistency, calculability, rule-governed nature, etc.) are independent of any substantive ends—this distinction is called to account for a critique of modernity as a social order increasingly governed by the formal rationality embodied in the impersonal norms of the market, bureaucracy and law, but which is substantively irrational from the viewpoint of values of equalitarianism, fraternity, and caritas. (Dean, 1994, p. 69)

Without doubt Weber's thought is difficult and often not easy to follow. He might be seen as providing some kind of theoretical framework for Ritzer in *The McDonaldization of Society*. This, however, is something needing further work by the reader. A brief introduction to a few facets of his thought can only suffice to whet the reader's appetite for further study.

THE READINGS

Each of the essays in this book are original in this volume. Because, as mentioned above, the contributors are from both the United Kingdom and the United States, and we anticipate broad readership in several countries as well, we have left the essays with either British English or American English spellings. More differences might have remained (we had considered allowing contributors to keep to local conventions in punctuation and reference style), but in the end we standardized these elements and adopted APA (American Psychological Association) reference guidelines. Perhaps this act itself was a form of rationalization. However, this choice was made to assist readability and avoid confusion.

We begin this exploration of consumer culture with an essay by Martin Parker entitled "Nostalgia and Mass Culture: McDonaldization and Cultural Elitism" in which he admires Ritzer's *The McDonaldization of Society* as a strange and marvelous book that manages to be both academic and popular, but Parker goes on to say why he is unconvinced about Ritzer's cultural politics. Particularly, Parker argues that Ritzer's argument rests on a rather old and essentially reactionary brand of elitism that is really no more than a condemnation of modern forms of organization and culture and not at all like Weber's grander thesis. For Parker, Ritzer is more concerned with pointing to cultural decline than theorizing rationality. Parker presents a view of mass or pop culture that is at odds with Ritzer's description of modern consumer culture. He argues that popular culture would be a site for possible resistance and not simply the terrain on which the vanquished modern citizen accepts his or her fate as postmodern consumer. Popular culture would be a site for subversion and pleasure.

In the next essay, "It May Be a Polar Night of Icy Darkness, but Feminists Are Building a Fire," Jane A. Rinehart talks about the "sociological imagination" and the importance of transformative social practice in the teaching of sociology to college and university students. She critiques Ritzers's McDonaldization thesis as a bleak and deterministic perspective and sees it as a roadblock or dead end. As a feminist sociologist, Rinehart believes Ritzer's book is not a useful tool for teaching students the virtues and rewards of serious social analysis and makes a persuasive argument for postmodern pragmatic theorizing, especially as articulated by feminist theorists. In her analysis she focuses on the significance of gender in shaping understandings and responses to McDonaldization, and rather than the "raging against the dying light" that Ritzer suggests, advocates serious engagement in consciousness-raising and promotion of social change.

John S. Caputo in "The Rhetoric of McDonaldization: A Social Semiotic Perspective" takes a communication theory approach to look at the commodification of culture. Caputo suggests that Ritzer used the wrong lens in examining McDonald's and, hence, the McDonaldization thesis applied to other examples of fast-food restaurants, quick eyeglass shops, amusement parks, and so forth, is hopelessly flawed. The essay looks at the concept of narrative paradigm and the rhetorical vision that McDonald's creates that attracts customers to come in, or drive through, and consume Big Macs. He proceeds through a detailed empirical analysis of a McDonald's commercial advertisement, and uses semiotics to explain the international success of McDonald's and critique the McDonaldization thesis. Finally, Caputo explains how looking at communication messages, in this case McDonald's ads, from a narrative perspective is radically democratic and enables the reader to see if a story holds together or rings true and to possibly discover "the lie."

In "McDonaldization and the Global Sports Store: Constructing Consumer Meanings in a Rationalized Society," Steven Miles argues that consumers actively and intentionally use McDonaldized consumption as a means of asserting some sense of stability in an everyday world that they actually perceive as being risky and unpredictable. He believes that Ritzer underestimates the creative abilities of individuals by exaggerating the extent to which they lose their own agency in a consumer culture. Miles, as a participant-observer, empirically studies consumers in a contemporary sports store and finds that in some ways McDonaldization is positively embraced by young people. The consequence then is that for young people the everyday reality of the consuming experience is not of being controlled, but of being in control. Miles asks this final question, "What is often appropriate [for young people to consume] is often McDonaldized, and if as a consequence young consumers lives are happier and more stable then who is Ritzer to argue otherwise?"

Philip D. Holley and David E. Wright's essay "A Sociology of Rib Joints" examines the place of rib joints in popular culture and analyzes rib joints within the context of McDonaldization. They argue that barbecue restaurants, and rib joints in particular, represent a part of contemporary culture worthy of close sociological examination and go on to do an ethnomethodological, dramaturgical, and phenomenological analysis of rib joints, their proprietors, and their patrons. In specifically examining patrons they utilize Ritzer's/Weber's typology of the "velvet cage," the "rubber cage," and the "iron cage." Lastly, they argue that in spite of the perpetuation of modernization and a tendency to "McDonaldize" everything, the rib joint will not disappear. Rib joints, in fact, are a backlash to the modern and find a niche in an effort to correct some of the alienating effects of modernity.

The next essay, "Old Wine in New Bottles: Critical Limitations of the McDonaldization Thesis—The Case of Hospitality Services," is written by Roy C. Wood. In this work, Professor Wood attempts to place Ritzer's work in a specific analogous context and, in so doing, to demonstrate that the novelty value of his [Ritzer's] arguments have been exaggerated and are seriously flawed. He uses Harry Braverman's book *Labor and Monopoly Capital* to demonstrate his argument and then looks at the hospitality industry in an effort to evaluate the likely durability and utility of McDonaldization as a concept and framework for analysis. He argues that Ritzer's thesis is primarily illustrative rather than analytical in its understanding of processes of social and economic rationalization and believes the McDonaldization thesis represents little more than "old wine in new bottles."

In their essay "McDonaldization and Consumer Choice in the Future: An

Illusion or the Next Marketing Revolution?," Stephen Taylor, Sheena Smith, and Phil Lyon posit, "Has product and service standardization reached the point where we are starved of consumer choice?" They critique Ritzer by arguing that ever-increasing rationalization is unlikely because of the complexity of human needs and the markets that serve them. They believe that rather than eliminating alternatives, there exists the possibility that the fast-food restaurant is actually providing a product/service that customers want. This is an antielitism argument made earlier in Parker's essay and will be found in others as well. The writers argue that fast-food menu/service innovation is not illusory or superficial as Ritzer would suggest, but rather gives rise to better consumer choice. Taylor and colleagues look not only at the fast-food dimension to Ritzer's thesis, but its application to hotel accommodation and find Ritzer's thesis an unnecessarily depressing portrayal of the future and an exaggerated half-truth. Their contention is that there is "as much room for optimism as there is for pessimism."

Thomas M. Jeannot's essay, "The McCommodification of Society: Rationalization and Critical Theory," tries to discern the best philosophical foundation, within Marxism and critical theory, for the McDonaldization thesis. By taking us through Habermas's reading of Weber, Jeannot shows how the "clash of Titans" in Marxism (and social theory)—Habermas's effort to trump Marx in *The Theory of Communicative Action*, Lukács's retrieval of Weber's theory of rationalization for Marxism, and Marx's own theory of commodification—can also be thought of as a contest for the best philosophical foundation for McDonaldization. In the end, Jeannot gives us compelling reasons for assimilating McDonaldization to a classical Marxist theory of commodification, hence "McCommodification."

Ngure wa Mwachofi's essay links the tools of communication theory used earlier in this collection by John S. Caputo, with the linguistic orientation of Mark Alfino's essay, and the concern for "ideology" critique. "Missing the Cultural Basis of Irrationality in the McDonaldization of Society" develops a criticism of Ritzer's work by showing how it misses the rhetorical role that language plays in constructing our cultural notion of rationality. Wa Mwachofi argues that there is no simple way to distinguish rational and irrational systems without engaging in an analysis of the ideology underlying our conception of what is reasonable. He argues that even reason is rhetorical. By providing such an analysis, the author shows how a more decisive normative stance toward McDonaldization may be taken.

Perhaps the next essay, Robin Wynyard's "The Bunless Burger" could have been retitled "Weber Revisited." Wynyard hoped that, through his reading on the literature of McDonald's and specifically his reading of Ritzer's book, he would find an interesting way to introduce his students to the finer points of postmodernity and postmodern thoughts. Although he found Ritzer readable and an interesting look at the fast-food industry, he also decided that Ritzer had got it wrong on the theoretical level. Wynyard criticizes Ritzer by saying the McDonaldization of society is not sociology and specifically that he [Ritzer] has misused Weber's theory on rationality. He goes on to provide a clarification of Weber that contrasts sharply with the way Ritzer has applied Weber to his theory of McDonaldization. In essence then, Wynyard sees Ritzer's work similar to the previous essays of Parker and Taylor and colleagues—a general discourse concerning the decline of high culture replaced by mass culture, appealing to the lowest common denominator in people and society. Wynyard believes that Ritzer's thesis cannot answer the question, "Why does a Muscovite quite willingly invest a week's wages in the purchase of a Big Mac and fries?" This is a similar question to that explored in the essay by Caputo. Wynyard goes on to answer this question by adding the theoretical underpinnings of (Wynyard calls them the three chefs or short-order cooks) Jean-François Lyotard, Jean Baudrillard, and Sharon Zukin. Again there are parallels that can be drawn between this work and that of Caputo. Although Wynyard does not see any overarching theory here for understanding McDonald's, nonetheless he believes this analysis offers more insight and awareness then the inherent flaws in Ritzer's application of Weber.

Mark Alfino's "Postmodern Hamburgers: Taking a Postmodern Attitude Toward McDonald's" is the final essay of the book and takes up many issues that are raised in the previous readings. He begins by discussing Lyotard's reference to McDonald's in *The Postmodern Condition* and considers what postmodernists can contribute to an understanding of the consumer culture of McDonald's and specifically what he sees as Ritzer's "McDonaldized" version of Max Weber. Alfino casts postmodernism as an attitude and leads the reader to his theses that 1) there is a distinctly postmodern attitude toward contemporary commercial culture in general and McDonald's in particular; 2) from that perspective McDonald's is not the villain in a cultural drama of bureaucratic rationalization, but 3) postmodernism encourages us to accept a qualified version of Weber's main concerns about rationalization in general and McDonald's in particular. In this essay, with clear links to the previous essay by Wynyard, Alfino explores postmodern social theory in the works of Derrida, Baudrillard, Lyotard, Foucault, May, and Saussurean semiotic theory previously described in Caputo's essay. Alfino once again picks up the theme expressed by Caputo that eating at McDonald's is about the consumption of the message of McDonald's rather than the food. Alfino suggests that a postmodern attitude mixes the best of two tendencies: critical awareness of the insidious character of rationalized bureaucracy and a healthy skepticism about the permanence and sustainability of the rationalized message.

REFERENCES

Billen, A. (1993, April 25). The beefy world of big mac. *The Sunday Observer*, pp. 49–50.
Dean, M. (1994). *Critical and effective histories*. London: Routledge.
Kracauer, S. (1995). *The mass ornament*. Cambridge, MA: Harvard University Press.
MacRae, D. G. (1974). *Weber*. Glasgow, UK: Fontana.
Merton, R. K. (1952). *Reader in bureaucracy*. New York: Free Press.
Weber, M. (1930). *The Protestant ethic and the spirit of capitalism*. London: Allen and Unwin.

McDonaldization
Revisited

1

Nostalgia and Mass Culture: McDonaldization and Cultural Elitism

Martin Parker

INTRODUCTION

> The Fish Filet Deluxe has a complex build. First I want your tongue to get a crispy seafood flavour from the pollock fillet coated with premium Japanese bread crumbs. Then, as you bite down, you sink into the welcoming crown of the potato roll, the creamy dill remoulade, a bit of flavour from the chopped onions. Then the cool contrast of crispness from leaf lettuce, the rich, melted American cheese and a little pepper note as a surprise. (Andrew Selvaggio, chef, describing one of the three new sandwiches he has created for McDonald's.) (*Newsweek*, 1996, p. 40)

George Ritzer's *McDonaldization of Society* (1996) is one of those strange and rather marvellous books that manages to be both academic and popular, but without doing particular violence to either genre of writing.[1] Like Vance Packard's *The Hidden Persuaders* (1957), Desmond Morris's *The Naked Ape* (1967), Germaine Greer's *The Female Eunuch* (1971) and a few others, it has sold more copies and been cited more often than most academics could dream of in a lifetime. That in itself is quite a feat, and one to be admired for crossing some boundaries that are usually rather impermeable. However, despite my sincere and considerable admiration for what Ritzer has achieved as a writer, in this essay I will attempt to show why I am rather less convinced by his cultural politics.

Basically, I wish to argue that this book has been so successful simply because it trades on a rather old and essentially reactionary brand of elitism. It encourages us to laugh at Andrew Selvaggio's description of his new burger. Perhaps this is because *McDonaldization*'s combination of cultural conservatism and nostalgic reformism is a form of politics that is particularly attractive to disenchanted middle-class liberals. Of course, for academics, one of the reasons this has not been particularly clear is because Ritzer claims to rest much of his argument on a contemporary restatement of Max Weber's rationalisation thesis. However, I will suggest that Ritzer does not really share Weber's deep *ambivalence* about modernity. This means that the McDonaldization thesis is really no more than a condemnation of modern forms of organisation and culture, not at all like Weber's rather grander thesis about the political relativity of bureaucratic and other forms of thought.

In order to demonstrate what I have asserted above I want to make some comparisons between different forms of mass culturalism. For well over a century now many intellectuals have condemned mass culture, and modernity itself, for the dangers it presents to high-cultural values. From both the left and the right the story is essentially the same, and "Americanisation" often plays the same role in both accounts.[2] Arnold, Leavis, Eliot, Nietzsche and others on the right have suggested that the masses threaten to submerge "the best that has been thought and said." For these authors, industrial societies tend to homogenise the cultural distinctions, or more accurately hierarchies, that allow elite (or supposedly "authentic" folk) artefacts and practices to exist. The mass suffocates individual genius. A parallel set of arguments can be traced for the left. Adorno, Horkheimer, Marcuse, Haug, and others make the claim that mass culture somehow drugs the common people into oblivion and pollutes the ground from which genuinely innovative cultural practice can spring. These are usually variants on a Marxist ideology and false consciousness argument—radical cultural change is stifled by feeding the people bread and circuses. In other words, the mass suffocates change because the ruling classes want it to. Though these condemnations are similar, the causes are considered to be slightly different. In the former case it is industrial society, modernity itself, that is the problem, but for the radical theorists a particular variant of modernity is to blame—capitalism.

Now, if we compare these two versions of mass culturalism, it seems that certain points can be made about Ritzer's thesis. If we translate right mass culturalism into Ritzer's terms, the McDonaldizing threat is one of levelling—the danger that everything becomes the same. If we similarly translate the left form of mass culturalism then the interests of multinational capital are best served by McDonaldizing goods and services. Now it seems to me that both statements might be true—and they are not necessarily incommensurable—but that Ritzer places much more emphasis on the former than the latter. In other words, he is more comfortable with cultural elitism than a political economy of capitalism. Further to this, an alternative view of McDonald's is given no space at all. After all, popular cultural approaches—from Gramsci, Hoggart, Williams, Hall onwards—are more likely to attempt some anthropological empathy with the so called masses who use McDonald's. Against the structural determinisms of mass culturalism it might be asserted that it is not possible to assume exactly what McDonald's is and means in specific places and for specific people. It might be that any set of artefacts and practices that is as global and complex as this organisation deserves a rather more careful and sympathetic reading than Ritzer's.

In sum, this essay will be broadly critical of the book, but I want to end asking some questions about cultural critique itself. It might be said that Ritzer seems to see resistance as eating with a knife and fork. I think this nicely expresses my disagreements with much of the stance he takes, but it still leaves me wondering how one might articulate a critical position on contemporary culture that does not fall into cultural elitism. Is it possible to come out against an institution like McDonald's without simply being nostalgic for "a world we have lost"?   In contrast, what would a progressive, or postfoundational, cultural critique look like? Presumably it would avoid the easy simplicities of "false needs," the "masses," and so on but, at some point, it is surely going to require a condemnation of something that billions of people seem to enjoy. To put it simply—who has the right to take this kind of position? What foundations do we have for criticising McDonald's or is there, as Kant put it, of taste no disputing?

MASS CULTURE

> If it is art, it is not for all, and if it is for all, it is not art.
>
> Schoenberg

Any formulation of "the masses" reflects an assumption of prescriptive elitism. This is simply because the writer, and the assumed reader, are implicitly or explicitly, not of the mass. The division that is performed requires that "we" are defined as culturally different, more discriminating, less likely to be duped and so on. Despite this rather obvious snobbery, there are many commentators from both the left and right who have attempted to articulate the dangers of mass society and shown a concern with the manner in which modern collectivities degrade the inhabitants of modern society. The language is all too often remarkably similar. Compare Denys Thompson (a cultural conservative and compatriot of Leavis) with the key work of the Frankfurt school.

The controllers' measure of success is profit, and they argue that what is sold is the most profitable, or what their tunnel vision envisages as the most profitable. . . . In these circumstances the individual does not matter, so long as the figures of people serving the system by consuming its products are high enough. He is thus part of a statistical nought, and as such the object of the controllers' contempt. (Thompson, 1973, pp. 15–16)

The public is catered for with a hierarchical range of mass-produced products of varying quality, thus advancing the rule of complete quantification. Everybody must behave (as if spontaneously) in accordance with his previously determined and indexed level, and choose the category of mass product turned out for his type. (Adorno & Horkheimer, 1972, p. 123)[3]

Both right and left mass culturalists formulate the same problem and use the same descriptions—the difference is in the way that they explain whose interests are served, and whose are damaged, by a mass society.

For the cultural conservatives the loss is that of the superior culture of a preindustrial past. An early example is Matthew Arnold's 1867 *Culture and*

Anarchy which defended a definition of culture as a set of preferred beliefs and practices against the danger of moral anarchy if these practices are submerged in mass culture. In England, this aesthetic defence of a high cultural tradition was developed through books like F. R. Leavis's 1930 *Mass Civilisation and Minority Culture* or T. S. Eliot's 1948 *Notes Towards the Definition of Culture* and, to this day, finds populist expression in the moral outrage that has greeted elements in commercial popular culture from cheap fiction and fish and chips (Walton, 1992) to cinema and pop music. All too often this contest is played out on the disjuncture between rural and urban cultures, an organic, "natural" culture is formulated as under threat from an urban trash aesthetic. Bennett (1981, p. 23) adds to this spatial dimension a temporal one—the notion of "cultural fall." After the fall, which is dated according to the interests of the author at hand, mass culture and its artefacts are inevitably debased and worthless, to be righteously condemned and not apologetically condoned. At the same time, high culture is seen as in some way transcendent of the merely contemporary, since it is so obviously aesthetically superior and also the mediator of a social comment or expression of the human condition that is somehow timeless and hence canonical. To put it another way, nostalgia for the imagined practices of another time and place are the key to this kind of mass cultural critique (Stauth & Turner, 1988).

From an opposed political perspective comes the tradition that stems from a version of the ruling-class ideology thesis. It has both its "hard" and "soft" versions, the former being represented by the Frankfurt school (particularly Adorno, Horkheimer, and Marcuse) and its later development into the area of commodity aesthetics (Haug), cultural critics like Postman or gleefully pessimistic postmoderns like Baudrillard. The "softer" version can be seen to originate in the socialist utopianism of individuals such as William Morris and John Ruskin and leading to the social commentary of George Orwell and Richard Hoggart's early cultural studies work. Both approaches are united in condemning consumer capitalism's construction of false needs. Whether it is revolution or reform that is required, the "Society of the Spectacle" (Guy Debord) that exists at present is condemned equally vehemently. For Hoggart it is a series of "Invitations to a Candyfloss World" (1958, p. 169), for Haug (1986, p. 99) it is "a world of multi-coloured surfaces and manifold forms which functions as bait for the buyers and their money." In comparison to the cultural conservatives, though mass culture is here still compared unfavourably with high culture, this is now because the best of the latter is potentially more critical of the social order than the former. Mass production and consumption are seen as an opiate for the wage slaves of capital, and thus a contribution to political quietism through distraction. As Neil Postman (1987) puts it, we are always in danger of "Amusing Ourselves to Death." Even more pessimistically, Jean Baudrillard sees the masses as an inert dead weight, hyperconsuming their way to the destruction of everything.

He can no longer produce the limits of his own being, can no longer play or stage himself, can no longer produce himself as mirror. He is now only a pure screen, a switching centre for all the networks of influence. (1985, p. 133)

Matthew Arnold may not have understood this as a liberation, but the cultural diagnosis would not be so strange to him.

Of particular relevance for the argument in this chapter is that European mass culturalists, of either form, are often united in articulating the United States as the source or epitome of all that is most debased and dangerous in popular culture. From de Tocqueville and Gorky to Eco and Baudrillard, the United States has been a source of sobering lessons about the European future—Baudrillard's "tragedy of an utopian dream made reality." In this sense, American-style language, clothes, music, and, of course, food all become powerful signifiers of modernity and consumer culture. If two areas can be singled out in recent writing, they would be the West Edmonton Mall and Disneyland—both key Archimedian points around which recent cultural critique has revolved. Whilst the mass culturalist could not consider these to be "culture proper," they can be used to tell cautionary tales to warn us against cultural totalitarianism or imperialism. It must be remembered that these are "mythical" accounts. As Tomlinson (1991) notes of both Madonna and McDonald's, it does not matter if they really represent the United States, or exist as a real cultural threat. If people believe those things to be true then they are true in their consequences.

In summary, and as Raymond Williams (1976, p. 87) seminally argued "culture," that is to say "real culture," is used in a highly prescriptive and selective sense within mass cultural arguments. Only certain artefacts and practices are allowed into the cultural canon and only certain people, those with cultural capital, are allowed to decide what counts. Again from opposite sides of the English political spectrum, this sense of culture might include

all the characteristic activities and interests of a people: Derby Day, Henley Regatta, Cowes, the twelfth of August, a cup final, the dog races, the pin table, the dart board, Wensleydale cheese, boiled cabbage cut into sections, beetroot in vinegar, Nineteenth Century Gothic churches, and the music of Elgar. (Eliot in Williams, 1961, p. 230)

solid breakfasts and gloomy Sundays, smoky towns and winding roads, green fields and red pillar boxes. (Orwell in Chambers, 1986, p. 53)

But what it could never include is something alien, new, or brashly commercial. Chronology aside, in neither Eliot's nor Orwell's landscape could you imagine the familiar golden arches ever attaining the status of "Culture."

TO POPULAR CULTURE

The rise of the "popular" as a description of culture suggested a very different assessment of the value of the artefacts and practices in question than did the term "mass" culture, though the distinction was initially not as watertight as I render it here—see Adorno's use of the term for example. Mass theorists placed an emphasis on

apocalyptic denunciations of all forms of "levelling," "trivialization" or "massification," which identify the decline of societies with the decadence of bourgeois houses . . . and betray an obsessive fear of number, of undifferentiated hordes indifferent to difference and constantly threatening to submerge the private spaces of bourgeois exclusiveness. (Bourdieu, 1984, p. 469)

As Bourdieu's tone suggests, it is rather easy to accuse mass culturalists of no more than middle-class elitism combined with a romanticism about the past. This is exactly what the popular culturalists attempted to counter in articulating a much more positive assessment of the value of—what were initially called—the "popular arts." Just as "mass" implied the culture of someone else, and an inferior culture at that, so a "popular" cultural perspective came to suggest a description or analysis from the inside, as a fan, or at least a sympathetic observer. In Williams's (1976) second definition, "culture" itself is then formulated in a comparative or anthropological sense, as a whole way of life and not simply an exclusive or elite set of beliefs and practices.

In England, figures like Richard Hoggart, Raymond Williams, and Edward Thompson, are now seen as important early articulators of what was later to become a "cultural studies" approach. All, to a greater or less extent, provided sympathetic reconstructions of the "structures of feeling" of ordinary people. Initially implicit, but later explicit, is the sense in which this sort of approach is directly opposed to the aesthetic and political judgements that are so central to mass culturalism. The central social-theoretical difference here could be said to be the analytic and descriptive stress on human agency, ensuring the evasion of various determinisms by characterising structure as no more than a set of "limits and pressures." This was important, particularly with regard to Althusserian structuralist Marxist formulations, which reduced culture to no more than a function of the economic base and therefore potentially no more than an epiphenomenon of the mode of production. Instead, if culture were seen as a product of a humanist "creative mind," then any cultural product becomes as worthy of investigation as any other, the capitalised "Arts" deserving no particular priority over the lower-case "popular," or vice versa. In practice, however, the dominant route that what became capitalised and institutionalised as Cultural Studies has taken is the investigation of nonelite cultural forms, whether these be the leisure habits of the Victorian working class, the practices of spectacular youth subcultures, or more lately, the search for resistance in shopping malls.

The work of the Centre for Contemporary Cultural Studies (CCCS) has itself rapidly become canonised as an exemplar of the popular cultural approach. Authors like Hall, Willis, and Hebdige attempted to synthesise forms of social constructionism and semiotics with a neo-Marxist conception of the way these meanings are ranked in power and influence. The point is made that we should not refer to culture but cultures, describing the

relationships of domination and subordination in which these configurations stand; to the processes of incorporation and resistance which define the cultural dialectic between them; and to the institutions which transmit and reproduce "the culture" (i.e., the dominant culture) in its dominant or "hegemonic" form. (Hall & Jefferson, 1976, p. 13)

For CCCS popular culture became a terrain on which opposition to the oppressive order of things is displayed or "magically resolved." The influence of Gramsci is vital in these writings. If hegemony is conceived as a shifting set of fractional alliances, then there is space for popular culture to exist both inside and outside the ideologies of particular locales. It can be, at one and the same time, oppositional and yet co-opted, existing within the spaces of the hegemony but still dependent on it economically, politically, and socially. In a now classic text, Dick Hebdige (1979) developed this work on youth and resistance by focusing on practices of consumption. Consuming (whether it be pop music, clothes, or food) becomes a process of "bricolage," in which the self is actively constructed by particular individuals in specific situations but within the constraints of particular sociohistorical circumstance. Products are copied, changed, and reframed. There is no necessary determination here because, for Hebdige, style is a signifying practice involving the continual capture and rearticulation of items within various semiotic fields.

A central connection for the development of the popular consumption literature in the 1980s was pleasure as resistance. As John Street puts it, "In taking pleasure, we grasp what is ours alone, and we deny the right of the greedy and the powerful to some part of ourselves" (1986, p. 226). In the most obvious examples, modern urban characters like Walter Benjamin's *flaneur* or Michel de Certeau's "producer-consumer" were invested with enough oppositional agency to subvert the meanings being generated by industrial society. For example, Iain Chambers (1986) provides a description of the popular that theorises it as constructed against high culture both in terms of aesthetics and everyday practice. Using Benjamin's notion of "distracted reception" to describe the individual's engagement with popular culture, he stresses localised, particular liberations and partial triumphs over the constraints of a generally oppressive whole. Thanks to an odd mixture of market economics and heroic romanticism, the consumer becomes empowered both to make and choose.

The previous authority of culture, once respectfully designated with a capital C, no longer has an exclusive hold on meaning. "High Culture," becomes just one more subculture, one more option in our midst. (Chambers, 1986, p. 194)

More recently, many of these formulations of resistant consumers have been now been joined to a grand historical periodisation. Within some theories of postmodern society it is suggested that consumption has replaced production as the central site of identity construction. "Affirmative" postmodernists promote the actor to a position within which he or she is empowered to challenge the supposed permanence of social structures. There are no master narratives anymore, merely a series of possible positions from which we can pick and choose in a democracy of equivalent lifestyle tastes. "Today there is no fashion: there are only fashions," "no rules, only choices" (Ewen & Ewen in Featherstone, 1987, p. 55). Local, weak, knowledge is celebrated as an alternative to the intellectual authority of traditional centres. The old rules are breaking down and cultural production and consumption involves playing with the codes, cutting and mixing, sampling, and stealing. The distinctions between claret and milkshake, Filet 'o Fish and filet mignon, politics and hedonism are now fragmented and replaced with "reflexivity, irony, artifice, randomness, anarchy, fragmentation, pastiche and allegory" (Ryan, 1988, p. 559).

So, for many contemporary academics, culture in its various manifestations is very often seen as an arena for displays of mundane agency in subverting dominant flows of meaning. The image of inert masses constituted by, and within, structures is replaced by a version of the social that is constituted by a process of ongoing struggle to comprehend and live through a world in which everything that was solid is melting into air. Popular culture would therefore be a site for possible resistance and not simply the terrain on which the vanquished modern citizens accepts their fate as postmodern consumers. In terms of the topic of this essay, the moral of the story so far should be fairly clear. Mass culturalists might view McDonald's as a prime example of suburbanisation, Americanisation, and degradation and assume that those who eat there are, by and large, dupes and victims. On the other hand, for popular culturalists McDonald's—and any other similar phenomena—would be a site for possible resistance, subversion, and pleasure. Elitist romanticism versus subversive hedonism. So, back to Ritzer.

ASSESSING MCDONALDIZATION

In terms of the chronology of approaches to culture that I have covered so far, it seems to me that George Ritzer's book is remarkably old fashioned. As I hope is evident, the McDonaldization thesis fits rather well into the mainstream of mass cultural approaches. On the specific level it is motivated by a nostalgia for the ethnically diverse "home cooking" cuisine of New York in the 1940s and 50s (Ritzer, 1994, p. 132). At a more general level it can be seen as an exemplar of a certain form of cultural elitist position, particularly outside the United States where "Americanisation" is so often a synonym for cultural decline. However, to argue this convincingly I need to first deal with Ritzer's version of Weber. After all, at various points in his argument Ritzer claims that McDonaldization is akin to the rationalisation process. In that sense, he claims that he is not hostile to McDonald's itself as a cultural form but rather to the iron cage it exemplifies, to the inexorable spread of bureaucratic systems that the metaphor so neatly captures. In addition, on many occasions he uses the "it has been said" rhetorical strategy in order to put forward a point of view or quotation without actually endorsing it himself. I will argue below that neither strategy—theoretical or rhetorical—actually conceals Ritzer's sustained hostility towards modernity.

Ritzer suggests that Weberians see efficiency, calculability, predictability, and control as the key symptoms of formal rationality. They reflect a social world in which nothing is left to chance, where systems have almost entirely routinised human action and producers and consumers are trapped in the wheels and cogs of the machine. Yet, it is essential to note that this Weberian argument is not a judgement about the value of McDonald's as a product or service. To do Weber's arguments justice, the corporation could only be regarded as a rhetorical prop—perhaps an ideal type—for demonstrating the dominance of formal rationality and the marginalisation of value rationality. Whether McDonald's is good or bad is irrelevant; the problem is what rational systematisation does to human responsibility. The problem is that means become ends, and hence real ends are no longer able to be legitimate subjects of discussion. The bottom line is delineated, and it prevents exploration of what lies beneath it.

Well, this is what Weber argues, and it is sometimes what Ritzer claims to argue. At several points in his book, Ritzer is clear that he is not "against" efficiency, calculability, predictability, and control—and hence "for" inefficiency, incalculability, unpredictability, and loss of control (1996, pp. 11, 14, 121). After all, Weber was also clear that bureaucracy provided huge benefits in terms of both the impartiality of the state or organisation and the coordination of labour. It attempted to ensure equal treatment and to avoid nepotism and the whims of the powerful. But, for Ritzer, McDonaldization is not merely a metaphor for rationalisation but also a practice of cultural impoverishment which he judges and condemns. In the simplest terms, the food and service are not as good as they used to be in "traditional" restaurants.[4] Yet, in order to dress this argument in ways that make it less mundanely elitist, he needs to assert that he not judging burgers, but the systems that make burgers. If Ritzer had only rehearsed Weber, or only denigrated the Big Mac, I doubt that his book would have been as successful. It is the blend of academic cultural capital and mass cultural elitism that makes for such a winning combination.

Let me give some examples of the judgements that seem to illustrate my contention that Ritzer (1996) is more concerned with pointing to cultural decline than theorising rationality. He suggests that the abridged *War and Peace* on tape is inferior to the book version, *USA Today* is inferior to the *Washington Post* (pp. 49, 76), microwave food and TV dinners are inferior to freshly prepared food (pp. 51, 95), and that package tourism is inferior to real travelling (pp. 56, 76). Similarly baseball and baseball fields are not what they were (p. 74), neither are motels (p. 80), camping holidays (p. 96), family meals (p. 134), universities (pp. 64, 138), houses (p. 98), or even birth and death. Film sequels are condemned (p. 91), as are theme parks (p. 132), the Internet (p. 147), and popular TV programmes (p. 70). In a particularly ringing passage Ritzer notes that even the French have allowed the "sacred" croissant to be "demeaned" by "obscene" rationalisation (p. 136). McDonald's itself is described as "sterile" (p. 58) and "superficial" (p. 156), having "mediocre" food (p. 59) which customers know is not the "highest quality" (p. 61). He also suggests that customers are wrong if they think that they are getting good value or eating efficiently (pp. 62, 123). Finally, he tells us that he only goes to fast-food restaurants if he has no alternative (p. 83) and that "the best that can be said is that . . . it is over quickly" (p. 131).

So, the book is hardly neutral about contemporary cultural practices and artefacts but is instead continually seeking to condemn them. Ritzer, and many of the authors he quotes, seem deeply nostalgic for an older, quieter, slower world. Ritzer's home-baking, museum-visiting, antique-hunting bourgeois (p. 178) is the revolutionary in this hostile environment. Of course, it takes economic capital to successfully resist the corrosions of modernity. As he acknowledges, "higher status occupations offer people the most opportunities to create non-rationalised niches" (p. 196). The list of subversion strategies—live in an architect-built house, watch public broadcast TV, read the *New York Times*—effectively reads like a description of the middle-class intellectual. Generalising these cultural practices then becomes the answer to the social problems of rationalisation. As Stauth and Turner suggest:

The cultural elite, especially where it has some pretension to radical politics, is thus caught in a constant paradox that every expression of critique of the mass culture of capitalist societies draws it into an elitist position of cultural disdain and refrain from the enjoyments of the everyday reality. To embrace enthusiastically the objects of mass culture involves the cultural elite in a pseudo-populism; to reject critically the objects of mass culture involves distinction, which in turn draws the melancholic intellectual into a nostalgic withdrawal from contemporary culture. (1988, p. 524)

Explicit cultural politics aside, the argument that connects most of Ritzer's examples is that "rational systems serve to deny human reason" (1996, p. 13). Yet, it is not reason—the practice of rationality—that Ritzer is referring to here but rather a denial of humanity, the encouragement of practices of dehumanisation that produce anonymity in workers and customers. Hence, he suggests, working like a robot is irrational and consuming Big Macs is irrational. This does not mean arational or antirational but instead irrationality seems to mean "mind numbing" or corrupting of intimacy. In a key sentence he suggests that rationality and reason are antithetical phenomena (p. 121). For the definition of rationality we need only to look to Weber, whilst reason, the key to this opposition, is left untheorised. I would suggest that Ritzer's reason is untheorised simply because he assumes that a shared bourgeois common sense, presumably provided by other "homeless intellectuals" (Turner, 1987), will fill the gap. After all, the outcome of reasonableness is surely something that we could all agree upon.

But of course we do not—and that is Stauth and Turner's paradox. If we did, then values, ethics, politics would never be matters of debate. Ritzer, like all mass culturalists, is alarmed about the "illusion of fun" (1996, p. 125) yet has to acknowledge that the fast-food restaurant gives people "precisely what they want" (p. 133). In other words, there is no agreement about reason. For myself, Ritzer's assertions then become rather hollow. He wishes to use the scales of reason to condemn, yet apart from an assumed rhetorical consensus, gives the reader no clarification as to where he is condemning from, in whose name he engages in his critique. It seems rather obvious to have to say this, but not everybody agrees that culture is being commodified. This is simply because it is not clear to many, including this author, where and when culture ends and commodities begin. I will return to these issues below, but first I want to contextualise some of the metatheoretical assumptions that lie behind his sociology.

DUALISMS AND EVIDENCE

As I have suggested above, one of the central features of a sociological analysis of culture over the last twenty years has been the gradual establishment of a new hegemony. However, despite the current popularity of versions of the popular, I have suggested above that mass cultural approaches have not disappeared but are merely being presented differently, as Baudrillard's hyperconsumption or the McMass society thesis. However, it is important to remember that in terms of the language of sociological theory, mass and popular are certainly related to Dawe's (1987) "two sociologies." That is to say, they assume very different models of social system and social action. An account of structural determination and constraint is found in the massification perspectives. However, to counter the generally unsympathetic and determinist reading of cultural practices provided by structuralists, action-oriented notions of popular culture are deployed to stress the role of agency in cultural production and consumption. Just as the former macrosociology stresses that culture is a determined product of systems, the latter insists that these structures are the products of the actions of individuals. In the starkest terms, Big Macs are the systematised products of capital but are also consumed as one element in the idiosyncratic and contingent lives of millions of individuals (see Law, 1984).

This "two sociologies" dualism is reflected in the general distinction between reactive and proactive conceptualisations of the relationship between message and recipient that are made in media studies. In the former, it is assumed that individuals simply respond to the injection of information in a stimulus/response fashion. McDesires are simply manufactured in order that the numerically popular sells even more units. The latter assumes a far more user-oriented view of cultural products, one in which the producers can never guarantee exactly what kind of gratifications their products will satisfy. Widespread and mundane semiotic terrorism ensures that the clockwork of mass marketing never really works.

The dualism can be seen as a linguistic metaphor too. As Saussure observed, language can seen as both langue and parole—predictable grammatical system and spontaneous individual utterance. Mass theories generally focus on langue, people are elements in a structure and hence appropriately categorised as types. For the structuralist and/or cultural elitist then, typification and generalisation are both a means and an end. "Standing back" is hence necessary in order to study surface manifestations of supposed deep structures. However, this must inevitably clean the account of all reference to situated use and reflexive agency. It is to assert, "I know why you bought that burger and what pleasures you will get from it." As opposed to the mass emphasis on langue, descriptions of the popular would be embedded in the parole of a particular situation. The liberation of the particular is preferred to the constraints of generalisation. However, often embedded in this latter position is an amplification of the actor to the status of a superagent with the power to challenge and change the permanence of structures. As I have suggested, this often appears to be the position of affirmative postmodernists who assert that since language and culture is in increasing flux the actor can play with increasingly radical intent. In other words, eating at McDonald's becomes an idiosyncratic and potentially subversive activity.

Whilst the latter positions in each dualism—heroic agency, proactive consumption, local parole—are clearly unsatisfactory on their own, they do help to dramatise Ritzer's metatheory as equally one-sided. His version of McDonald-ization is one that is heavily structuralist, assumes consumers simply react to marketing and follow determined semiotic scripts. Rather more simply I think it can be said that Ritzer just overgeneralises the reach and meaning of McDonald's because he thinks he already knows what it means. This is not to deny that the institution and the process are fairly global signifiers, but rather to suggest that they might mean different things to different people in different places. If the world is being revolutionised then, contra Ritzer, perhaps the revolution has no agreed manifesto. Law quotes a Burger King advert that makes the same point rather more succinctly,

'Two hundred million people
No two are quite the same
Each doing things their own way
Each plays a different game.' (1984, pp. 183)

I can illustrate this by suggesting that, in empirical terms, his thesis is simply an overdrawn view from a U.S. freeway. I do not know most of the other food, supermarket, holiday, child-care, garage, and other chains he mentions, and yet I live in one of the most "coca-colonised" European states of all. Indeed, I can think of local fast-food chains, even burger ones, that are not, at the time of writing, to be found in the United States—unless there are fish and chip shops in Maryland? In any case, McDonald's itself has expanded outside North America by adapting to local circumstances—selling new products, supplying beer with meals, avoiding local taboos like beef, and customising its architecture to match native styles. Indeed, expansion outside the United States is not a rationalising inevitability, but a strategy that is organisationally necessary because the United States market for the product is on the decline. In other words, the golden arches mean different things in different places. For Russians, this is new food, exotic food, and rich people's food at that. For Americans, the Big Mac is common food, poor food—certainly not worth queuing around Pushkin Square for (see Caputo in this volume). Similarly, the responses of Chinese, Singaporeans, or Filipinos (Sklair, 1995, pp. 172, 189, 237) will be different, as will those of parents with toddlers, the elderly, vegetarians, public transport users, travellers, people who live far from a large town, sociologists writing an article about McDonaldization, and so on. Whilst I can suggest that all these groups might have different attitudes towards McDonald's, I can no more predict what they might be than can Ritzer. As Sklair neatly puts it, the attraction of the two "Mc's" explanation—McDonald's and McLuhan—should not lead us to think that globalisation means homogenisation. Ritzer's own example of the personalisation of the identical houses in Levittown or the diverse use of malls (1996, pp. 28, 29) illustrates my point. People make diverse uses of the same spaces and products within the same culture. Yet, in this case, the spaces and products are actually quite different globally, and even (again as Ritzer suggests) locally (1996, p. 180). Why then should we assume that we know what a Big Mac means everywhere (see Miles in this volume)? Why should we assume that we already know what forms cultural imperialism takes (Tomlinson, 1991)?

In writing of a programme for cultural sociology, Stuart Hall (1982, p. 72) writes of the necessity of "historicizing the structures." That is to say, inserting specific histories into the theoretical explanations that grow from varieties of structuralism. It seems to me that Ritzer has a substantial amount of historicizing to do before his thesis about an institution and a process becomes more than a view from Maryland. In comparison, for example, Mark Prendergrast's (1994) book on Coca-Cola is both more historically nuanced and less judgmental. One of the historical stories that could have been told is about the rise of franchise capitalism—an organisational structure common to McDonald's, Coca-Cola, The Body Shop, and many other companies—and which raises many interesting questions about boundaries, negotiation, and control (Felstead, 1993). In general, it seems curious that Ritzer is so negative about the supposed spread of bureaucratic rationalisation when, for many years now, management practitioners and academics have been developing and theorising "postbureaucratic" forms of organisational structure. For example, Ritzer does not dwell on the way that accountability and surveillance structures have recently been used to open up various professional monopolies from higher education to spectacle making. It can easily be argued that these McUniversities and McOpticians are now costing less and doing more because various forms of unwarranted occupational control have been removed (Parker & Jary, 1995). It is also because Ritzer is simply negative about McDonaldization that he also ignores the debates on the complexity of deciding what "deskilling" is, or sustains such an odd enthusiasm for management guru versions of the committed Japanese worker. I do not intend to resolve any of these questions—I simply wish to point to them as ambivalent and complex issues that are given no space in a book on contemporary organising.

But, to follow this line too far is to be in danger of marginalising possibly the most important question that is raised by *The McDonaldization of Society*. How can we judge McDonald's, or, how can we not judge McDonald's? Never mind whether the thesis is empirically validated, or relies on a balanced metatheory, does the book convince as an intervention into some kind of public discourse? This, after all, is Ritzer's claim for his volume (1996, p. xix), and it is also one of the reasons that—despite what I have said above—I still admire it. It is to these matters that I wish to return in my conclusion.

ON CULTURAL CRITIQUE

For the nostalgic, the world is alien. (Turner, 1987, p. 149)

Reading Ritzer one might have the idea that McDonald's is an inexorable steamroller crushing all the world into dull similarity. An attitude of detached fatalism is possibly the most dignified response to a world that will end, not with a bang, but with a Wendy's. Not that Ritzer would be likely to agree with my reading of his stance here. He does claim that his is a future-oriented critique, not a nostalgic one (p. 15), and concludes the book by quoting Dylan Thomas, not pastiching T. S. Eliot—"Rage, rage against the dying of the light." The problem for me is that I find very little evidence to back up his claim. I assume that a humanist argument about distorted potential should be able to provide some systematic suggestions for, either what the utopia might look like or how we might get there. These suggestions are, after all, the essence of the most historically potent future-oriented critique of all—Marxism. Ritzer does neither. He does not seem to believe that the world might be better if intellectuals like him sponsored an anticapitalist politics. Indeed, he seems to assume that capitalism is the end of history and that resistance is a matter of lifestyle choices. If history has ended then presumably all we are able to do is look backwards.

But both Ritzer and Marxism share the structuralist sense that they already know what McDonald's means. As I have suggested, structuralisms tend to homogenise local practices and specificities. If you already know that rationalisation and capitalism are shaping the world, then there is little point in looking for evidence—hence phrases like "false needs" or "false consciousness."
On the other hand, if you agree with the popular cultural counterargument set out above, then McDonald's is a contingent and polysemic set of practices—a process of permanent social construction that demands astonishment and fascination not condemnation. We could never summarise what McDonald's is or does, simply because we make and remake it every time we enter a restaurant or write an essay. So is the mundane task of flipping burgers after forty-five seconds transformed into a magical celebration of social construction.

Well, the arguments should be clear enough by now, but it seems that choosing one side simply strengthens the attractions of the other. If I condemn, then I am a prescriptive elitist who underestimates the diversity of local practice. If I celebrate, I am a naive subversive who underestimates the coercive and routinising power of organisation and structure. But perhaps we do not need to choose on the grounds that I have presented above. If modern cultural theory was characterised by the normative use of the dialectically related terms mass and popular, both are intended to be superseded by a postmodern epistemology. This may, or may not, be connected to postmodern theories of social change (Parker, 1992 and Wynyard, in this volume) but is first and foremost a relativism of judgement. It occupies what Hebdige (1985) terms a different planet, a world with a plurality of gods and an eternal flat present. This approach would make discussions of whether a cultural practice or particular historical epoch is postmodern or not effectively irrelevant. The point is how we justify our judgements of those practices or epochs. The philosophical base of this approach is in the exhaustion of structural metaphors and the movement into poststructuralism. If the structuralists said that "X" had to be "not Y" to mean anything, the poststructuralists pointed out that it also had to be "not the rest of the alphabet." The meaning of one term resides in all the others so signification is uncontrollable and undecidable. The author no longer has control over the text, the cook over the food, the global manager over global consumption. If all we do is tell stories that mean different things in different places, then perhaps there are no grounds for any cultural judgements. If you like a Big Mac, then who am I (or Ritzer) to tell you otherwise?

Of course the term "postmodernism" is not consistently deployed as a description of a relativist epistemology. In Ritzer's book it is treated as a new form of society, after the modern (1996, p. 153–159), and one that he largely rejects. In terms of cultural politics, and as I have suggested previously, those sometimes called postmodernists have often mirrored the modernist mass-popular opposition that they sought to avoid. The lexicon may be different but the author is often still either looking out of the study at the distant seething mass or outside happily eating with them. This may well account for the widely divergent accounts of postmodern politics (Ryan, 1988)—either doing capitalism better than the capitalists (hyperconsuming) or subverting the system altogether. It seems to me that the conflation of wildly divergent social theories and political commitments under one banner is simply unhelpful. In any case, as Featherstone (1987) observes, the use of the term postmodernity, is itself a signifier that locates persons within the cultural field. Using Bourdieu's (1984) model of class distinction suggested that it reflects an attempt to define a new area of legitimate taste and intellectual interest. In other words, using the term effectively positions you as culturally avant garde (or at least it used to), even if your cultural politics reflect some even more elderly dualisms.

As Jameson (1985) notes, the erasing of distinctions, between intellectual and mass, Shakespeare and Egg McMuffin, agents and structures is particularly dangerous for academics. They earn a living by policing boundaries. But, following epistemological postmodernism, how could we condemn or locate responsibility? On what grounds could our cultural judgements, our claims to critique, our stories be justified? Well, the simple answer is that they cannot—if by justification we mean impartial empirical evidence or good reasoning. What would count as compelling evidence about a cultural phenomenon as complex as McDonald's is by no means obvious, and in any case, the stories we tell about it can make no claim to be disinterested. Both George Ritzer and Martin Parker are fascinated by Big Macs, and we both tell very different stories about them by using different citations, rhetorical strategies, and cultural backgrounds. As for reason, well that takes us back to Ritzer's untheorised claim to consensus against rationality. To me, there seems to be little or no consensus on these matters. As Weber insisted, what is reasonable for one person is not for other. A possible solution to this impossible question is hence to refuse such claims, to attempt not to engage in the normative dualistic thinking that characterises what is now usually called modernism. So, against either nostalgic or revolutionary romanticism:

The subversion that pop culture has often imagined, the subversion of activity, infiltration, revolution, eruption of repressed desires, can be forgotten. All that's possible today is the renunciation of agency, varieties of refusal to recreate power, to be yourself: simply disappearance from or discrediting of the places where power and resistance keep propagating each other. (Oldfield, 1989, p. 265)

Perhaps this is a kind of an answer—the refusal of either condemnation or affirmation. But, for myself, this is to leave the field of debate to others. It effectively means engaging in intellectual practices that encourage a kind of political quietism and which would allow Ritzer to speak loudly and unopposed. It would allow his particular combination of nostalgia and elitism to define modernity as being a departure from a "golden age," a fracturing of values, a loss of real freedom and authenticity and so on (Turner, 1987, pp. 150–151). Unfortunately, I do not have a rabbit to pull out of my hat at this point. I do not believe that my judgements about the commodification of culture, the merits of *The McDonaldization of Society*, the employment practices of McDonald's, or the "correct" way to read Weber can ever be justified either in some final sense. Instead, perhaps all we can do is to continually acknowledge the location where one's own thought comes from. Acknowledge it both for ourselves and for our audiences. On these terms, if Ritzer's book does have a failing, it is that he allows the reader so little space to make other kinds of judgements (see Rinehart in this volume). By assuming that we all agree what "reason" is, he seduces his audience into believing that there could be no other way of considering these matters. This is not to say that I do not concur with many of his cultural and political judgements, though not all by any means, but rather that I do not believe he is at all reflexive about where those judgements come from. [5]

To conclude, there are many things that I wish to condemn about McDonald's. I believe that it is an organisation that does not reward its workers well and has been hostile to worker organisation, that is complicit in farming practices that do not benefit the citizens of many states, that it encourages a reliance on meat which is both ecologically and morally questionable, and that relies on transportation technologies that are polluting. However, it also supplies employment to millions and enjoyment to billions and (from my point of view) is cheap, convenient, and child friendly. Like Andrew Selvaggio perhaps, I also happen to like the food, but then perhaps essays on the commodification of culture should not begin or end with such admissions of bad taste?

NOTES

1. I thank participants in a Popular Culture group seminar at Keele University for their comments on an early version of this paper and to Steve Brown, Valerie Fournier, Peter Kramer and Robin Wynyard for their detailed responses.

2. It is important that the reader, and the author, should not forget that this essay is written by a European and reflects this in a variety of ways. I am, for example, well aware that "Americanisation" may mean something rather different in the home of McDonald's. The local specificity of meaning and understanding is important to my argument at points in this essay.

3. In passing, the reader might like to know that I got this quote from a book entitled *Key Quotations in Sociology*. These books are becoming very useful for McAcademics who

are too busy to bother with too much reading.

4. See Ritzer (1994, pp. 131–138) for an account of a how "a New Yorker with a sophisticated palate" learned to dislike McDonald's.

5. The McTextbook style of *McDonaldization* is a curious illustration of this point. Whilst it has enabled the book to reach a very wide audience, it also glosses over the contested political and theoretical issues that I have been discussing. Ritzer's own self-publicity for McDonaldization as "a key idea in sociology" (1994) further abbreviates the possibilities of public discourse by radically simplifying the issues at stake. Of course, as Ritzer himself acknowledges, getting cited does not guarantee quality in academic publications—just as personal marketing does not guarantee good publicity.

REFERENCES

Adorno, T., & Horkheimer, M. (1972). *Dialectic of Enlightenment*. New York: Seabury.

Baudrillard, J. (1985). The ecstacy of communication. In H. Foster (Ed.), *Postmodern culture* pp. 126–134. London: Pluto.

Bennett, T. (1981). *Popular culture: Themes and issues 2*. U203 Popular Culture course, Block 1, Unit 3. Milton Keynes: Open University Press.

Bourdieu, P. (1984). *Distinction: A social critique of the judgement of taste*. London: RKP.

Chambers, I. (1986). *Popular culture: The metropolitan experience*. London: Methuen.

Dawe, A. (1987). The two sociologies. In K. Thompson, & J. Tunstall (Eds.), *Sociological perspectives* (pp. 542-554). Harmondsworth, UK: Penguin.

Featherstone, M. (1987). Lifestyle and consumer culture. *Theory, Culture and Society, 4*(1), 55–70.

Felstead, A. (1993). *The corporate paradox*. London: Routledge.

Greer, G. (1971). *The female eunuch*. St. Albans, UK: Paladin.

Hall, S. (1982). The rediscovery of ideology. In M. Gurevitch, M. Curran, T. Bennett, & J. Woollacot (Eds.), *Culture, society and the media*. London: Methuen.

Hall, S., & Jefferson, T. (1976). *Resistance through rituals*. London: Hutchinson.

Haug, W. (1986). *Critique of commodity aesthetics*. Cambridge, MA: Polity.

He put deluxe in the arch. (1996, October 7). *Newsweek,* 40.

Hebdige, D. (1979). S*ubculture: The meaning of style*. London: Methuen.

Hebdige, D. (1985). The bottom line on planet one. *Ten, 8*(19), 40–49.

Hoggart, R. (1958). *The uses of literacy*. Harmondsworth, UK: Pelican.

Jameson, F. (1985). Postmodernism and consumer society. In H. Foster (Ed.), *Postmodern culture*. London: Pluto, pp. 111–125.

Law, J. (1984). How much of society can the sociologist digest at one sitting?, *Studies in Symbolic Interaction*, 5, 171-196.

Morris, D. (1967). *The naked ape*. London: Jonathan Cape.

Oldfield, P. (1989). After subversion: Pop culture and power. In A. McRobbie (Ed.), *Zoot suits and second hand dresses* (pp. 256-266). London: Macmillan.

Packard, V. (1957). *The hidden persuaders*. London: Longman.

Parker, M. (1992). Postmodern organisations or post-modern organisation theory. *Organisation Studies, 13*(1), 1–17.

Parker, M., & Jary, D. (1995). The mcuniversity: Organisation, management and academic subjectivity, *Organisation, 2*(2), 319–338.

Postman, N. (1987). *Amusing ourselves to death*. London: Methuen.

Prendergrast, M. (1994). *For God, country and Coca-Cola*. London: Phoenix.

Ritzer, G. (1994). *Sociological beginnings: On the origins of key ideas in sociology*. New

York: McGraw-Hill.

Ritzer, G. (1996). *The McDonaldization of society* (Rev. ed.). Thousand Oaks, CA: Pine Forge.

Ryan, M. (1988). Postmodern politics. *Theory, Culture and Society*, *5*(2/3), 559–576.

Sklair, L. (1995). *Sociology of the global system*. Hemel Hempstead, UK: Prentice-Hall.

Stauth, G., & Turner B. (1988). Nostalgia, postmodernism and the critique of mass culture. *Theory, Culture and Society*, 5(2/3), 509–526.

Street, J. (1986). *Rebel rock*. Oxford, UK: Blackwell.

Thompson, D. (1973). *Discrimination and popular culture*. Harmondsworth, UK: Penguin.

Thompson, K. (1996). *Key quotations in sociology*. London: Routledge.

Tomlinson, A. (1991). *Cultural imperialism*. London: Pinter.

Turner, B. (1987). A note on nostalgia. *Theory, Culture and Society*, *4*, 147–56.

Walton, J. (1992). *Fish and chips and the British working class*. Leicester, UK: Leicester University Press.

Williams, R. (1961). *Culture and society 1780–1950*. Harmondsworth, UK: Penguin.

Williams, R. (1976). *Keywords*. London: Fontana.

2

It May Be a Polar Night of Icy Darkness, but Feminists Are Building a Fire

Jane A. Rinehart

MISUSING THE SOCIOLOGICAL IMAGINATION

One of the cover blurbs on the 1996 revised edition of Ritzer's *The McDonaldization of Society* states that this book "genuinely succeeds in communicating the sociological imagination" and is "a wonderful catalyst for an extended discussion on rationalization, modernity, and a number of related issues" (Peter Kollock, cited in Ritzer, 1996b). Having taught Max Weber's theory for a decade, I was perhaps more vulnerable to this promise than others might be. My experience in exploring Weber's ideas about modern society with sociology majors is that many interpret his work as a *negative* advertisement for practicing the sociological imagination. In other words, when they read that Weber said he became a sociologist because he "wanted to see how much he could stand" (Ashley & Orenstein, 1995, p. 267), they understand why he would say that and question why they would make the same choice. For them, Weber becomes "gloomy Max"—hardly a positive role model—either because he does not assist them to imagine fundamentally altering the imprisoning forces of the iron cage, or because he attributes severely negative effects to what they regard as positive or neutral. Not all students are persuaded that Weber is correct in his characterization of bureaucratic rationality and its consequences, but even among those who do agree with him, there is an intense resistance to Weber's tragic vision in which acceptance of what is and will be can, at best, be combined with political engagement to limit the worst effects of what he called the "polar night of icy darkness and hardness" (Gerth & Mills, 1958, p. 128) that is modern life. They are sociology majors, after all, and they want to believe that practicing the sociological imagination does not inevitably lead to despair.

I thought Ritzer's work might be a vehicle for responding to the desire of some students for theorizing that promises pathways for change. Instead,

Ritzer's elaboration of Weber, which replaces the bureaucracy with the fast-food restaurant as the model of formal rationality, produces even more resistance. The students who do not agree with the negative evaluations of Weber and Ritzer, the ones who find the modern world of bureaucracies and golden arches mostly benign (Ritzer's "velvet cage" occupants), are even more emphatic in their position because Ritzer has given them a familiar reference point toward which they feel accepting and affectionate. Criticizing bureaucracies is one thing, but taking on McDonald's is another. These students cannot accept that the fast-food paradigm is dangerous. They may agree that reducing its plastic waste and fat content are laudable goals, but these do not require characterizing its basic principles as dangerous.

The students on the other side, those who share Ritzer's position that the fifth dimension of McDonaldization is degradation of the natural environment and dehumanization, become even more depressed than they were after reading Weber because they now have an unavoidable sign to remind them of rationalization's widening path through human societies. Ritzer's work seems to work against engaging students in the sociological imagination, unless we understand that as resignation to overriding social forces, accompanied either by a smile or a scowl. Ritzer is correct when he suggests that these differences in student reactions can produce heated debate in the classroom, but I am not convinced that he is right to describe such debate as both good teaching and good sociology.

My doubts spring from my conviction that insight and rethinking should be connected to conceptualization of alternatives and hopefulness about how these can be achieved. Ritzer and Weber leave my students and me in the same place that they describe; that is, their analyses reproduce the iron cage. While both Weber and Ritzer strongly criticize bureaucratized or McDonaldized society, their analyses indicate that these processes are encompassing and irreversible. Weber is often described in secondary discussions of his work as sober, bleak, and pessimistic (Lemert, 1995; Rossides, 1978; Seidman, 1994). Ritzer ends his book on a somber note, acknowledging that while protesting and resisting McDonaldization are possible and worthwhile, a future of more McDonaldization seems inevitable (1996b, p. 204). I concede that Ritzer does more than Weber to indicate specific possibilities for resistance by closing with a chapter about strategies for surviving within McDonaldized society that do not depend on wholesale acceptance or revolutionary change. However, strategic survival seems to me insufficient reward for the rigorous practice of the sociological imagination. I want critical social analysis linked to promising examples of transformative social practice. I resist the irony I find in Ritzer's position whereby he has made the system less mysterious, but no less determining.

My resistance is echoed in Denzin's critique of Mills's formulation of the sociological imagination (Denzin, 1990). Whereas Mills's definition claims that the sociological imagination seeks to portray the connections between biography and history, between private troubles and public issues, between individual experiences and the forces of social structures and culture, Denzin argues that too often sociologists (Mills included) have contributed to the death of the social by replacing the experiences of ordinary members with their own dominant master narratives. This eliminates the movement back and forth between biography and history, individual life and social structures, or the conversation that sociologists desire to enrich and enlarge. Only sociologists are talking, mostly to themselves. Denzin proposes that we replace social theory with efforts to understand the stories of members as they struggle to interpret the signs of the times, to make sense of their lives.

I do not believe, as Denzin does, that theory itself should be abandoned, but I share his skepticism about virtuoso accounts, expert tellings of how things are and what will happen that seem to render the actions of individuals and groups irrelevant. I am eager to rescue theorizing from the experts, following Lemert's understanding of it as a basic social practice—the public activity of putting into words what we know about the worlds we live in, figuring out what is going on and why (Lemert, 1993, pp. 2–3). It is not enough, however, just to move theory building by professional social analysts closer to the experiences and articulations of society's members—to local knowledges and local communities. Often, members' accounts of what is going on resemble quite closely the master narratives that Denzin criticizes and the kind that Weber and Ritzer have developed. Their resemblance lies in constructing a version of the "big picture" as all encompassing and determining. The claim of this type of theorizing, whether done by professionals or ordinary folks, is that theory actually explains how the world works, shows us what is *really* going on, but stops there. In this view, the theory of McDonaldization's warrants are in the "real world" of spreading fast-food franchises, with their detailed training manuals for employees, their ability to dominate numerous markets, the "obvious" relationship between their principles and their capacity to produce profits. I hear accounts from my students that echo Ritzer's, students for whom the metaphor of McDonaldization is clarifying, but not transforming. In other words, Ritzer's theory appeals because it gives a name and an image to previously held assumptions and expectations about what counts and succeeds.

But, if you wish to go further than this, to move toward significant changes, the theory of McDonaldization is a roadblock or dead-end street. Ritzer exposes what the organized routines and taken-for-granted values of McDonaldization conceal, but the exposure is hollow. Ritzer's "Practical Guide for Living in a McDonaldized Society" (chap. 10), his effort to be concrete and specific about avenues for change, is not meaningful because the suggestions it contains are undercut by the preceding nine chapters. In those chapters, Ritzer has articulated his moral assessment of McDonaldization and linked this to what he admits is "a dark and pessimistic outlook" (Ritzer, 1996b, p. 178). The complete story is both Ritzer's telling of what is happening "out there in the world" and his interpretation of it. His favorite readers, presumably, are those who have been persuaded by his analysis, who have assented to his full account and share his "iron cage" position.

For those who go all the way with Ritzer, the "practical guide" is a terrible contradiction that renders the analysis pointless at best, perhaps even destructive; we see our situation's deep flaws and know ourselves to be powerless against its continuation. Overall, the resistances described by Ritzer do not have a political character. The closest he comes to identifying a possibility for political action is his suggestion that readers "organize groups to protest abuses by McDonaldized systems" (Ritzer, 1996b, p. 200). This is just one on a list of twenty-five recommendations, and he offers no indication of what such groups might be or do. Ritzer has crafted a grim narrative of how American society is developing, but he has not shown how we can be anything other than characters constrained by its foreordained plot line. Knowing we can be different kinds of characters—some content, some pressing for small escape routes, and some despairing—is no consolation.

I agree with Seidman that theory often assumes the form of story-telling:

Social theory as moral inquiry often assumes the form of story-telling. Theorists craft social narratives of the origin, meaning, and possible future outcomes of the present. They alert us to potential social dangers and to the possible remedies and prospects for social progress. There are stories of class conflict, male dominance, the decline of religious faith, the crisis of solidarity, and the bureaucratization of society. The aim of this sociology is to educate the public in order to prompt or guide social and political action. (Seidman, 1994, p. 5)

In order to achieve the aim that Seidman has identified, I think it is necessary that these social narratives be connected with those of members and pose possibilities for constructive action. Decisions about how to tell social narratives have ethical and political implications (Rosaldo, 1989). Ritzer's decisions contradict his objective of ameliorating the worst effects of McDonaldization because there is an enormous gap between his narrative of McDonaldization and its consequences and his list of alternatives.

This gap cannot be explained as the necessary difference between telling a general story and making specific recommendations. In advocating social theory that presents a practical moral vision, Seidman is clear that he is not proposing giving up the effort to tell general stories:

general stories are still needed. This is so because in all societies there occur certain events and developments that prompt highly charged social, moral, and political conflicts. The various parties to these conflicts frequently place them in broad conceptual or narrative frameworks. . . . These narratives offer alternative images of the past, present, and future; they can present critical alternatives to current dominant images; they can provide symbolic cultural resources on which groups can draw in order to redefine themselves, their social situation, and their possible future. (Seidman, 1991, p. 139)

Seidman goes on to state that these general narratives should not emulate several characteristics of the great modernist narratives: they should not disregard complexities and ambiguities in seeking to tell one unified story of progress or decadence, they should avoid the dichotomous construction of domination versus liberation, they should abandon the fixed essentialist view of the human subject, and they should eschew foundational concerns (Seidman, 1991, pp. 140–145). Seidman proposes that theorists encourage "open public moral and social debate" (Seidman, 1991, p. 144). Social theory is social criticism that is connected to important public debates; that is, it is socially relevant and accountable.

Ritzer's analysis matches Seidman's proposal in intention, but not fully in execution. In Ritzer's work, domination and liberation are not presented dichotomously because Ritzer does frequently acknowledge that McDonald-ization is both beneficial and detrimental. He lists fourteen positive changes associated with McDonaldization (Ritzer, 1996b, p. 12). While his focus is on the negative consequences—the irrationality of formal rationality extended everywhere—Ritzer does try to avoid constructing McDonaldization simply as oppressive. He perceives the mixture of progress and decline in a McDonaldized society, but he does tend toward a unified story nonetheless, one that denies heterogeneous experiences of and reactions to McDonaldization. The efforts that Ritzer makes to enunciate practical alternatives to McDonaldization are dwarfed by the comprehensive account he draws of its pervasive and irresistible growth, so that finally he is forced to admit that such countering moves may just be futile cries against fate.

It is Ritzer's goal to tell a story about McDonaldization as a step in fostering resistance to its spell. But I believe that the impact of his work often takes the opposite direction; that is, *The McDonaldization of Society* is interpreted as a story told behind our backs (Denzin), over which we, the McDonaldized, have no control. Ritzer has created a story that backs us all into corners, places where we may complain or enjoy our efficient and predictable experiences, but away from public spaces of engagement and reinvention. His story has the flawed logic of the debate in modernist social theory that directs readers either toward resignation (Weber) or redemption (Marx). It is clear that Ritzer does not believe in redemption, but he accepts that these are only these two possibilities. His suggestions for resigned resistance, then, are a feeble anticlimax. If I accepted Ritzer's terms, I would have to resign myself to teaching students to view the society they inhabit as both destructive and unchangeable. I am not willing.

SPECIFIC CRITICISMS AND RESOURCES

In this essay, I will show that Ritzer's theory of McDonaldization is not a useful tool for teaching students the virtues and rewards of serious social analysis. My perspective is rooted in my own experiences as a feminist sociologist in the academy. I hope to make a persuasive argument that Ritzer's form of theorizing is less useful for attracting students to the work of social analysis than the perspective of postmodern pragmatic theorizing, especially as this is articulated by feminist theorists.

I will focus on two basic difficulties that I have with Ritzer's presentation of McDonaldization. The first of these is its level of generalization that allows Ritzer to ignore individuals' construction of meanings and the significant differences in these related to varied social positions negotiated in terms of race, ethnicity, social class, sexuality, and gender. Any one of these is worthy of analysis, but I will focus here on the significance of gender in shaping understandings and responses to McDonaldization. It is telling that Weber declared sociology's main purpose to be the understanding of such diverse meanings and resisted characterizations of "society" that were forgetful of these complexities.[1] This view is echoed in Denzin's criticism of virtuoso renderings of social life that are constructed at great distance from the experiences and interpretations of society's members. The distance of Ritzer's analysis from individual and group reactions to McDonaldization constructs his readers as passive victims of social forces, rather than as engaged participants in constructing social meanings. If formal rationality's worst effect is to limit or even erase possibilities for thoughtful action by society's members, then Ritzer's analysis compounds that negative consequence.

The second difficulty is the resignation that Ritzer's analysis effects, illustrated in his decision to end with the Dylan Thomas quotation about raging against the dying light. In my view, this assumption that all we can do is express anger against the inexorable (the analogy between McDonaldization and death) is connected to the first problem concerning the level or distance of the analysis. Ritzer's theory of McDonaldization is so general, suppresses heterogeneity to such a degree, that it prevents recognition of complexities or the many-sided nature of the domination/liberation nexus. Because his work does not include an account of the many possible ways that people understand and respond to the spread of the McDonald's model, Ritzer's analysis does not draw attention to resources that might be deployed to counter its influence.

My reading of Loeb's (1994) analysis of the current college student population has influenced these two criticisms of Ritzer's work on McDonaldization. Loeb found a majority of the students he talked with on more than one hundred campuses are in political retreat, believing the world is indeed unfair and the future precarious, but that they have little possibility for altering it. They are not conservative in their politics or callous about suffering, but withdrawn: "apolitical students find it hard to imagine how their common efforts might shape a more humane world" (Loeb, 1994, p. 4). The minority who are activists have stories that awaken their moral imagination and models of commitment that show them their actions can matter (Loeb, Chapter 14). Ritzer's story is not such a model; rather it is a sweeping narrative that represses the resources needed to act on what it reveals.

My principal resource for encouraging students to take a less pessimistic stance is the example of feminist thinking and activism and all the stories and models these provide. Feminism offers an important critique, in different voices speaking from different positions, of McDonaldization both as narrative and as social process. This is not to say that feminist theorizing is immune to the difficulties I have attributed to Ritzer's work. Bell hooks has admitted this:

I have taught feminist theory courses where students express rage against work that does not clarify its relationship to concrete experiences, that does not engage feminist praxis in an intelligible way. Student frustration is directed against the inability . . . to make the work connect to their efforts to live more fully, to transform society, to live a politics of feminism. (hooks, 1994, p. 88)

So, students can find feminist theories disappointing in the same ways that I have found Ritzer's analysis of McDonaldization to be a letdown. But hooks's comment also indicates that students have an alternative example that gives shape to their desires for something else: feminist models for living differently and acting politically.

FEMINIST THEORIZING

Several strands of feminist theory can be interpreted in relation to Ritzer's model of McDonaldized America. This section will focus on the work of Dorothy Smith as showing the importance of connecting theorizing to politics, the theorist's ability to identify agents of social and cultural change and their possible actions. Smith has created a modernist narrative that imagines the transformation of society. She produces a disruptive reading of rationalization by introducing the differences made by gender; she contests the level of generalization that renders women invisible. By bringing in women's perspectives, Smith addresses the collective category of women as a political agent on the side of liberation. Feminist thinkers influenced by postmodern forms of theory have identified problems with these two categories: women and liberation. The feminist critique influenced by postmodern themes is not a surrender of transformational goals, but a reinterpretation of how these are defined and pursued. Postmodern theorists construct the difficulty of generalization in terms of the heterogeneity and instability of *all* categories, rather than in the identification of a unified, stable, previously excluded category called "women." Postmodern perspectives entail a view of politics that refuses a fixed clear contrast between oppression and liberation and general (or total) proposals to accomplish the better outcome. In place of these, postmodern feminist politics advocates acceptance of multiple and changeable identities, continual negotiations, a plurality of forms of resistance, and a lack of closure or certainty. In each aspect, postmodern feminist theory and politics are at odds with Ritzer's assumptions, methods, and recommendations. Smith's work is less of a complete contrast to Ritzer's and, therefore, serves as a device for indicating the insufficiencies of his project in its own terms.

Dorothy Smith has sought to reinvent sociology from the standpoint of women. Her work criticizes the sociological tradition as male-centered:

presenting a distorted, limited view as the general one, and denying its grounding in men's interests. Men's practices are the "relations of ruling" that organize existence in all parts of modern capitalist societies. Smith claims for women a "bifurcated consciousness" which is the product of the domination of women's worlds of households, children, and neighborhood by the worlds of men. Women inhabit a primary world of "locally situated consciousness" that serves as a necessary ground for the governing consciousness, is subjugated to it, but not cancelled by it. Smith argues for the necessity of a sociology done from the standpoint of women:

From this standpoint, we know the everyday world through the particularities of our local practices and activities, in the actual places of our work and the actual time it takes. In making the everyday world problematic we also problematize the everyday localized practices of the objectified forms of knowledge organizing our everyday worlds. (Smith, 1990, p. 28)

Smith's bifurcated consciousness is a tool that allows us to understand McDonaldization differently, both as part of the dominant relations of ruling that structure existence and as not all there is. There are experiences and knowledge that are not completely shaped by the principles of McDonaldization, although they are certainly affected by them. In Smith's hands, feminist sociology aims to articulate bifurcated consciousness in order to create resistance to the dominating structures. These dominating structures include sociologies formulated as objectified knowledge, but more accurately viewed as centered in men's commitments to generalizing, abstract, impersonal characterizations of the social world. Sociological knowledge has moved away from social relations as they are lived and toward interests in controlling through its own connections with various bureaucratic organizations. For Smith, social experience is gendered and cannot be understood unless this is recognized. Women sociologists are in a position to grasp the disjunction between official accounts and actual experience because, as women, they are engaged in domestic responsibilities and relations that cannot be expressed in the texts and language of sociology.

Smith, then, would challenge the meaning of the word "society" in the title of Ritzer's work because it does not include women as subjects of the process it describes and evaluates. Women are subjects of McDonaldization in two senses: they experience its subjugation as consumers and workers, and they are capable of formulating a distinctive perspective on it. While Ritzer is intent on showing that McDonaldization first focused on key aspects of daily living—providing food, drink, entertainment for children—and has moved into more and more arenas—the workplace, housing, sports, medicine, funerals—he discusses all of these without noting their gendered properties. Ritzer states that fast-food restaurants and other McDonaldized institutions are advantageous for single-parent and dual-career families pressed for time (1996b, p. 146). Using Smith's framework reveals more complications than Ritzer acknowledges. The pervasiveness of fast-food opportunities, as well as omnipresent advertising for them, may escalate pressures on busy mothers in terms of fitting in frequent trips to them, emulating their "efficiency" and "fun" in their cooking at home, or worrying about whether boxed "Happy Meals" can truly substitute for more traditional family ones.

For example, a recent television commercial depicts a mother using a packaged sausage product in order to meet her three children's demands for different dinner dishes. She is able to do this quickly and efficiently because she has purchased the right solution. What makes it right is that it allows her to reproduce at home the experience of taking her children to eat at a fast-food restaurant. Each child can have maximum control over her/his choice of entrée, and their mother can deliver their exact requests efficiently. The commercial, of course, represents this as a gain for both the children and their mother, and Ritzer seems to agree. Ritzer allows the reader to believe that McDonaldization is compatible with the entry of more women (especially wives and mothers) into the paid labor force. In effect, this is one of the messages conveyed in McDonald's television commercials: busy parents find relief by taking their kids to McDonald's. The commercial described above simply has to draw on this understanding to further extend the market for McDonaldized solutions; now it also includes numerous kinds of foods available at the supermarket that require minimal cooking time and effort at home. By creating a critique of McDonaldization that accepts one of the main claims of this enterprise, Ritzer weakens the impact of his argument.

Smith's analytic tools, on the other hand, allow us to pose questions about the neatness of the fit between the needs of working parents and the efficient, predictable, calculable, and controlled McDonaldized solution. Ritzer presents McDonaldization as ideological; it is a system of beliefs and values, as much as it is a system of actions. The beliefs and values of McDonaldization are marketed relentlessly, sold as attractive, desirable, a positive part of the way we live now. Ritzer seeks to challenge that characterization, but concedes that McDonald's and other similar organizations offer significant advantages to harried parents. His analysis is constrained by the self-promotion of the McDonaldized world. Smith provides tools for establishing some distance from the advertised virtues of McDonaldization. In writing about "conceptual strategies that obliterate women as active agents" (Smith, 1987, p. 164), Smith might include Ritzer's approach to McDonaldization. An analysis of the connection of fast-food, and so on, to the increase of dual earner households using Smith's theory would begin in suspicion of how neatly everything is tied together. Such an analysis would be open to discovering that women may have something else to say about how they manage the standards and expectations reinforced by McDonaldization. In Smith's sociological practice, the question "What do women make of McDonaldization?" is just as important as what McDonaldization makes of and for them. If we can imagine that women might speak of the fast-food model as a burden rather than as a benefit, then even without knowing what their answers are, we nevertheless have a basis for finding Ritzer's perspective limited. After all, he never seems to have even considered the possibility of asking.

In addition, Smith's perspective directs our attention to how McDonaldization and Ritzer have erased gender by substituting "parents" and "families" for mothers. While this move appears nonsexist, it may be interpreted as the opposite: a continuation of the silencing of women's voices and exclusion of women's experiences. Commercials that make it appear equally likely that children will be taken to McDonald's by their fathers or mothers and Ritzer's characterization of McDonaldized institutions as advantageous for single-parent and dual-earner families ignore the gender-based division of labor in regard to caring for children. This division of labor continues to assign more responsibilities for children to their mothers; for example, the majority of single custodial parents are women and the "second shift" or "double day" concepts point to employed women's larger share of domestic tasks. Acknowledging this brings up questions that do not appear in Ritzer's analysis: questions about how women in different economic circumstances respond to the challenges posed by "opportunities" to spend money and time in fast-food restaurants, rather than in other ways; or what it means when women stay home to catch up on the week's laundry, while their husbands take the kids out for "Happy Meals." It seems likely that some women might regard our McDonaldized society as yet another way to feel inadequate ("I don't have the money for another trip to McDonald's this week") or excluded ("McDonald's is the place my husband gets to play with the kids while I do the housework. No one seems to consider staying home and preparing a meal together"). Ritzer only examines the McDonald's "solution" for busy families superficially; therefore, these and other possibilities do not enter his account.

Another striking example of Ritzer's neglect of gender, and the difference it makes, is found in his discussion of the McDonaldization of childbirth. Here, it would seem, the standpoint of women as Smith understands it is highly relevant. Ritzer's presentation of technological innovations in reproduction as a means for reducing uncertainties and developing more control over pregnancy and childbirth is critical; that is, he does endeavor to show that maximizing control comes at the expense of wonder and humanity (Ritzer, 1996b, p. 170). He includes some criticisms that have been voiced by women patients and physicians, criticisms that seem to reveal the bifurcated consciousness of women. In other words, women do appear briefly in Ritzer's analysis as subjected to McDonaldization and as subjects with a critical perspective. But the dominant voice is Ritzer's and his message emphasizes the unstoppable march of McDonaldization transforming a natural human process into a bureaucratically and technologically managed set of events controlled by administrators and doctors.

The effects of this are to erase gender from a domain in which its influence is crucial and to ignore many examples of resistance. A narrative of how birth has been subjected to an ever-increasing emphasis upon efficiency, calculability, predictability, and control that does not give a place of importance to women's perspectives (for examples of the opposite approach, see Corea, 1985; Diamond, 1994; Gordon, 1990; Martin, 1987; Oakley, 1980; O'Brien, 1989; Rich, 1979; Trebilcot, 1984) and women's collective efforts to change these values (e.g., the movements toward minimal intervention childbirth, birthing centers outside hospitals, home births, and midwives) is a distortion of the sociological imagination. Ritzer's reader is denied access to the parts of this story that contain the strongest criticisms and to the examples of successful construction of alternatives. The most significant actors are missing in Ritzer's formulation of McDonaldized birth, and they do not show up in his final chapter on examples of escape routes from the McDonaldized world. Again we can perceive the irony in Ritzer's position: he has shaped a critique that mimics the conditions he decries in its failure to attend to the construction of meaning by members, the role gender plays in this, and the encouraging stories and models that show McDonaldization's rule is not omnipotent. As Dorothy Smith might say, this is a "peculiar eclipsing" (Smith, 1987, pp. 17–43).

PROBLEMS IN THE MODERN EPISTEME

Even though Ritzer's explicit intention is to raise consciousness of the negative side of McDonaldization and promote its subversion, this is undercut by his adoption of the authoritative voice. This voice gives his critique qualities of impersonality, detachment, abstraction, and standardization which are aspects of the four principles he identifies with McDonaldization. Even critics of the legacy of the Enlightenment, such as Weber and Ritzer, are vulnerable to entrapment within its values.

Smith also is not immune to the spell of modernity's promise of objective truth in the service of human progress. While her work is deeply critical of the uses to which objectified knowledge has been put, she identifies this knowledge that serves the relations of ruling as male in origin and interests. This means that she preserves the hope that knowledge generated from the "standpoint of women" will provide a fuller and more accurate representation of the world. Smith argues that knowledge is both situational and objective. While it is not possible to arrive at one true version of the social world because knowers have different positions in it and different interests, Smith believes that contextual knowledge can represent the world reliably. She is unwilling to let go of a representational concept of truth, even as she asserts that how such representations are made will be affected by position and declares her own desire to build a sociology for women that will enable a critical, feminist politics.

Smith shares with Ritzer a commitment to the Enlightenment version of reason. She is akin to Ritzer in the search for comprehensive, general theories that diagnose reliably and prescribe with authority. She also differs from Ritzer and contests this modernist project, in her move to reveal the universal subject as male, to assert the voice and experience of women (including her own), and to describe the invasion of women's domestic world by forces of rational control. Though Smith strives for credibility within the established model of analysis, this tendency is offset to some degree by her necessary skepticism about universalizing descriptions, her investment in feminist practice, and her decision to be accountable to readers working for social transformation (to create a sociology *for* women).

Ritzer does not acknowledge the contextual nature of truth; that is, he presents us with "the truth" about McDonaldization, which reveals "the truth" about the present and future of industrial capitalist societies such as America. Ritzer's analysis does admit that there are two other positions that one can assume toward the process of McDonaldization: the "velvet cage" and the "rubber cage"—alternatives to his "iron cage" metaphor. But these are not portrayed as aspects of a plural account, a portrait of McDonaldization as viewed from multiple vantage points, each having part of its truth; rather, Ritzer is concerned to show that the iron cage metaphor is the accurate one, case closed, even though he knows that some will deny that "fact" either wholly or in part.

Ritzer has given us an authoritative critical account animated by a moral vision, but rooted in despair. His critique is not anchored, not addressed to people in a specific historical context who might collectively act to alter the direction of his story. Ritzer's version of McDonaldized America is apolitical: there is no contest of viewpoints, no mobilization on behalf of shared interests, no imagination of a future much different than the present and worth working for. Smith's works reveal her accountability to organized feminist groups. She seeks to subvert academic discourse and institutional practices and to link this subversion to women whose lives are outside the "ruling apparatus," opening up to women's gaze the forms and relations determining women's lives, and enlarging women's powers and capacities to "organize in struggle against the oppression of women" (Smith, 1987, p. 225). This type of accountability is absent from Ritzer's analytic practice.

Borgmann offers an explanation of our current situation that explains this absence in Ritzer. He identifies prediction and control as the dominant features of modern discourse:

It is as though we had taken ourselves out of reality and had left only objectified and disavowed versions of ourselves in the universe we are trying to understand and to shape. We vacate our first-person place and presence in the world just when we mean to take responsibility for its destiny. Surely there is deprivation and helplessness in this. (Borgmann, 1992, pp. 2–3).

In vacating our place and abdicating responsibility, we exile ourselves from "communal conversation and action" (Borgmann, 1992, p. 3). This is Ritzer's position, I believe, and I do not wish to teach students to follow him there.

Borgmann's analysis rightly associates this flight from politics with modernity, rather than with postmodernity as has often been suggested. The modern project, centered on science and bureaucracy as the apotheosis of knowledge and organization respectively, has replaced citizenship with submission to experts and formal systems that render communal reflection and decisionmaking unnecessary. All that is left are consumer "choices," and Ritzer shows how these are narrowing, converging into a routine of entering and exiting rationalized structures that leave little room for spontaneity, originality, creativity, meaningful relationships with others, and serious attention to values—in short, thoughtful, energetic living. The difference—and it is a big difference—between Borgmann and Ritzer is that Borgmann does not leave us in Ritzer's cage decorated with proliferating golden arches. Borgmann encourages us to ask what lies beyond this on the "vast intricate mountain range" of postmodernism. His own answer is that there is

a way of life beyond sullenness and hyperactivity. It is a recovery of the world of eloquent things, a recovery that accepts the postmodern critique and realizes postmodern aspirations. I call this recovery postmodern realism and point up its emerging characteristics—focal realism, patient vigor, and communal celebration. (Borgmann, 1992, p. 6)

PROMISING SHIFTS IN POSTMODERN FEMINISM

These are the qualities I find in the theories and commitments of some feminists whose work draws upon postmodern perspectives and in the practices of some feminist organizations. Postmodern[2] feminists move away from "the view from nowhere" (Bordo, 1993, pp. 225–229) and "the truth." Both feminism and postmodernism criticize the Enlightenment legacy, especially its dualistic category scheme (mind vs. body, objective vs. subjective, culture vs. nature, rational vs. irrational, masculine vs. feminine, etc.), with its attendant hierarchy privileging the first partner in each of these contrasts, and its absolute version of truth (Hekman, 1990). For all feminists, the minimum change necessary is a reconstruction of this version of the world and of knowing so that women are no longer marginalized and discredited. Postmodern feminists reject the Enlightenment paradigm more thoroughly, arguing that all knowledge is contextual, multiple perspectives are desirable, and secure foundations unattainable.

Differences arise about what this rejection means; that is, what can feminists know and do? Some feminists (Bordo, 1993; Di Stefano, 1990; Hartsock, 1990) worry that feminists who adopt a postmodern position will lose credibility, will not be able to make strong knowledge and political claims in the name of women. But others (Butler, 1992; Flax, 1990, 1992; Fraser & Nicholson, 1990; Hekman, 1990) argue that feminist projects, both theoretical and political, benefit from incorporation of postmodern insights. Postmodern perspectives offer feminists a way out of masculinist epistemology and individualistic morality (liberal feminism) and essentialism (radical or cultural feminism), without entailing a sacrifice of political engagement (as some socialist feminists, following Hartsock, fear).

I think Hekman (1990) is correct when she argues that what feminists need is a view of the subject as constituted (shaped by language and history, located within discourses, always limited) and as capable of effective resistance to prevailing social arrangements. Nonfoundational knowing does not mean that there are no standards, but that these standards are chosen, negotiated, and continually reexamined. Postmodernism offers feminism a richer, fuller model for thinking and acting than that provided within modern narratives of liberation. It is the glorification of instrumental reason at the heart of the modern view that eviscerates political imagination and engagement. Politics is about values (as Weber recognized) and formally rationalized structures eliminate consideration of values, thereby curtailing possibilities for nonconformist thinking and acting. A postmodern position opens up multiple opportunities for considering values (what we might want and do) and attending to a variety of perspectives. Those who worry that postmodernism means no basis for political action have not been looking closely at the modern situation in which the public square is empty, political rhetoric irrelevant, and citizens distracted by the standardized entertainment of television, malls, and fast-food restaurants. The modernist understanding of knowers as independent, autonomous, objective, and certain—as experts who know better than the rest of us what policies are necessary—does not serve feminist politics that seeks transformation.

Ritzer's analysis gives us an account in which we are exiled from our capacity to act collectively. Postmodern feminists present accounts that reveal manifold possibilities to return and take up places within communal conversations, to recognize our embeddedness in discourse and our stake in using this as a resource for exposing its contradictions and silences. For Nancy Fraser (1995), postmodernism means turning away from the view that our minds reflect reality to the position that our understandings of the world are culturally constructed. This makes language central to understanding how we know, and it makes all inquiry located, changeable, and nonneutral. According to Fraser, thinkers who operate within this understanding of their activity are postmodern, and she believes that this basic position can be fruitful for feminist theorizing, although she does not argue that every aspect of postmodernism is compatible with feminist thought.

For Fraser, feminist theorizing should have these qualities:

a. It should focus on the ways that sociocultural meanings of gender are constructed and contested. In doing this, feminist thinkers have to pay attention to the connections between language/discourse and social institutions (especially the political and the economic).

b. It should offer alternatives to the dominant meanings given to gender.

c. It should recognize that gender dominance is huge and complicated, affecting all aspects of human life, and that its forms vary in relation to other axes of power such as class, race, sexuality, nationality, and age. Because of these variations, feminist theorists should be wary of easy generalizations, while also not avoiding the task of understanding large patterns. We have to respect contexts without giving up on finding connections among different ones.

d. It should reach for provisional generalizations that we treat as fallible—open to being challenged.

e. Finally, feminist theory must be able to critique injustice and envision liberation. This means feminist thinkers must identify norms for judging what is right or wrong and why, but it does not entail that these norms must be universal and transcendent. Power operates unchallenged within sociocultural constructions because we treat these as necessary and unalterable when they are not. The way things are must be delegitimated; this is possible because all of our understandings are historical and subject to change. We are constituted by our sociocultural constructions, but not imprisoned by them permanently. We are always simultaneously constrained and capable of maneuvering. Knowing the historical origins of our social practices and cultural rules fosters emancipation, which is understood as incomplete and open to revision.

Fraser believes that adopting a pragmatic approach allows feminists to say that there is a plurality of different angles from which to understand sociocultural phenomena. Which angle you adopt depends upon your specific purposes. These vary in relation to what needs to be done, where we are located, and what resources are present. Feminist theorists need a pragmatic approach because we have many tasks and many different situations. This makes it necessary for feminist theories to be multiple. They are properly regarded as tools, rather than as all-or-nothing positions in which we reside. Fraser states clearly that an impure, eclectic feminism will not be unprincipled or shallow. Feminists still face difficult decisions about what to do, how to define our locations, and how to mobilize resources. There is no single set of theoretical or political choices that is absolutely right, but Fraser does posit three basic standards that can guide feminist efforts: addressing both discourse and social practices, honoring the views of different women and respecting their differences, and promoting greater freedom and well-being for women (while recognizing that these have no simple, universal definition).

The difference between Fraser's ideas and Ritzer's approach is plain. Fraser believes that it is not necessary to settle for rage against the forces of McDonaldization because those forces are not completely dominant. There are other possibilities in play and no determined direction fixed. Unlike Ritzer, Fraser displays a sociological imagination that encourages us to see not an all-encompassing cage, but spaces for reflection and action. We settle for a mechanistic construction of our present when we discount our capacities as historical actors and stand to the side to gaze at "the system." Ritzer invites this passivity whereas Fraser reminds us of our creativity.

Fraser's pragmatic, fallibilistic feminism is amply documented in studies of feminist organizations (Bookman & Morgan, 1988; Ferree & Martin, 1995). A key practicality to consider in organizing women for social change is their existing networks. It is conventional to interpret the current political malaise in America in terms of rampant individualism (Bellah et al., 1984, 1991). Each of us is then viewed as confronting dehumanizing rationalized structures as isolated selves. This isolation—a retreat into our private lives for therapy and/or satisfaction makes us unable to imagine creating different structures and institutions. But many women are not isolated, but connected—in their workplaces, neighborhoods, churches, and so forth. These networks often provide bases on which organized activism can be built:

the existence of these networks suggests that women do not necessarily enter the public arena as "individuals." Networks and community associations develop from women's responses to issues that confront them not as isolated individuals but as members of households, and, more important, as members of the communities in which these households are embedded . . . the "problem of politics" is less that of creating an allegiance to something other than the self—building community out of isolated individuals—than of finding ways to link the concerns, visions, and perspectives they share with their neighbors and coworkers to the "political system" that stands apart from them and seems to control their lives. (Ackelsberg, 1988, p. 303)

It is important that feminist thinkers have also been networked. Lengermann and Niebrugge describe "the women of Chicago" in the early part of the twentieth century as centered on Jane Addams and Hull House. These women undertook both theoretical and activist projects, using sociological analysis to lead political struggles for protection of women workers, better urban sanitation, child labor laws, and other progressive causes (Lengermann & Niebrugge, 1996, pp. 308–310). Similarly today, many feminist thinkers collaborate to create theoretical perspectives that bear on social policies (Fraser & Gordon, 1994). Commitments to collaboration foster relationships among theorists and activists that are already politicized; that is, these relationships are based on sustained conversations about common concerns and the actions to which these lead.

Formulating the problem of politics in this way takes us beyond the limits of Ritzer's analysis and toward possibilities for transforming the dehumanizing system he delineates. Ritzer cannot conceive of resisting power that can match the power of McDonaldization because his analysis is not oriented toward the existence of genuine and meaningful connections among people. He does not see himself as accountable to produce an analysis that can be translated into collective action to create change. Lacking that form of accountability, he delivers the bad news in a glossy package. Ritzer seduces readers with the familiar image of McDonald's that seems to promise social analysis linked to everyday life, but retreats instead to a detached and pessimistic of a relentless system we cannot hope to influence. *The McDonaldization of Society* offers no empowerment; as individuals we can move away from it in various ways, but we cannot hope to make it move away from us. It seems terrible to me that a gifted social analyst would settle for inducing deeper depression and cynicism about our society.

It is commonplace for introductory texts in sociology to tell students that social institutions are not "given," but rather human creations; this is often characterized as the "liberating" effect of studying sociology. Learning to regard the structures and forces of the social world as the products of our decisions is supposed to nurture a sense of responsibility. How can this happen if sociologists like Ritzer stifle the ability to respond by developing analyses that present the social world as fixed in its pattern and direction, impervious to our criticisms? Social analysis that shows us the awful costs of the way we live now while also denying our capacities to act on that awareness is worse than cheerleading for the success of the McDonald's model; both are complicit in maintaining the status quo. At least the cheerleader version is honest in admitting the desire to do so. In my view, social analysis should open up our practices, help us to examine them, and provide us with tools for addressing what seems troubling about them. We cannot do this in one conversation, one semester, even in the whole set of major courses; it is a lifelong project of creating continuing conversations about things that matter and acting on what these teach us. We are not likely to undertake this project if we are accustomed to the way things are and numb to their bad effects. Ritzer seeks to wake us up, to help us recognize the irrationality of McDonaldization, but his analysis leads us to desire stronger anesthesia because paying attention to terrible things we cannot do anything to change is decidedly worse than being unaware of them.

Audre Lorde's often cited dictum, "The master's tools will never dismantle the master's house" (Lorde, 1984, p. 123), supplies a framework for summarizing this essay's analysis of possible positions. Ritzer neither discards the tools nor leaves the house of Weber's master narrative. Smith wants to create new knowledge based on listening to the silenced voices of women, to expand what is represented in the master's story, but her project is constrained by her attachment to the master's tools. Fraser and many feminist activists regard the house and its familiar story as occasions to ask questions that destabilize their solidity. They make different kinds of dwellings, built with different tools, and they tell many kinds of stories.

Fortunately, Ritzer's stance of "See it, become enraged, but know that you cannot stop it" is not the only option. Fraser's formulation of feminist theorizing and the examples of empowering relationships and actions within feminist projects offer encouragement that models and movements to resist rationalization and reinvent politics do exist, and that participation in these local stories of resistance "often engenders a broader consciousness of both the nature and dimensions of social inequality and of the power of people united to confront and change it" (Ackelsberg, 1988, p. 307). I have not heard yet of organized collective resistance to McDonaldization per se, but I think it is probably already occurring in numerous group efforts to resist efficiency, predictability, calculability, and control. Most of the time, if we are bothered by something, others are as well, and it is good to remember this. Otherwise, all we have is a giant system out of our reach and the company of others who think everything is fine or could be if we just tinker with details. That is not how I interpret our situation, or I would have to give up teaching sociology.

NOTES

1. Weber defined society in terms of the understandable actions of its members. This does not mean that he avoided structural explanations (Gerth & Mills, 1946, p. 57), but that he resisted any effort to regard structures independently of individual actions. His resistance was imperfect, however. In *Classical Sociological Theory*, Ritzer develops this contradiction in Weber's thought well in his discussion of the difference between Weber's methodological stipulations and the thrust of his substantive sociology. Ritzer points out that Weber's methodology emphasized the individual's motives and meanings, but that in his substantive sociological investigations Weber focused on large-scale social structures that he did not explain in terms of the actions of individuals (Ritzer, 1996a, p. 232). In his own theory of McDonaldization, Ritzer has chosen to follow the structural emphasis of Weber.

2. Judith Butler has criticized this term and the category to which it refers as masking significant differences among thinkers, as a "gesture of conceptual mastery" grounded in misunderstandings and a false authority that purports to discover unity. In her view, this is a continuation of the disguised power plays in efforts to establish universalizing categories (Butler, 1992, pp. 5–7). While I am sympathetic to her point, I cannot find a way to do without the term "postmodern" in this essay in that it allows me to name a way of proceeding to think about society and politics that criticizes Ritzer's method by raising questions about his assumptions. Perhaps it helps to acknowledge that it is just a name and a loose, somewhat misleading one at that.

REFERENCES

Ackelsberg, M. A. (1988). Communities, resistance, and women's activism: Some implications for a democratic polity. In A. Bookman, & S. Morgen (Eds.), *Women and the politics of empowerment* (pp. 297–313). Philadelphia: Temple University Press.

Ashley, D., & Orenstein, D. M. (1995). *Sociological theory: Classical statements*. Boston: Allyn and Bacon.

Bellah, R. N., Madsen, R., Sullivan, W. M., Swidler, A., & Tipton, S. M. (1991). *The good society*. New York: Alfred A. Knopf.

Bellah, R. N., Madsen, R., Sullivan, W. M., Swidler, A., & Tipton, S. M. (1984). *Habits of the heart: Individualism and commitment in American life*. Berkeley, CA: University of California Press.

Bookman, A., & Morgan, S. (Eds.). (1988). *Women and the politics of empowerment*. Philadelphia: Temple University Press.

Bordo, S. (1993). Feminism, postmodernism, and gender skepticism. In *Unbearable weight: Feminism, western culture, and the body* (pp. 215–243). Berkeley, CA: University of California Press.

Borgmann, A. (1992). *Crossing the postmodern divide*. Chicago: University of Chicago Press.

Butler, J. (1992). Contingent foundations: Feminism and the question of "postmodernism." In J. Butler, & J. W. Scott (Eds.), *Feminists theorize the political* (pp. 3–21). New York: Routledge.

Corea, G. (1985). *The mother machine: Reproductive technologies from artificial insemination to artificial wombs.* New York: Harper & Row.

Denzin, N. K. (1990). The sociological imagination revisited. *The Sociological Quarterly, 31,* 1–22.

Diamond, I. (1994). *Fertile ground: Women, earth, and the limits of control.* Boston: Beacon.

Di Stefano, C. (1990). Dilemmas of difference: Feminism, modernity, and postmodernism. In L. J. Nicholson (Ed.), *Feminism/postmodernism* (pp. 63–82). New York: Routledge.

Ferree, M. M., & Martin, P. Y. (Eds.). (1995). *Feminist organizations: Harvest of the new women's movement.* Philadelphia: Temple University Press.

Flax, J. (1990). *Thinking fragments.* Berkeley, CA: University of California Press.

Flax, J. (1992). The end of innocence. In J. Butler, & J. W. Scott (Eds.), *Feminists theorize the political* (pp. 445–463). New York: Routledge.

Fraser, N. (1995). Pragmatism, feminism, and the linguistic turn. In S. Benhabib, J. Butler, D. Cornell, & N. Fraser (Eds.), *Feminist contentions: A philosophical exchange* (pp. 157–171). New York: Routledge.

Fraser, N., & Gordon, L. (1994). A genealogy of dependency: Tracing a keyword of the U.S. welfare state. *Signs: Journal of Women in Culture and Society, 9*(2), 309–336.

Fraser, N., & Nicholson, L. J. (1990). Social criticism without philosophy: An encounter between feminism and postmodernism. In L. J. Nicholson (Ed.), *Feminism/postmodernism* (pp. 19–38). New York: Routledge.

Gerth, H. H., & Mills, C. W. (Eds.). (1958). *From Max Weber: Essays in sociology.* New York: Oxford University Press.

Gordon, L. (1990). *Woman's body, women's right* (2nd Ed.) New York: Penguin.

Hartsock, N. (1990). Foucault on power: A theory for women? In L. J. Nicholson (Ed.), *Feminism/postmodernism* (pp. 157–175). New York: Routledge.

Hekman, S. J. (1990). *Gender and knowledge: Elements of a postmodern feminism.* Boston: Northeastern University Press.

hooks, b. (1994). *Teaching to transgress.* New York: Routledge.

Lemert, C. (Ed.). (1993). *Social theory: The multicultural and classic readings.* Boulder, CO: Westview.

Lemert, C. (1995). *Sociology after the crisis.* Boulder, CO: Westview.

Lengermann, P. M., & Niebrugge, J. (1996). Early women sociologists and classical sociological theory: 1830–1930. In G. Ritzer (Ed.), *Classical sociological theory* (2nd Ed.) (pp. 294–328). New York: McGraw-Hill.

Loeb, P. R. (1994). *Generation at the crossroads: Apathy and action on the American campus.* New Brunswick, NJ: Rutgers University Press.

Lorde, A. (1984). *Sister outsider.* Freedom, CA: Crossing Press.

Martin, E. (1987). *The woman in the body: A cultural analysis of reproduction.* Boston: Beacon.

Oakley, A. (1980). *Women confined: Towards a sociology of childbirth.* New York: Schocken.

O'Brien, M. (1989). *Reproducing the world: Essays in feminist theory.* Boulder, CO: Westview.

Rich, A. (1979). *Of women born: Motherhood as experience and institution.* New York: W. W. Norton.

Ritzer, G. (1996a). *Classical sociological theory.* (2nd Ed.). New York: McGraw-Hill.

Ritzer, G. (1996b). *The McDonaldization of society (Rev. ed.).* Thousand Oaks, CA: Pine Forge Press.

Rosaldo, R. (1993). *Culture and truth: The remaking of social analysis.* Boston: Beacon.

Rossides, D. W. (1978). *The history and nature of sociological theory.* Boston: Houghton Mifflin.

Seidman, S. (1991). The end of sociological theory: The postmodern hope. *Sociological Theory, 9*(2), 131–146.

Seidman, S. (1994). *Contested knowledge: Social theory in the postmodern era.* Cambridge, MA: Blackwell.

Smith, D. E. (1987). *The everyday world as problematic: A feminist sociology.* Boston: Northeastern University Press.

Smith, D. E. (1990). *The conceptual practices of power: A feminist sociology of knowledge.* Boston: Northeastern University Press.

Trebilcot, J. (Ed.). (1984). *Mothering: Essays in feminist theory.* Totowa, NJ: Rowman and Allanheld.

Weber, M. (1958). Politics as a vocation. In H. H. Gerth, & C. W. Mills (Eds.), *From Max Weber: Essays in sociology* (pp. 77–128). New York: Oxford University Press.

3

The Rhetoric of McDonaldization: A Social Semiotic Perspective

John S. Caputo

> You see, but you do not observe.
>
> Sir Arthur Conan Doyle, *Scandal in Bohemia*

This essay is about the commodification of culture, particularly the culture of McDonald's and the process of McDonaldization as described by George Ritzer in his book *The McDonaldization of Society*. Although Ritzer (1993, p. 1) says: "this is *not* a book about McDonald's or the fast-food business," he does use McDonald's as a "paradigm case of a wide-ranging process I [Ritzer] call McDonaldization." Ritzer extends his metaphor of McDonaldization to other aspects of the twentieth century including other fast-food restaurants, newspapers, medical care, schools, and so on, that he sees as "an inexorable process as it sweeps through seemingly impervious institutions and parts of the world." Ritzer's argument of this process he calls McDonaldization rests with his analysis of McDonald's and how others have taken on this model. Ritzer explains: "Overall, the central thesis is that McDonald's represents a monumentally important development and the process it has helped to spawn, McDonaldization, is engulfing more and more sectors of society and areas of the world" (1993, p. 16). For Ritzer, it is McDonald's that he sees as a cultural icon and uses this metaphor to extend all his arguments. For this reason I will focus my discussion on McDonald's. If the McDonald's "process" can be seen differently, then perhaps the whole argument of McDonaldization collapses, or at minimum should be looked at differently.

I approach this subject as both a consumer who partakes of McDonald's hamburgers and as a communication theorist. As a consumer, I grew up within a few miles of one of the original McDonald's hamburger stands in California, and with the globalization of McDonald's, have visited their restaurants in several countries. As a communicologist, I am interested in what Bormann (1985) has called "symbolic convergence." Symbolic convergence theory suggests that sharing of group fantasies creates symbolic convergence. For McDonald's this sharing of a fantasy takes place through a rhetorical vision, a vision that is spread and reinforced through recurring media messages. These messages come to us as stories and, as Fisher (1987, p. 2) points out, "All forms of human communication need to be seen fundamentally as stories." I will come back to Fisher a bit later in this essay, but to understand the rhetorical vision of the McDonald's story, I will begin this analysis with a story of my own. It is a story about the almighty hamburger, or so the story might seem.

THE STORY

In 1981 I went on sabbatical from California to Canterbury, Kent, England. Accompanying me were my wife and (then) three children, ages five, three and four months. Although many people thought we were silly to move to a foreign, albeit English-speaking country for six months with small children, we looked at it as an adventure and a fulfilled wish.

We landed at Heathrow airport outside London on a Saturday morning shortly after the Royal Wedding between Prince Charles and Lady Diana. We rented a car and drove to Canterbury following what is called the South Circular Route (this was before the new and now outdated M 25 was built). Although this distance is somewhere near seventy miles, it took nearly five hours to drive the route that passed through practically every south London town and highway repair project. Because by California standards, a seventy-mile car trip translated into one hour (no one in California says how far something is, but rather how long it takes to get there), I had not prepared for miles of snarled traffic and a hungry family. Although the children expressed their hunger during the journey, we did not notice one restaurant that seemed appropriate to stop at on the entire trip. Of course I kept thinking we would get there any minute and then find a place to eat.

When we got to Canterbury and drove down the heavily crowded High Street (that kept changing its name every few blocks), we felt claustrophobic, hungry, and tired, but our adventure was just beginning. It being Saturday, the city was very crowded with shoppers, and in addition (we learned later), shops were closed not only on the next day, Sunday, but on the "bank holiday" Monday. Since we were going to be staying in Canterbury for six months, we had arranged to rent a "modern" (built in this century) house. We went to the estate agent who then directed us to the house. By this time it was nearly 3:00 in the afternoon. After an intensive and exhaustive inventory of the house, the estate agent wished us luck, but not before I asked him about a supermarket (we were now getting in desperate need of diapers/nappies) and a restaurant to get some food for the children. He couldn't think of a nearby restaurant where they welcomed children, but there was a supermarket on the outskirts of town that had a small canteen where one could purchase prepared food. But he told us we better hurry before they closed for the rest of bank holiday weekend.

We proceeded to find our way around the city ring-road several times before we finally saw the road to the supermarket. Although we were hungry and tired, there was a momentary joy of finding the market. We got our shopping trolley and decided we better shop before we ate because the market was only going to be open for about another hour. With a tiny baby and two small toddlers we went from aisle to aisle, and after twenty minutes or so we had only located about three or four products to purchase. Nothing seemed to be what we were looking for. We couldn't find milk, diapers, napkins, or most other products we thought would be crucial. Finally, in desperation my wife said we better go over to the canteen and eat before we all passed out.

At the canteen we didn't recognize many of the food items either, but the children saw a picture of a hamburger and french fries and that is what we all decided to eat. Although the canteen was rather empty, I waited at the counter quite some time before someone came to take my order. My wife and children were seated at a table. I asked for the all-American favorite, "four cheeseburgers and fries, with water to drink." The server asked did I mean beef burgers and chips and told me they didn't sell water. I said yes and okay. I went back to the table and eventually the server came over with four hamburger patties and a small pack of greasy "chips." My wife said to me, "Didn't you ask for buns with the hamburgers?" No, I hadn't, but I didn't think I needed to. I proceeded back to the counter to ask for buns, but the server seemed to have no idea of what I was asking about. Eventually I showed her the picture on the wall, and she said, "Oh, you mean baps." "How many would you like?" I replied, "Four." A few minutes later she collected the beef patties and returned with four beef burgers on baps! My wife asked if I had requested any lettuce and tomatoes or ketchup and mustard. I told her I had assumed it would come that way but I would go back and ask. When I asked the server for ketchup I was told that would be "5p for a sachet." When I asked for lettuce and tomatoes, she asked, "Oh, did you want salad with the beef burgers?" To add brevity to the story, the entire day was a fiasco. Yes, I learned quickly that when I wanted a hamburger or cheeseburger, I would always ask for a beef burger on a bap with salad, and a portion of chips with a sachet of ketchup. But, oh, where was McDonald's when we needed it?

A FIRST GLANCE

This story took place nearly fifteen years ago. At that time Canterbury's only equivalent of a fast-food restaurant was a few fish and chips shops, a Wimpy Bar (which sold a type of beefburger unlike the American hamburger), and a shop that sold chicken and chips. For the most part, it was unusual to see children in restaurants except pubs that had gardens for children. And everyone would talk about customer service in England by saying "service with a sneer" instead of the Americanism "service with a smile." I know, the reader may be saying to herself, "If you wanted American service and fast food, you should have stayed in America." But the fact is, in the past fifteen years Canterbury has changed. There is now a McDonald's, with a Burger King just opposite. There are several pizza chains and a second larger McDonald's out on the (almost, by American standards) suburban highway, and that McDonald's has a drive-through window.

Was all this to cater to the odd American academic on sabbatical with family? I give that a resounding no. Or perhaps to serve the hordes of French and Italian tourists who flock to this historical Cathedral city, the heart of the Anglican church? Not hardly. Well, perhaps then these establishments have been so successful because of what Ritzer has pointed out using Max Weber's theory—efficiency, calculability, predictability, and control. Certainly, these are factors worth considering, but are they the primary factors in this McDonaldization process that Ritzer sees? And if they are, do they have a negative effect on the "English way of life"?

A SECOND GLANCE

In attempting to answer these questions, I would like to look at McDonaldization from a narrative perspective. What is the story of McDonaldization? What ideals does it construct? What rules does it prescribe? What is its source of authority? And how does it give us a sense of continuity and purpose? What about the McDonaldization narrative has sufficient credibility, complexity, and symbolic power to hail us through its "golden arches"? From a communication perspective, what is it about McDonald's, or Disneyland, or my university, that hails one to come in, to spend one's money and to consume a product? Although McDonald's is hugely successful on an international basis, most Americans would not consider McDonald's to make the "best" hamburger in their home towns. McDonald's hamburgers are just that, McDonald's hamburgers. One does not go to McDonald's expecting the best hamburger in town. One goes to McDonald's expecting McDonald's. So what is the story of McDonald's?

As Postman says, "Our genius lies in our capacity to make meaning through the creation of narratives that give point to our labors, exalt our history, elucidate the present, and give direction to our future" (1995, p. 7). He goes on to suggest that in order to work, narratives do not have to be true but rather "Does it provide people with a sense of personal identity, a sense of community life, a basis for moral conduct, explanations of that which cannot be known?" (p. 7). Narratives then are a form of storytelling and may go by the name of myth to use the term of Joseph Campbell and Rollo May. In Freud's terminology, narratives may be referred to as "illusions," or from a Marxist analysis they might be called ideology. To this extent then, Ritzer's work has provided us a narrative about McDonaldization based upon his understanding of the theories of Max Weber. All narratives are imperfect. Ritzer tells us a compelling story, but to use Fisher's concepts, one that lacks "coherence and fidelity." For Fisher, all stories are not equally good. He believes we tend to judge stories for coherence and fidelity, and with a bit of common sense, almost any of us can spot a good story based upon narrative rationality. To that extent I would like to provide a different narrative analysis of McDonaldization, one that looks at the McDonaldization "story" from the perspective of semiotics.

Semiotics is the study of signs and how signs are used to create meaning. Meanings are not located in the text itself, be that words, images, aesthetics, and so on, but are produced in the interactions between the text and audience. As Fiske (1990, p. 165) states, "The reader and the text together produce a preferred meaning." Therefore, when I see a McDonald's or Burger King commercial, I create a meaning that is influenced by a particular set of dominant values. This is how ideology works. Semiotics is well suited to the analysis of narratives because narratives are constructed from signs, signs that move a reader to symbolic convergence with a text.

Williams (1977) finds three main uses of the term ideology. The first use is as a system of beliefs characteristic of a particular class or group. The second use is as a system of illusory beliefs or false ideas or false consciousness which can be contrasted with true scientific knowledge. In this sense, a fast-food commercial cannot be taken on its own but rather as part of our cultural experience: the reading is affected by readings of other fast-food commercials. This "intertextuality," to use Fiske's (1990) term, suggests that the meanings generated by any one text are determined partly by the meanings of other texts to which it appears similar. The third use of the term ideology is to describe the social production of meanings, or what Barthes (1977) refers to as "the rhetoric of ideology."

Semiotics, as a "school of communication," has grown from the works of Pierce (1931–58), Saussure (1966), Barthes (1968), and Eco (1976), among others. Although semiotics has been taken down many roads to understand the generation of meaning, I will look at semiotics as a form of structuralism that argues that we cannot know the world on its own terms, therefore, we must look to the underlying conceptual and linguistic structures of our culture. It is these underlying conceptual and linguistic structures of our culture that hold for us insight into what is the essence of the stories we are told—what is the myth. "For Lévi-Strauss a myth is a story society tells that is constructed of a specific and local transformation of a deep structure . . . that are [sic] important to the culture within which the myth circulates" (Fiske, 1990, p. 122). The myth is thus examined for both denotative and connotative meaning. At the denotative level, one looks at signs for the first order of signification, the first order of syntagm. At the connotative level, one looks for the second-order syntagm: the underlying myth. As Fiske writes,

Once we start thinking about the signifieds, we realize how unreal is the distinction between the first and second orders: it is of analytical convenience only. For the signifieds slide imperceptibly into the second-order myths. (1990, p. 106)

SEMIOTIC ANALYSIS OF MCDONALDIZATION

By providing a semiotic analysis, I hope to discover and make visible the ideological practice that helps drive the process of McDonaldization. For this essay I am going to analyze a television commercial for the McDonald's restaurant chain. Television advertisements are helpful in exploring aspects of commodification. A commodity is a "good," something that is bought and sold, something with intrinsic value that can be traded economically. Commercial advertisements are produced to sell commodities to the public. Western society is saturated with advertisements, particularly on commercial television. Brummett (1994) suggests that advertisements blend into regular programming, because

1. ads have production values that are as high or higher than the shows themselves, so that ads are interesting and eye-catching and therefore resemble the program;

2. the same actors will appear on both programs and advertisements, thus linking the two ("I'm not a doctor, but I play one on television");

3. ads and programs often employ the same formats, such as that of music video, thus blurring any clear distinction between the two; and

4. ads and shows are interspersed with each other with increasing frequency. The end result is that the selling of commodities becomes increasingly inseparable from what one sees in general in watching television. (p. 140)

Additionally, in television advertisements, the audience is a commodity as well. Programmers sell advertisers audiences based on ratings. In essence, the audience is sold to the advertiser for fifteen seconds at a time, on the expectation that we will be there in front of our television sets to watch a commercial message at that time (Brummett, 1994).

Although ideally it would be better to show you the video, I will do my best to describe the commercial message from both an audio and video perspective. Although this commercial will not have been seen by all consumers of McDonald's hamburgers or other fast-food restaurants, or urgent-care clinics, or one-hour eyeglass shops, it does make up and fit within the general narrative of technology and leisure, and hence is part of the intertextuality of ideology as mentioned by Williams (1977).

THE VIDEO

This video consists of approximately ten frames and lasts fifteen seconds. It is shot in color and through a "soft-focus" lens filter, giving it a rather "grainy textured" image. There are three main actors in this video, an adult male approximately thirty-five years old, an adult female approximately thirty years old, and a female child approximately four years old. The video is shot in three locations: (1) the driveway of a home, (2) a drive-through window of a McDonald's, and (3) a zoo.

Frame 1: Adult male dressed in suit and tie with a large smile on his face gets out of a car in a driveway.

Frame 2: As he alights from the car, a young, clean, well-dressed child runs into his arms calling out, "Daddy." He raises the child up, while an adult well-dressed female comes up as well.

Frame 3: The car drives off with two passengers, daddy and child, with the woman smiling, waving, and saying "good-bye."

Frame 4: The daddy and child are sitting in the front seat of the car with the child in a safety seat. They are parked at a McDonald's drive-through window, and there is a McDonald's worker handing a bag of food to the dad. The dad, who now has his suit coat removed and is dressed with a tie and suspenders (braces), hands the food bag to the child who is laughing.

Frame 5: The dad and child walk through a turnstile and a sign over their shoulders reads "zoo." The father now has his tie removed and the daughter has balloons tied to her right wrist. Both dad and child are carrying McDonald's bags and have large smiles on their faces.

Frame 6: Dad and child are sitting on a wooden bench seat. The child still has the balloons tied to her wrist and they are consuming drinks from McDonald's cups, french fries, and hamburgers.

Frame 7: While still sitting on the bench, the child feeds french fries to her dad. Both again are smiling.

Frame 8: A small elephant walks across the screen.

Frame 9: Still sitting on the bench, the child with a look of wonder on her face, points her finger and calls out "Daddy!" The dad looks in the direction of the pointed finger, and they both smile.

Frame 10: Father and daughter are walking together holding hands apparently leaving the zoo. The balloons are still tied to her right wrist, her left hand is holding her daddy's right hand, and his left hand is holding a McDonald's cup. In the lower left corner of the screen is a small (approximately three-inch square) McDonald's logo.

FIRST-ORDER SYNTAGM

The general ambiance of this commercial is fun, relaxation, and togetherness. With the use of a soft-focus lens, it is almost dreamlike. There is little dialogue, only exclamations like "Daddy." In essence, the commercial is constructed as a series of signs that tells a narrative story about a father and daughter getting away without Mom, sharing easily purchased food, and having fun together. There is very little written material in the advertisement. The McDonald's name shows on the bags of food, the beverage cups, and the superimposed logo in the last frame. The only other written material is the word "zoo," which appears as a location sign. Each frame of the video contains a full image, most in two-shot form. When a long-shot is used, it is mostly to show location and fun. The action takes place in the daytime so lighting "appears" natural but soft. With essentially no dialogue, the only sound in the commercial is the soft background music. Even when words are expressed, they are very soft. Again, this adds to the "dreamlike" mood of this piece.

The signs and symbols of this advertisement consist of the few actual words spoken, the nonverbal expressions on the faces of the three characters, the dress of the characters, the physical contact, the car, the outdoor activity, the McDonald's food, the balloons, the grainy soft picture, the soft music, and the absence of dialogue. The signs intimate affluence, independence, joy, familial relations, and leisure. The story is about a busy father taking off time from work to spend with his daughter. Statistics in America currently show that the average father may spend as little as five minutes per day in direct contact with his child. But in this story, the dad seems to be spending a lot of time, and this time will not be interrupted by needing to prepare food. However, the food can be brought along, by driving through McDonald's. McDonald's not only does not get in the way of the outing, but adds to the fun of it. The father and child have the same expression on their face in nearly every frame, a smile. The only other facial expression is the child's when she looks off in wonder at the zoo, closely followed once again by smiles from dad and daughter. Joy and happiness are constantly expressed. This is consistent with McDonald's ad campaigns. Their consumer research indicated that a trip to McDonald's was an event for each member of the family that could be likened to an escape to an island of enjoyment. Kids could see the mountain of french fries, moms could escape from meal planning, and dads could escape from the grind of work (Love, 1995).

The family has a "nice," middle-class sedan. The father is dressed in a conservative business suit (even with braces/suspenders). The child is dressed casually but nicely. The mother has short hair and is dressed in a soft sweater. These items of clothing add up to an image of the comfortable middle-class American family, an American success. The car adds independence by providing "easy" travel to McDonald's and the zoo. McDonald's makes it easy for the consumer to use that independence by driving his or her car through the drive-through lane instead of having to come in and wait for his or her food.

This commercial does not spend any time presenting information about McDonald's or the quality of their food. The commercial is a "lifestyle" commercial, and McDonald's is part of that lifestyle. What is being sold here is the centrality of McDonald's to the family. In a busy world where one does not even have time to change out of his work clothes to spend "quality" time with his or her daughter, McDonald's is there to help. This commercial does not even describe the food that McDonald's sells. The food is necessary to have the fun and companionship, but what the food consists of is irrelevant. Love (1995) points out that as McDonald's started to expand in the late 1960s it realized that to cultivate a national mass market, it needed to develop a media campaign that focused on the family rather than the product and price. As Love explains it:

but [Paul] Schrage and creative executives at D'Arcy took aim at a far more elusive but potentially more rewarding target: image. They wanted to sell hamburgers the way Miller sells beer. McDonald's now was attempting to extend to network advertising an old Kroc homily: "We're not in the hamburger business; we're in show business." (1995, p. 303)

The chain's advertising campaign was not about the product, but rather the enjoyment it creates, and became "food, folks, and fun" and remains so today. The commodity then is food, folks, and fun.

Another important sign of this advertisement is the notion of a "break." The father is taking a break from his work to share this "special" time with his daughter. The notion of a "break" is central to McDonald's success. A break indicates moving from the world of work to the world of leisure. This is indicated by the dad slowly stripping off the uniform of the businessman, to achieve the look of a relaxed dad whose little girl rains down smiles upon him. McDonald's has worked on this break issue in several ways: break from the routine, break from preparing meals, break on prices, and so forth. But most importantly was its theme, "You deserve a break today, so get up and get away—to McDonald's." This theme became the best known commercial music on television.

This commercial is very subtle. The "food, folks, and fun" of McDonald's commercials are "soft sells" portraying the character of McDonald's as helping the family have fun. As Love explains, "the product reference became so subtle that . . . the McDonald's logo [would be there] so there would be no mistaking who the ads were for" (1995, p. 307).

SECOND-ORDER SYNTAGM: MYTH AND CONNOTATION

The signs used to construct this narrative carry through the message of commodification. We learn to understand our desires in terms of commodities made to meet them. So the problems of having fun with our children are framed and solved in commodities—clothing, house, car, smiles, McDonald's drive-throughs and food, balloons, zoos, and elephants all serve to define the family and fun by middle-class prosperity. This is a commodified family—a family that consumes. And we consume the message as well. Eating at McDonald's, even when driving through, becomes a "naturalized" event, perhaps even more natural than eating at home.

On one level then this McDonald's commercial advertisement operates around the McDonald's strategy of "food, folks, and fun." On a deeper structural level, however, the essence of this advertisement works to circulate around three main clusters of meanings. And it is these three clusters of meanings that serve to globalize McDonald's by exporting Americana. The first can be associated with hard work and leisure. Hard work has provided the family with "nice" clothes, a "nice" car, a "nice" home, and a "nice" family. Additionally, the value of work provides the opportunity for leisure and enjoyment with the family. The dad has earned his "break today," his leisure time to bond with his daughter and just generally have fun. The second is a set of associations around Americana. The aesthetics of the film in lighting, filters, relationships, artifacts, and affluence all portray "the American dream"—a spouse, job, child, house, car, freedom, naturalness, informality, and self-sufficiency. The dad does not even need the mother to go along to the zoo. She can have her own break today, and he can serve as a model to single dads who need to learn how to "bond" with their children. A third set of meanings cluster around American culture and consensus. In this advertisement, the product appears primarily in the bags and cups. In only two of the ten frames are the hamburgers, or french fries, or drinks being consumed. However, the reader of the commercial message already knows that McDonald's products are the hamburger sandwich, french-fried potatoes, and "cokes" (used to name all types of soda pop flavors). Hamburgers are the United States' unique contribution to international cuisine. Whereas the American consumption of the hot dog originated from German sausages and the pizza emerged from southern Italian immigrant's old-world recipes, the hamburger is "all American." In fact, McDonald's calls one of their hamburger combinations the "all American meal deal." Hamburgers are eaten by all social classes, races, genders, and ages. They transcend all social categories by carrying the myth of freedom and equality. In the recent O. J. Simpson trial, O. J. reported that on the evening Nicole Brown Simpson was murdered, he and another person who lived at his residence had taken his Rolls-Royce to the drive-through windows at McDonald's, for dinner. Here is a multimillionaire, former all-American football player, former all-star professional football player turned actor, driving one of the most expensive cars in the world, going to McDonald's for dinner. Anyone can go and eat at McDonald's.

DISCUSSION

Thus, the combination of these two orders of syntagms help to create a myth. This myth is what hails one into McDonald's, and this myth has intertextuality with other myths that are part of an American consumer culture. But how does this myth travel with the globalization of McDonald's? McDonald's success abroad is well known at one level and at the same time one of the best-kept secrets of American business. As Love points out:

When McDonald's began expanding internationally . . . [m]ost countries had no locally based fast-food outlets, either. Indeed, eating out—an increasingly routine experience for Americans—was an uncommon experience in most foreign markets. In Europe particularly, restaurants were still locked into traditions of full linen service, waiters in black tie, wine stewards and multicourse meals. There were virtually no family restaurants, and thus for the middle class eating out was always a special occasion. (1995, pp. 414–415)

How could McDonald's sell a hamburger to the Japanese whose diet consisted primarily of fish and rice? How could McDonald's sell a hamburger to the Australians who would instead want their fish and chips? Or to the Germans who love their beer, but not children? "The German public is not a kid-loving public. There are restaurants where a dog is more welcome than a kid" (Love, 1995, p. 434). How could McDonald's sell a hamburger to the Swedes who were proud of their traditional foods, and even questioned the need for bulk food in plastic environments? How could McDonald's sell a hamburger to the Irish who resented McDonald's nonunion stance for service workers? How could McDonald's sell a hamburger to the English, who knew hamburgers (or I should say beefburgers) tasted so much like cardboard, and already had low-cost food service available at fish and chips shops, Wimpy (hamburger) bars, and pubs with family gardens? How could McDonald's "naturalize" eating out?

This list could go on and on. McDonald's now exists in Taiwan, the People's Republic of China, Russia, Puerto Rico, Costa Rica, Panama, the former Czech Republic, Brunei, Guadeloupe, Iceland, Belgium, Israel, Poland, Morocco, Monaco, Saipan, Saudi Arabia, Slovenia, Oman, Kuwait, New Caledonia, Trinidad, Bulgaria, Latavia, Bahrain, United Arab Emirates, Egypt, and India. I could name more, but the fact is by the turn of this century, McDonald's international sales are expected to exceed their domestic sales. This is in spite of a rather rocky start in which McDonald's attempted to modify their menus and environment to meet local traditions. When McDonald's returned to their complete American menu, altered their buildings to be more similar to their American architecture, and modified their ad campaigns to "food, folks, and fun," the second-order syntagm—the myths of hard work and leisure, Americana and American culture and consensus—did their work. In Britain the McDonald's ads proclaimed, "The United Tastes of America." In Japan, the McDonald's spokesman discussed that by eating McDonald's hamburgers and potatoes, the Japanese would grow taller, develop white skins, and blond hair (Love, 1995, p. 423). In both Japan and the UK, adverts were aimed in the middle of the biggest market, the family segment. If children wanted to have fun at McDonald's, their parents would take them, and they would be McDonald's customers for life. This, in spite of the fact that in many countries the price of McDonald's food is quite expensive by local standards—not at all the notion of inexpensive food that first saturated America. So what is all this money buying?

Here I return to my brief story at the beginning of this essay. What I was experiencing in the supermarket in Canterbury was not a craving for McDonald's hamburgers, but rather I was in the early throes of culture shock. I wanted not my Big Mac, but rather my American experience. I wanted to buy my happiness, buy my commodity. This Americana experience, the second-order syntagm, pulls upon me just as it pulls upon consumers in other countries. The reader may question, however, if others do not see these commercial messages, then how could this order of myth prevail? Quite simply, the second-order syntagm travels well. So well that the myth is larger than the ads that carry them. The clusters of hard work and leisure, Americana, and American culture and consensus, are part of the intertextuality of the American myth. Just as most small towns in America feel they made it on the map when they open their McDonald's, or Wal-Mart, or Colonel Sanders, many foreign cities feel the same when they are able to attract their own McDonald's. This is true even if prices seem high, the food strange, and the taste lacking. Again the product is not hamburgers and fries, but rather "food, folks, and fun" all carefully wrapped within its second-level syntagms—hard work and leisure that earns us our "break" today, "the American dream"—a spouse, job, child, house, car, freedom, naturalness, informality, and self-sufficiency and American culture and consensus—the myth of freedom and equality in which anyone can and does go and eat at McDonald's.

CONCLUSION

So what does this essay say in relation to Ritzer's analysis of McDonald-ization? I began this essay with a short story about a stay in England and an attempt to buy a hamburger and I asked why, over the years, has McDonald's been successful in building up its business in England. From my perspective, the McDonald's success is based upon its ability to tell a story, a story that does not make sense from a logical perspective but rather from an aesthetic one. The story has coherence and fidelity and helps one solve his or her problem through the purchase and possession of commodities. This narrative offers a little bit of American culture to up-market Brits. In Canterbury, as well as in many cities around the world, you will find people who want to drink American Budweiser and buy their kids triple-thick chocolate milkshakes at McDonald's. McDonald's is successful in creating and fulfilling this need not through the components of a rational system that includes efficiency, calculability, predictability, and control, but through its advertising campaign that hails each of us to come in and buy its product of "food, folks, and fun," to come in and fulfill our American dream. This campaign is successful on the global market not through specific ads at this point, but rather the second-order syntagm of intertextuality with the American myth. This myth—the McDonald's narrative—has sufficient credibility, complexity, and symbolic power to hail us through its golden arches. Although most Americans would not consider McDonald's to make the "best" hamburger in their home towns, McDonald's is hugely successful on an international basis. One does not go to McDonald's expecting the best hamburger in town. One goes to McDonald's expecting the image. McDonald's success is due to their creation of a narrative that is not necessarily true but rather provides us with a sense of personal identity, a sense of community life, a basis for conduct, and explanations of that which cannot be known. The McDonald's narrative—the story—is an illusion that contains our ideology. The McDonald's narrative is imperfect. But it is a narrative quite different from Ritzer's. If this interpretation of the narrative rings true, the process of McDonaldization is not based upon rationalization, but rather the role of the "story" in human experience, in human behavior. McDonald's must, in fact, be seen as unique in its story and not seen as a monolithic process being followed by others. This story is one of culture, economics, equality, and family. It is an American story, but it transcends time and space. It shares intertextuality which helps to add to its cumulative effect. It may be transmitted through modern communication media, but it is a story as old as time. Using semiotics and the narrative paradigm of Walter Fisher, we come to understand the story by understanding what goes on in human communication. This approach is radically democratic by suggesting that when viewing communication as a narrative, people do not need specialized training to figure out if a story holds together or rings true. Each of us can be a competent rhetorical critic by looking closely at the stories we are told—or to use Eco's (1976, p. 7) term, the discovery of "the lie."

REFERENCES

Barthes, R. (1968). *Elements of semiology*. London: Cape.

Barthes, R. (1977). *Image-music-text*. London: Paladin.

Bormann, E. (1985). Symbolic convergence theory: A communication formulation. *Journal of Communication, 35* (4), 128–138.

Brummett, B. (1994). *Rhetoric in popular culture*. New York: St. Martin's.

Eco, U. (1976). *A theory of semiotics*. Bloomington, ID: Indiana University Press.

Fisher, W. R. (1987). *Human communication as narration: Toward a philosophy of reason, value, and action*. Columbia, SC: University of South Carolina Press.

Fiske, J. (1990). *Introduction to communication studies*. (2nd Ed.). London: Routledge.

Love, J. F. (1995). *McDonald's: Behind the arches*. New York: Bantam.

Pierce, C. S. (1931–58). *Collected papers*. Cambridge, MA: Harvard University Press.

Postman, N. (1995). *The end of education: Redefining the value of school*. New York: Alfred A. Knopf.

Ritzer, G. (1993). *The McDonaldization of society*. Thousand Oaks, CA: Pine Forge.

Saussure, F. de (1966). *Course in general linguistics* (Wade Baskins, Trans.) New York: McGraw-Hill.

Williams, R. (1977). *Marxism and literature*. Oxford, UK: Oxford University Press.

4

McDonaldization and the Global Sports Store: Constructing Consumer Meanings in a Rationalized Society

Steven Miles

Consumers actively use, and, arguably *need*, the stabilities and predictabilities that characterize the everyday experience of a "McDonaldized" society. As Ritzer (1993) sees it, the essential problem with living in a McDonaldized society appears to be that although people have the potential to be thoughtful, creative, and well-rounded human beings, they are unable to fulfil that potential as a result of the constraints characteristic of a rationalized world. Focusing, in particular, on the nature of youth consumption, the argument that I will present in this essay is that Ritzer (1993), and Weber (1958) before him, tend to underestimate the extent to which individuals can negotiate their own sense of reality within the structures that are laid down in a so-called "McDonaldized" society. Ritzer's conception of McDonaldization, as Wynyard argues elsewhere in this volume, underestimates some of the more subjective complexities of the everyday experience of modern or postmodern societies. In this context, I will argue that consumers actively and intentionally use McDonaldized consumption as a means of asserting some sense of stability in an everyday world which they actually perceive as being risky and unpredictable.

MCDONALDIZATION AND CONSUMPTION

Consumption plays a key role in Ritzer's (1993) discussion of McDonald-ization, as well as his more recent work on the global credit card society (Ritzer, 1995). As such, he implies that people's roles as consumers have emerged as a fundamental focus of the modern life experience. In this context, it can be argued that consumption has itself developed into an increasingly influential domain in which McDonaldization is becoming more and more evident. As the productivist bias, so long associated with Marxist conceptions of modernity, has broken down, there has emerged a debate concerning whether consumption provides consumers with the feeling or illusion that they can escape from the drudgery of everyday life when what it perhaps does is ensure that consumers are locked within an "iron cage" of consumerism.

Relative to this "iron-cage" there exists a common-sense, though as yet unproved, notion that consumption has become so fundamental to the modern life experience that it *must* have some role to play in the construction of people's identities. From Ritzer's point of view this may imply that the nature of the modern consuming experience is so constricting that the impact on identity formation is necessarily a negative one. In this context, Dittmar (1992) refers to the existence of a materialism-idealism paradox; that is, the commonly accepted idea that every individual has a unique personality independent of material circumstances, alongside the paradoxical notion that material possessions are central regulators, not only of large-scale social processes, but also of interpersonal relations and impressions. The problem with Ritzer's overtly negative thesis is that he fails to comprehend the interdependence of these two issues. My research amounts to an attempt to come to terms with the meanings with which young consumers endow what it is they consume, and, by implication, to address the relationship between structure and agency. In doing so it will subsequently be possible to explore the *active* negotiation of McDonaldized experience. Are consumer meanings any more than the mere afterthought of a McDonaldized society?

BACKGROUND

As a means of addressing the sorts of arguments that Ritzer presents, I will discuss the findings of a research project that specifically focuses on the relationship between youth consumption and the construction of identity. I therefore intend to analyse how far the consuming experience is, in fact, characterized by some of the features that Ritzer associates with McDonaldization. In order to address the nature of consumer meanings among young people, I conducted a participant observation in a multinational sports store located in the north of England. Given the apparent significance of brandnames among young people, and the close identification with high-profile sports stars advertising such goods, the sports store seemed a likely context in which the meanings with which young people endowed consumer goods might prove accessible.

By working over a period of ten weeks as a sales assistant, I was able to gain access to the sorts of meanings young people applied to these types of consumer goods, as well as the structural and personal contexts within which such meanings were constructed. Although I worked as a conventional member of staff (who made copious notes on visits to the store room) and although my fellow store assistants were aware of my research role, customers were not. As such it was possible to observe the shop as a site of consumption. Customers were asked various questions, the intent of which was to address the significance of consumption in their lives, most particularly in relation to the training shoes they were considering purchasing. The meanings with which these shoes were endowed, the role that these meanings played in the construction of personal identities, and the cultural context in which such meanings operated, were therefore the issues addressed. For this purpose, preprepared questions were used as a means of stimulating discussions with customers. For example, customers would be asked what it was that attracted them to a particular pair of training shoes or, indeed, why they thought that a given brand was popular amongst their peers. However, at no point did the store's customers appear to be suspicious of my research role. Rather, I was perceived to be an especially enthusiastic member of staff who was showing particular interest in customers and their purchases.

The priority here, then, was for the customer to discuss the role that training shoes (and often, as the conversation developed, other types of consumer goods) had in their lives, and what factors they believed influenced that role. The intention was to allow the customer to set the agenda of the discussion as much as possible. The data was, therefore, analysed qualitatively according to the assumption that the meanings that consumers express are potentially worthy of serious consideration. From this basis it might be possible to begin to consider empirical evidence of the impact of what Ritzer (1993) describes as McDonaldization.

THE SPORTS STORE AS "SELLING MACHINE"?

Ritzer notes how in recent years shopping has become an increasingly *efficient* process (1993, p. 49). With the emergence of department stores and more recently shopping malls, it is now possible for consumers to visit several shops in one vicinity and thus be entertained, fed, and educated in a single visit. The store in which I worked was efficient in the sense that though it was not located in an actual mall, it was in a prime location: a pedestrianised collection of high-order stores in the centre of a northern English industrial town. Indeed, it is worth pointing out at this point that British shopping centres are extremely predictable and uniform, perhaps even more so than their North American counterparts. The town in which my research was located is overwhelmingly dominated by the ubiquitous chain store. This, as Ritzer (1993) points out, has the advantage of predictability, in as much as during a shopping excursion the consumer knows what to expect and where to expect it (p. 30). However, the converse effect is that both the shopping centre and the individual consumer using that centre lose the opportunity to impart a certain degree of spontaneity and creativity into the shopping experience.

The convenience of predictability is reemphasised within the actual setting of the sports store itself. The store concerned, which I will not refer to by name in order to protect the anonymity of it's employees, is part of a multinational American-owned corporation and has approximately 5000 stores worldwide. To ensure the familiar nature of the company's corporate image, branches are supplied with vast amounts of training literature, illustrating in fine colourful detail prescribed standardized ways in which the shop floor should be presented. The customer should not be surprised if he or she were to enter one branch of the store in North America and another on his or her vacation in Great Britain, only to find the same items on sale in the same replicated layout. This sort of predictability is closely associated with notions of globalization and Americanization, both of which have been discussed by Ritzer (1995, p. 22). Ritzer argues that the latter term is more appropriate in describing the way in which the worldwide influence of American consumerism has spread. Subsequently, as avenues of communication broaden their influence, so does the ubiquitous global nature of Americanized consumption habits.

The predictability of the shopping experience is personified by the actual sales assistants themselves. Local colour and flavour simply do not fit in to the rationalized world of the sports store sales assistant. The store concerned abides by a very strict dress or uniform code, the nature of which is determined by Head Office. Uniforms are provided by the company and there is a definite determination on their part to portray a common image throughout its stores. There is no room for any display of individuality in this context.

As for the actual stock, this too displays some of the characteristics Ritzer associates with rationalization. The manager of the branch in which I worked has limited control over the stock coming into his store. The company as a whole has a universal stocking policy within which there is little room for flexibility. The manager pointed out that on the rare occasions that he felt that a new line would be particularly useful addition to his stock, or if he needed to replenish a line that had sold out more quickly than expected, then the ordering system simply could not cope and it may take approximately six weeks for the new stock to arrive.

Once new stock does arrive and once the consumer sits down to try on a new pair of training shoes, he or she is not encouraged to hang around. Reminiscent of the uncomfortable seats that Ritzer (1993) argues are characteristic of the "get 'em in and get 'em out" mentality of McDonald's, the sports store offers its customers an extremely uninviting bench which discourages any intention to loiter, thereby maximising the efficiency of the "selling machine" (p. 110).

This notion of predictability is further emphasised when you consider the atmosphere that the management actively seeks to promote in its stores. All branches of the sports store concerned are dominated by a large TV monitor overlooking the shop floor. This acts as a magnet for passing customers. British branches of the store often broadcast MTV, though interestingly it is more common in North American branches to transmit sports channels. Either way, as far as the Head Office is concerned, this helps to create a relatively straightforward means of perpetuating a superficial feeling, on the part of the customer, of personal familiarity with what it is to experience this particular store. It gives the individual a sense of personal knowledge about the store, whilst apparently simultaneously denying him or her of any sense of individual creativity in that selfsame context. The experience of shopping in this sports store is a passive, as opposed to an active one. Meanwhile, the TV monitor provides an additional means of advertising the wares offered on the shop floor.

In many respects then, it could be argued that the foundations of rationalization, and in particular, predictability, are crucial to the sports store experience. What is also of interest is that paradoxically, measures are taken by the company to actively disguise the impersonal nature of the experience of shopping at this particular site of consumption. The most vivid example of such efforts are the detailed instructions sales assistants are given as how to best approach customers entering the store. Though on the one hand the company's training literature is entirely open about the importance of giving the consumer a common experience on entering the store in whatever country, on the other, any hint that efforts are being made to control such an experience are hidden from the consumer's actual perception of the shopping environment. As such, the store's "lease line operation"—the displays that confront the customer immediately on entering the shop—have a significant strategic importance as a means of controlling the customer from the minute he or she enters the store, whilst simultaneously giving the customer the impression that he or she is in control.

The company concerned adopted an unwritten law that all customers should be "greeted" (or should that read "controlled"?) within three minutes of entering the store. In this sense, the shopping experience is a predictable one, though the fact that assistants are encouraged to embellish such predictability with a personal edge is clearly intended to convince the consumer otherwise. Sales assistants receive a large amount of customer-service training and are told that under no circumstances should they approach a customer and say, "How can I help you?" The managerial preference is that they ask something like, "Hi, how are you doing today?," altering their tack according to circumstances and, more importantly, according to the "needs" of the customer concerned. This point is illustrated by the following extract from the company's internal training literature.

From the minute the gate or the door of the store opens one of us must be there to control the lease line. We must position ourselves as close to the lease line as possible . . . And while we are there on the lease line why not have fun and be a go-getter with an innovative style and creativity. Greeting is not just a job, it is an art, the art of public relations.

Indeed, the company actually goes on to describe its employees as "chameleons" in that they are expected to change and adapt to every situation and to treat each customer as an individual. This takes Ritzer's (1993) discussion of "false fraternization" one sophisticated step further (p. 134). Ritzer may indeed interpret these tactics as amounting to a rather disingenuous attempt to disguise some of the more unsavoury dehumanizing aspects of McDonaldization.

The above points clearly illustrate that the chosen setting of a sports store appears, superficially, at least, to exhibit many of the characteristics that Ritzer (1993) equates with McDonaldization. There appears, at this preliminary level of analysis, to be at least some basis for arguing that the store concerned actively deploys some of the processes characteristic of the social trends that Ritzer describes. But what is potentially even more interesting is that the actual process of purchasing an item from a sports store appears to have evolved in such a way as to reinforce the dehumanizing nature of McDonaldization. By its very nature, the process of buying a pair of training shoes, for instance, appears to be more rationalized than creative. An individual does not appear to have complete freedom of choice in deciding which model of training shoe to buy, but this choice is framed by a variety of intervening factors. In the rationalized society in which we apparently live, consuming decisions are determined by a wide variety of influences including those perpetuated by advertising and the media. Yet, consumers feel that they can freely choose the product of their choice. The fact that such choice is predicated by a variety of factors, including fashion trends which determine what item is popular and when, conflicts with this belief.

It is in the interest of multinational sports companies to channel consumers in certain directions in order to make the production process more straightforward and less costly. This, indeed, is the basic philosophy behind any mass production process which thereby ensures that the demand for a particular product is maintained at a particular level until such time as producers feel that in order to maintain such demand at a profitable level consumers should be encouraged to purchase an alternative product. This polarized process, whereby consumers feel as though they are free to choose as they see fit and yet at the same time can only choose goods from a selection constructed for them by rationalized forces beyond their personal control, lies at the centre of the consumer paradox which this essay attempts to explore. To imply, as Ritzer does, that the belief in their own agency which consumers have is a form of false consciousness is to ignore the creative abilities of individuals. As the following analysis will reveal, what Ritzer fails to do is conceptualise the active ways in which young consumers interpret rationalized social structures as part of their own conception of reality.

THE SPORTS STORE AS "MEANING MACHINE"?

Having briefly discussed the evidence for arguing that both the sales assistant and the customer are dehumanized by the rationalized environment which is created in the guise of the sports store, and more broadly by processes of consumption in general, I want to argue that as an overall assessment the McDonaldization thesis is, in fact, misleading, in that though at a superficial level the experience of the sports store may appear to be McDonaldized, the actual relationships young consumers have with that store and the products it offers are far more subjective than Ritzer is prepare to concede. I would suggest, in fact, that young consumers are at least partially aware of the rationalized nature of the consuming experience and actually use that experience to their own personal and communal advantage. McDonaldized experience is negotiated in the sense that young people use the goods available on the marketplace (which, in turn, are often produced, at least partly, as a reaction to what is acceptable to consumers 'on the street') as a means of constructing their own sense of everyday stability. Mc-Donaldized consumption offers producers the profits they aspire to, while serving a pragmatic function for the consumers they are targeting.

An overriding theme that emerged throughout my research was the way in which young people appear to deny the existence of any pressure to buy particular models of training shoe for their fashion value and yet readily become involved in the craze to buy them. This might be seen to reflect the standardized nature of contemporary forms of consumption, but what I want to argue is that, in fact, in this respect, McDonaldization is positively *embraced* by young people. Far from wanting to express their individuality through sports goods *per se*—thereby being ensnared by the standardized nature of the goods and the services provided for them—young people are more concerned with establishing their individuality according to youth cultural parameters that are already well established and therefore involve minimal risk on their part. They actively embrace the predictable nature of the consuming experience, and the actual process of consumption, because it gives them a sense of *control*. Young people gain benefit from their consumption experiences precisely *because* such experiences are rationalized. As I will explain in the following section, such an argument can be further developed in the context of debates regarding the existence of a "risk society."

YOUNG PEOPLE IN A RISK SOCIETY

Beck (1992) and Giddens (1991) contend that the contemporary experience of society amounts to one of late modernity in which the old scientific world is being challenged, where predictability and certainty become a thing of the past, and where a new set of risks are brought into existence at both a macro- and microscale. As far as young people are concerned, this argument reflects the ways in which, in recent decades, young people's life experiences have become increasingly diversified. A young person shares less and less in way of common biographies with his or her peers. With longer transitions into employment, longer transitions towards adulthood, more postcompulsory education and training, a more complicated mix of part- and full-time employment, a narrower range of employment opportunities, and higher rates of residential mobility, young people have emerged historically with increasingly diverse personal biographies (Roberts, 1995). Young experiences, notably patterns of schooling and routes into the labour market, are therefore argued to be very different to what they were a mere generation ago. This creates a growing sense of insecurity and unease for young people. That is, young people are in an increasingly precarious position where they make important life decisions unsure if they will reap the rewards or pay the penalties for their actions. Youth then, is a period of adaptation and adjustment (Roberts, 1995). A young person may undertake a university career, but there is no guarantee of a professional career afterwards. Young people may, in a sense, be liberated from the traditional support networks of the family, but such forcible emancipation brings with it risks, not least, the risks inherent, in the United Kingdom at least, of a rapidly rising divorce rate, which may in itself undermine a young person's sense of everyday stability (Furlong & Cartmel, 1997).

The argument that consumers are experiencing an increasingly unpredictable social life, appears, at first glance to directly contradict Ritzer's (1993) vision of a highly predictable rationalized world. My argument is that the trends that Ritzer actually describes are far more psychosocially beneficial than he is willing to admit. In effect, as I suggested earlier, Ritzer underestimates the ways in which structures of McDonaldization can be actively negotiated. The structures of McDonaldization are, in this sense, enabling, equally as much as they are constraining. In fact, the individual is constituted in an increasingly global culture which appears to offer a greater diversity of lifestyle choices. McDonaldization amounts to a means by which consumers can begin to assert some sense of control over the *diversity* of modern life.

In this context, Beck (1992) argues that it is possible to identify a new mode of socialisation, a "metamorphosis" or "categorical shift" in the make-up of the relationship between the individual and society. He suggests that in advanced modernity the individual becomes removed from traditional support mechanisms and support relationships, and that consequently the constraints of everyday life, as experienced by the worker and the consumer, take on new significance. Therefore, as Beck (1992) points out, the market comes to play an ever more active role in people's lives. Indeed, it could be argued that mass consumption provides an essential focus for young people in particular, in that they experience risk in its most dramatic form, in as much as questions of identity construction loom especially large during the teenage years. In conditions of late modernity the suggestion here, then, is that the individual is at a permanent disadvantage, in as much as he or she is under constant pressure to manipulate society in ways that will serve his or her reflexive biography. Potentially then, the individual becomes preoccupied with maintaining a particular personal image. Beck (1992) argues that this creates an ego-centred world view on the part of the individual. This opens the individual up to an increased risk of failure, in the sense that any failure is perceived on his or her part as implicating the inadequacies of the individual. Young consumers desperately need to identify aspects of their lives in which they can be reassured about their individuality, whilst enjoying the benefits of a communal social life. Rationalized forms of consumption readily fit the bill. They serve a valuable purpose in shielding young people from the instabilities of the outside world.

At this point it is worth reaffirming the belief underlying this chapter that consumption is "social, relational and active" (Appadurai, 1986, p. 31). It is, "part of the repertory with which users carry out operations of their own" (De Certeau, 1984, p. 31). However, as I will illustrate shortly in a further discussion of aspects of my research, in order to carry out such operations, young people need to have the confidence that what they are doing is a legitimate reflection of the cultural capital of consumption, as perceived by their peers. The adaptable and flexible nature of identity appears to be mirrored by the similar ways in which people use the active nature of consumer goods as a means of structuring social relations. In this context, consumption appears to provide young people with an invaluable source of confidence. This confidence is expressed in various ways, through the significance of fashion and in particular through branded goods as indicators of self-confidence and through the role of peer groups as arbiters of consumption patterns. Consumer meanings are culturally constructed and, as such, amount to an important resource by which young people can communicate and interact with one another. As such, they are also rational, in the sense that such meanings need to be endowed with more than a purely personal investment in order for them to have any value in communal contexts.

By immersing themselves in consumer-led experiences, young people appear to be able to forget about the stresses inherent in the prospects of a dilapidated labour market, divided families, and limited resources. Consumption, which is made possible through part-time employment and parental pocket money, appears to offer some form of an escape; an idea that John Caputo argues, elsewhere in this volume, is equally applicable to the more specific enjoyment children experience in a visit to McDonalds. But the use of the word "escape" should not imply that young people are simply leaving that risk behind. In viewing it in this way consumption could be perceived to be an easy option, a means of avoiding the harsh realities characteristic of an identity crisis. This, I believe, is an oversimplification. More than simply opting out of a risky lifestyle, consumption actually appears to provide young people with a sense of control, a means of offsetting risk. But the irony here is that the risks inherent in social pressures to consume are potentially riskier than everyday experience itself. Young people find themselves in a predicament where, to a large extent, they *have* to consume in particular ways. Ultimately, this does not simply mean that they are controlled, but rather that they choose to trade a sense of individuality for the sense of stability that is offered to them through their consumption habits.

As far as young people are concerned then, the McDonaldization of the sports store can, therefore, actually be perceived to be liberating. Upon entering the sports store the young people I observed were able to forget, indeed, escape from, their everyday concerns. They became immersed in another culture, a culture symbolised by the street life portrayed by MTV. In a world characterised by insecurity and uncertainty as to the future, as well as the present, young people can open this "window of stability" and enter a whole new world—a world in which, regardless of family background or work prospects, they can be treated as equals, in the sense that they have equal access, depending upon resources, to the cultural capital of consumption. In order to develop this argument, I will now focus upon a more specific illustration of the consuming experience—namely, the negotiated construction of meaning in the structured context of retro training shoe provision.

THE EXEMPLAR OF THE RETRO TRAINING SHOE

Shorthand for retrospective or retro-chic, retros are training shoes that originated from North America during the 1950s and which were singled out in Britain in the early 1990s, both as a result of the simplistic styles that they incorporate and because training shoes manufactured any earlier would not have been sturdy enough for modern everyday use (Windsor, 1993). The resurgence of this type of training shoe started in America in the late 1980s. By the early 1990s all the major manufacturers produced their own particular models (e.g., Adidas: "Gazelles," "Sambas"; Puma: "States"; Converse: "All Stars").

Retros were by far and away the best selling training shoes in the sports store in which I conducted my observation. They occupied a prominent position on the stores' shelves and appeared to act as a magnet for incoming customers. According to the manager, the Gazelle accounts for over 5 percent of Adidas's overall sales (a vast amount when you consider that Adidas produces hundreds of models of trainers a year, as well sports clothing, football boots, and so forth), and, in fact, Adidas intentionally avoids flooding the market with Gazelles, in order to maintain demand at a particular level. Adidas thereby avoids the mistake made by Puma towards the end of the 1980s, when Puma flooded the market with "States," thereby undermining their product's cult status (Windsor, 1993). In effect, sports shoe manufacturers actively construct and rationalize what is a captive market. Interestingly, the sports store manager was none too aware of the need to maintain this market: "If everybody buys 'em, nobody'll want 'em in three years time will they?" The sports store in which I conducted my research simply could not keep up with the demand for retro training shoes, but had to maintain that market at a certain controlled level in order to maximize profits. Retro training shoes therefore manage, despite, and arguably because of their apparently uniform and standardized nature, to retain their long term popularity among young consumers.

In as much as there appears to be widespread uncertainty as to the functional or aesthetic qualities of the retro training shoe amongst the consumers I interviewed, the consumption of retro training shoes appears, on the surface, to be peculiarly rationalized. Young people continue to purchase them as a "fashion statement," and the individual investment in such a product appears to be minimal in the sense that the product concerned is universally popular. The actual production of such training shoes is also rationalized in so far as the shoes themselves are constructed in a very standardized fashion. Retros tend to be suede and very plain in design and are usually finished off in bright colours. The rarer the colour the more desirable the shoe, as Windsor (1993) points out. However, the point here would seem to be that rarity is a relative term, in that individual meanings for such rarity can only be applied in the context of the vast numbers of any one model that is available on the market as a whole, at any one time. Originally used as basketball boots, retros are now self-evidently a fashion shoe. They give the minimum of support to the foot, and many customers, trying them on, describe them as uncomfortable, and yet they still buy them (although it must be acknowledged that the occasional customer described their slim fitting as comfortable). In this respect they might be described as "retrograde," a reactionary reversion to the past, whereby the customer actually pays for the *lack* of quality. One customer said that he had bought a pair of Gazelles a mere two years ago, in which time the same model had doubled in price. If anything, the excessive price tag acts as an extra incentive for young consumers to buy the product. In fact, it seems that according to any reasonable measure of quality retro trainers have very little to actually recommend them by.

Herein, however, lies the irony about retro styles. People like them precisely *because* they are standardized and predictable. It is this predictability that has made them so fashionable. It is often not the aesthetic style of the product, or the way in which that product will fulfill them individually, that matters to teenagers, but rather the rationalized meanings which that product is endowed by peers. One customer even said of Gazelles that, "For me they wear out too quick." Consumers are fully aware of the limitations of what it is they are consuming and are actively prepared to trade in the qualities and creativity they might invest in an alternative product if that product can offer them a sense of psychosocial stability. Indeed, one customer, a female in her late teens went as far as to say that, "They wear 'em if they like 'em or not, don't they." Ritzer's conception of McDonaldization is misleading in the sense that young consumers value a sense of predictability as a means a means of easing their passage through the uncertainties of everyday life.

In his discussion of the global credit card society, Ritzer (1995) is critical of postmodern theorists, who would in fact argue that retro styles are symptomatic of the nostalgic playful nature of contemporary consumer culture. There is, I agree, no doubt that such conceptions of playfulness tend to gloss over the global power of companies such as Adidas, Nike, and Reebok. By producing a subtle variation in the number of styles and often colour tones of retro training shoes such companies are able to uphold a vision of post-Fordist consumer-driven markets whilst actually maintaining a Fordist driven ideal of mass consumption in an environment where the supplier is slow to react to the needs of consumers, as I pointed out above. Ritzer might argue that this misleading image of post-Fordist industrial practice merely amounts to a rhetorical device which attempts to camouflage the actual day-to-day effects of McDonaldization. In this sense, it might be tempting to argue that contemporary forms of capitalism are essentially (post)Fordist (i.e., a subtle combination of the two) in that they play on the potential for freedom of choice by creating a superficial impression that a consumer's choice can be expressed by the product he or she purchases when, in the final analysis, individual meanings can only be established in the context of rationalized conformity. From the above point of view, retro styles are symbolic of the adaptable nature of consumer capitalism, that is the way in which it can perpetually identify and adapt to new markets when the need arises. Retro training shoes are Fordist products dressed in post-Fordist clothing. The illusion of choice is inherent in the superficiality of colour schemes which allow the consumer to believe he or she is an individual, when he or she is, in fact, from this point of view being "controlled." There can be no doubt that the global sports goods economy readily exploits the need on the part of young consumers to stabilise their consuming experience.

To take Ritzer's arguments to an extreme then would be to argue that identity cannot, by its very nature, be expressed individualistically, but only according to criteria laid down by fellow consumers, which, in turn, have been determined by the market. The market, in effect, might be seen to encourage consumption by conformity in order to simplify the production process and create long-term demand whilst convincing the consumer of his or her sovereignty. This amounts to a trade-off. The consumer can depend upon the certainty that retro styles of consumption already have historical precedents and therefore represent less of a risk on their part. Such styles already bear the stamp of historical authenticity and thereby boast a ready-made consumer cachet. In turn, retro gear gives the young person the sense that he or she is able, at least to some extent, to usurp the rationalized intent of the marketplace.

MCDONALDIZATION IN CONTEXT

The important point here is that the above is indeed a *trade-off* and in this respect I agree with Martin Parker's contention, elsewhere in this volume, that Ritzer's over-deterministic vision of rationalization is essentially misguided. Ritzer's analysis glaringly overestimates the power of rationalization, simultaneously underestimating the role that individual agency can play in interpreting social structures. Ritzer's approach is simply not subtle enough to explain what Mark Alfino, elsewhere in this volume, calls the "counter-measures of popular and local culture." The relationship young people have with consumer goods amounts to a subtle balancing act between elements of structure and agency and is therefore far more complicated than Ritzer's position allows. What is important here is that young people perceive the ways in which they consume sports goods to be individualistic. Such individualism is negotiated through the communal interpretation of rationalized social structures. Time and time again during my research, respondents acknowledged the fact that the sports goods available to them on the marketplace were essentially limited, offering little more than mass-produced communal acceptance. Young people exploit the so-called limitations of communal forms of consumption and, in this sense, far from a McDonaldized rationalized society robbing an individual of his or her creativity, such a society actively allows him or her to shield that individuality from the potential traumas of overstimulation.

Although, on the one hand, I would argue that much postmodern theory tends to underestimate the rationalized nature of contemporary society (see Mark Alfino's contribution below); on the other, I am suggesting that rationalized forms of consumption are actively used by young people as a means of adjusting to the fluidity of everyday life, of giving such fluidity a constant, though adaptable, focus. The stability engendered by such a focus is an essential ingredient for the construction of a satisfactory sense of identity. Such identity emerges out of a *sense* of control and thus, individuality. As far as the McDonaldization of society is concerned the structures are there; they do provide a framework within which young people conduct their everyday lives. But ultimately those young people construct their own realities within those structures, and such realities are as "real" and important to them in their everyday lives as any more global or structured versions of reality. In effect, "If men [*sic*] define situations as real, they are real in their consequences" (Thomas & Thomas, 1928, p. 572). The everyday reality that stems from the consuming experience for young people is not one of being controlled, but of being *in* control. Ritzer (1993) ignores this at his peril.

In one sense, Ritzer's analysis is correct in that the relationships that young people have with the goods they purchase illustrate that they are essentially modernists—modernists who recognise the breadth of the menu available to them, but pick out what they feel is appropriate in their given circumstances. What is often appropriate is often also McDonaldized, and if as a consequence young consumers lives are happier and more stable, then who is Ritzer to argue otherwise? Many contributors to this volume acknowledge the extent of Ritzer's contribution to the teaching of complex sociological concepts. This much should not be doubted. As for the value of a discussion of rationalization and McDonalidzation to broader theoretical debates, Weber, as Robin Wynyard also notes elsewhere in this volume, can be excused by the fact that the society he analyzed was very different from the one in which we live today. However, I can only conclude by suggesting that, ultimately Ritzer cannot be forgiven for presenting a theory which misunderstands a consumer society in which the complexities of structure and agency are played out and negotiated by consumers throughout the course of their everyday lives.

REFERENCES

Appadurai, A. (1986). Commodities and the politics of value. In A. Appadurai (Ed.), *The social life of things: Commodities in cultural perspective* (pp. 1–63). Cambridge, UK: Cambridge University Press.

Beck, U. (1992). *Risk society: Towards a new modernity*. London: Sage.

De Certeau, M. (1984). *The practice of everyday life*. Berkeley, CA: University of California Press.

Dittmar, H. (1992). *The social psychology of material possessions: To have is to be*. Hemel Hempstead, UK: Harvester Wheatsheaf.

Furlong, A., and Cartmel, F. (1997). *Young people and social change: Individualization and risk in late modernity*. Buckingham, UK: Open University Press.

Giddens, A. (1991). *Modernity and self-identity: Self and society in the late modern age*. Cambridge, UK: Polity.

Ritzer, G. (1993). *The McDonaldization of society: An investigation into the changing character of contemporary social life*. Thousand Oaks, CA: Pine Forge.

Ritzer, G. (1995). *Expressing America: A critique of the global credit card society*. Thousand Oaks, CA: Pine Forge.

Roberts, K. (1995). *Youth employment in modern Britain*. Oxford, UK: Oxford University Press.

Thomas, W. I., and Thomas, D. S. (1928). *The child in America: Behavior problems and programs*. New York: Knopf.

Weber, M. (1958). *The protestant ethic and the spirit of capitalism*. New York: Scribner's (Originally published 1904–5).

Windsor, P. (1993, October 23). But trainers . . . now they're another matter. *The Independent*, p. 36.

5

A Sociology of Rib Joints

Philip D. Holley and David E. Wright, Jr.

INTRODUCTION

Barbeque is fit for presidents and the condemned, and all in between. Ribs were shipped to Washington, D.C., from North Carolina for President Clinton's 1993 inauguration. Clinton, it is reported, "likes food"; and, among his most favorite is "barbecued ribs (from Sim's Bar B Que in Little Rock)" (Booth, 1993, p. 12). Another reported favorite, dating from his adolescence in Hot Springs, is McClard's (Carlton, 1993). According to *Newsweek* (1993, p. 6), Otto's BBQ is former President Bush's favorite Houston restaurant. For his last meal prior to lethal injection, Keith Hatch, Oklahoma death-row inmate, requested ribs (Hatch Requests Ribs, 1996, p. 7).

The contemporary renaissance of grilling, illustrated by the annual rating of restaurants in many cities by newspapers or magazines (*Oklahoma Gazette* 12th Annual Best of Oklahoma City, 1996), including those that serve barbeque, has been such that "grilled food has become an integral part of haute cuisine" (Davis, 1989, p. 6). But, restaurants serving barbeque as the primary entrée numbered fewer than 7,000 in 1986, fewer than 2 percent of all restaurants in the United States (Johnson & Staten, 1988, p. 17). Nevertheless, barbeque restaurants in general and rib joints in specific represent a part of contemporary culture seemingly worthy of close sociological examination.

This research is an ethnomethodological, dramaturgical, and phenomenological analysis of such rib joints, their proprietors, and their patrons.

Ethnomethodology, according to Ritzer (1992, pp. 371–413), primarily involves learning by doing and focuses attention on overt behavior. To this end, we frequented as many rib joints as possible. We have eaten at hundreds of restaurants. The first author estimates that during the last five years he has eaten barbeque in fifteen states and at nearly one-third of the top hundred barbeque restaurants, as judged by Johnson and Staten (1988). The second author estimates he has eaten barbeque in twelve states. We continue to take uninitiated people to these establishments. In all of this, the authors studied locale, menus, recipe books, food, proprietors, patrons, and behavioral practices.

Phenomenology is more concerned with the subjective meanings of events to those involved in them (Ritzer, 1992, pp. 371–413). To determine these meanings, the authors engaged proprietors and patrons in informal, unstructured discussions whenever possible.

Dramaturgical analysis is concerned with the techniques with which a "persona" is created, projected, and maintained (Goffman, 1959). The authors used Goffman's concepts as related to a "front" to describe and distinguish proprietors of rib joints. In all of this qualitative research, the subjects probably never knew they were being studied. The purpose of this research includes an analysis of rib joints as a type of barbeque restaurant within the context of Ritzer's McDonaldization, that is, the increasing rationalization of society. Within this framework, we examine the place of the rib joint in popular culture, exploring the location, architecture, and furnishings of rib joints, the rib-eating ritual, the proprietors, and patrons of rib joints.

FIRE, SMOKE, AND MEAT: HISTORY AND RITUAL

After fire was discovered, it is surmised that barbeque was soon discovered (Johnson & Staten, 1988, p. 4). Spontaneous sharing of the sacrificed animal at the completion of the hunt seems likely (Visser, 1991, p. 229).

While sometimes beneficial, language does not help us much in determining the origins of "barbeque." The French *barbe a que* refers to whole hog cooking. *Barbacoa* refers to a type of cooking in the West Indies, discovered by the Spanish, where game and fish were smoked over an open fire (Johnson & Staten, 1988, p. 5). Europeans were responsible for the diffusion of cooking meat in this fashion, in two respects. First, they brought the pig to the New World, with "literally thousands of pigs on this side of the Atlantic by 1550" (Sokolov, 1991, p. 29). Second, the Spanish both shared their discoveries with Southerners and learned from the Indians with whom they came in contact (Johnson & Staten, 1988, pp. 5, 6).

According to a source cited in Johnson and Staten, the first mention of barbeque in the United States is dated 1610 (1988, p. 198). George Washington's diary for 1769 mentions attending a "barbicue" in Alexandria (Johnson & Staten, 1988, p. 7). In 1822, Charles Lamb, an English essayist, published "A Dissertation upon Roast Pig," a fabled ancient history of barbeque (Johnson & Staten, 1988, p. 4).

Barbeque ultimately migrated to Texas, throughout the American West, and up the Mississippi River to Missouri and points beyond, even as cooking came to be an indoor rather than an outdoor activity, and as cooking increasingly meant subjecting meat to electrically heated elements in ovens, and today, to microwaves.

Outdoor cooking with fire has continued relatively uninterrupted for some pueblo dwellers, such as the Acoma and the Taos. For the rest of Americans, however, Johnson and Staten note two "barbecue booms," the first in the twenties and thirties with auto travel and the other in the post-1950s period with the increase in suburban dwellers and their backyard barbeques (1988, p. 7).

BACKGROUND OF BARBEQUE CULTURE

What is generally considered to be the South and perhaps part of the Southwest and Midwest is overrepresented with barbeque establishments. The region is bounded on the north by Missouri, Kentucky, and North Carolina, Texas and Oklahoma to the west, the Atlantic Ocean on the east, and the Gulf on the south. *Real Barbecue* by Johnson and Staten (1988), which rated the 100 best barbeque restaurants in the United States, discovered 70 of them in the thirteen states in this region.

By contrast, Egerton's discussion of barbeque in the South covered just seven states: Alabama, Arkansas, Georgia, South Carolina, North Carolina, Kentucky, and Tennessee. He found little in Florida, Louisiana, and Mississippi in the way of "barbeque history and tradition" (1987, p. 149).

The hog symbolizes the culture of the South, historically rivaling cotton for its economic value (Bass, 1995). The hog barbeque or festival, however, has had no rival. According to Reed (1990), barbeque is distinctly Southern, despite numerous and deep differences within the South, as it pertains to barbeque. While "(g)rits glue the South together," preference over "barbeque pits Southerners against one another" (Reed, 1990, p. 100). Reed highlights some of the variations within the South:

Barbeque drives a wedge between Texas (beef) and the Carolinas (pork), and completely isolates those parts of Kentucky around Owensboro (mutton). Even porcivores can't agree: barbecue divides western North Carolina (tomato) from eastern North Carolina (no tomato), not to mention from South Carolina (mustard). (1990, p. 100)

Two cities—Kansas City and Memphis—represent the main competitors in the friendly competition for preeminence in barbeque. According to The Kansas City Barbeque Society, barbeque is "part of the mentality" of Kansas City (1989, p. 1). Memphis, though, may well be the Mecca of barbeque. Not only does it boast of having over eighty barbeque restaurants, it also hosts the premier barbeque cooking contest, The Memphis in May World Championship Barbecue Cooking Contest (Wells, 1991, pp. xiii, xv). No other city quite compares to Memphis and Kansas City, although Atlanta has several highly rated commercial establishments, and as mentioned above, Owensboro's mutton barbeque is widely known. Cities like Oklahoma City, while not usually considered significant in any discussion of barbeque, may be deceptive. The authors recently counted over fifty barbeque restaurants in the metropolitan area.

Certainly barbeque, and good barbeque, is found elsewhere, such as in California, Colorado, and Kansas, as noted by Johnson and Staten (1988). It should also be mentioned that where barbeque restaurants exist outside the South, in places like Oakland, California (Floyd and Ila's Oklahoma Style Hickory Bar-B-Que), it is typically Southern folk who operate them (Johnson & Staten, 1988, pp. 154, 155). Daddy Bruce, of Daddy Bruce's Bar-B-Q in Denver, hails from Arkansas (Johnson & Staten, 1988, p. 161). Reed (1990) is at least willing to entertain the possibility that Johnson and Staten's review of barbeque in places like New England is reasonable. However, it is asserted that "nearly all of the great pit-folk come from the South, and most are still in it" (Reed, 1990, p. 101). One exception with which we are familiar is The Hickory Tree, located in Oklahoma City, run by a Bostonian transplanted to Oklahoma (Nachod, 1990).

A TYPOLOGY OF BARBEQUE ESTABLISHMENTS

A barbeque restaurant serves various cuts of beef, pork, chicken, turkey, lamb, or other meat usually cooked by some kind of indirect heat and/or smoke to which has been or can be added a special sauce, as opposed to grilling over a direct flame or heat. Bass (1995, p. 314) identified three types of barbeque establishments: (1) those with black proprietors, (2) upscale restaurants owned by whites, and (3) lower-class white joints. We developed a typology in 1993 (in an earlier version of this research) which took into account variables other than characteristics of the proprietor. We have identified four types of barbeque restaurants:

1. Fancy, upscale restaurants

2. Respectable, ordinary restaurants

3. Fast, temporary, and mobile places

4. Joints

Fancy, Upscale Restaurants

A rather uncommon type of barbeque restaurant is one which lacks the formality of a French or Continental restaurant, yet has rather expensive menu items, interior furnishings not unlike other establishments serving American fare frequented by middle-class diners, and an exterior that is esthetically pleasing. This is the "fancy, upscale restaurant," well illustrated by Rosie's Rib Joint, a very popular restaurant in Tulsa, Oklahoma, serving both beef and pork ribs. In addition to providing huge, disposable bibs for diners, the salad bar includes boiled shrimp and black caviar. In Oklahoma City, the Oklahoma County Line, serves beef and pork ribs in a relatively elegant setting.

Respectable, Ordinary Restaurants

The "respectable" barbeque establishment may be located in a shopping center, in a city or small town, is plain and ordinary in presentation both inside and out, and is perhaps run by a husband and wife. It offers up average fare at average prices, with patrons drawn from locals as well as travelers who stop in on the spur of the moment. This type barbeque restaurant competes with Mexican, Italian, Chinese, pizza specialties perhaps located nearby, as well as fast-food chains, such as McDonald's, Wendy's, Hardee's, Subway, and so on. The city in which we live, Weatherford, boasts of the Barbeque Shed, located in a high-traffic shopping area, heavily depending upon university students, other locals, and travelers who stop in as they pass along I-40. These establishments usually serve different types of meat—beef, chicken—as well as sandwiches, and so on. They may also have drive-up windows.

Fast, Temporary, and Mobile Places

"Fast, temporary, and mobile" barbeque operations display considerable variety and are increasingly common today. Several folk in our area of Oklahoma have mobile operations, with a booth on wheels containing a smoker, or a large portable smoker towed by a pickup, which serves double duty as the office. They are often located in the parking areas of shopping malls or grocery stores, or on main street in a vacant lot. And, they are often found at fairs and community festivals. Such operations may be relocated at intervals or remain in place for a considerable period of time. The service is typically take-out; no seating is available.

A recent "experiment" is the invasion of barbeque into food courts of shopping malls. This represents an attempt at offering barbeque in a "fast-food" fashion. Several malls in Oklahoma City recently had barbeque places in their food courts, blending in with all the other types of food, although none appear to have lasted. In Oklahoma today, some convenience stores retail barbeque, prepared on site, which may be consumed on site or taken out.

Rib Joints

The term "joint" is itself disreputable, sometimes used to refer to prisons or to a marijuana cigarette. The term also applies to certain rib places.

The "rib joint" is a disreputable establishment, judged so by architecture and location, as well as function and ownership. It is relatively rare in the barbeque scene.

The architecture of the typical rib joint is aptly characterized as "bizarrantine," evolving from anything: gasoline station, lean-to shed, backyard workshop, former picnic table, and more (Johnson & Staten, 1988). According to Johnson and Staten, the "original barbeque joint" was a building with "corrugated tin sides, bare concrete floors, and a tin roof," built in "Greasian style" (1988, p. 9). With success over time, additions are built and added on in a hodge-podge fashion. For some barbeque folk, the barbeque business starts in a grocery store, and ultimately takes over. The epitome of the barbeque joint, for Johnson and Staten, is the former fast-food restaurant, out of business, and converted into a barbeque joint

(1988, p. 10). We consider the classic joint to be located in a former service station, such as the original Leo's in Oklahoma City. Other buildings, formerly homes or something else, renovated, added to, and remodeled serve well as barbeque joints. John & Cooks in Lawton, Oklahoma, is housed in a former laundromat.

The bizarreness of the architecture is itself a statement of protest and independence by the rib joint proprietor and by his or her patrons. The style basically seems to say that there is no need for the trappings of the modern eatery. Barbeque proprietor Hubert Holman (now deceased) appears to speak for many when he said, "The fancier the place is, the more people think they have to pay for the building" (Fink, 1992, p. A-11). The building and its furnishings are not what is important.

The joint may share the facility with other enterprises. One place in McAlester, Oklahoma, shares a golf cart sales operation. One of the most unique is Smoklahoma, which has a ranch and farm supply operation along with the barbeque business, in a building that does not look like an establishment that prepares and serves food. Fortunately, it has a walk-up window for take-out orders.

Location and ownership may be considered together. For the barbeque joint, we are considering an establishment located in a remote rural area, a seedy part of town, in a lower-class neighborhood, perhaps in a residential area, off the main route (out of the way), or in a predominantly commercial area of mobile home dealerships or auto body shops. To be a joint, the establishment is typically located in a spot where it is least expected.

Given the location, the owner is often a black man of meager means, but a man with a passion, such as John Bishop Sr., of Dreamland in Tuscaloosa, Alabama. After commercial success was achieved, "Big Daddy" kept the joint in the original location, certainly with no intent to move, although other locations have been added. Or, it may be a white man of questionable reputation or uncertain background, about which rumors abound.

The barbeque joint is typically a single commercial operation, with the owner looking no further than personally supervising or overseeing the "pit" and the business element. Essentially, the owner may not have achieved acclaim that would allow expansion to other locations or, once achieving success, is unwilling to take the risk or make the effort involved with expansion. Or, he or she simply is not interested in business "success." The joint remains at the same level of development over time, envisioned by Whyte (1973) as the first stage of the business cycle: small in size, little division of labor, and no formal organization.

In recent years, it seems as though successful joints have expanded, so that in a city or limited geographical area, several operations are under way, owned and operated by the same person or other family members. Such is the case with Leo's in Oklahoma City. Leo's, one of the most popular barbeque places in Oklahoma City, had expanded to four locations, although only the original and one other remain open currently. In North Alabama, five barbeque places are run by siblings as a result of the earlier work of their now-deceased father, Big Bob Gibson, who began barbequing in 1925. These places are located in the Huntsville-Decatur area (Johnson & Staten, 1988, pp. 25, 26). Dreamland, of Tuscaloosa, Alabama, has opened a place in Birmingham. While the new location appears successful, it is too early to make a determination.

However, at that point of expansion, the joint loses its uniqueness; the "expansions," even when managed by a family member, seldom match the aura or quality of the original. With expansion, more attention than before is given to planning of location, decor, menu, staff, and cost-profit margins; this planning is the antithesis of the original joint and the joint becomes more ordinary and "respectable." Such evolution, whereby original success leads to a rational attempt to place the endeavor on a more routine basis and in the process diminishes the initial creativity, is similar to the treatment on bureaucratization by Weber (1947).

Only barbeque restaurants that feature ribs may be classified as "rib joints." Other cuts will perhaps be served, but ribs represent the basis for the reputation of the joint and the motivating force behind the customers' interest. Furthermore, to be a "real" rib joint in most parts of the country, it must feature pork ribs. For this study, the "rib joint" may also feature beef ribs. A few rib joints specialize in both pork and beef ribs. This ideal type includes the following deviant aspects.

1. A location that is usually difficult to find—as opposed to marketing trends today which emphasize accessibility such that one with routine predictability finds the standard array of fast-food and upscale eateries at every major intersection. It is as if a deliberate attempt were made to prevent people from finding the joint. This joint seldom advertises; patrons learn about it by "word of mouth" and by the occasional "lifestyles" section of some metropolitan newspaper or magazine written by a reporter looking for an "offbeat" story, or by an annual exercise of rating local restaurants. The best rib joints must be searched out. Johnson and Staten (1988) recommend utilizing referrals from locals, such as service station attendants.

2. The location may seem "shady," "suspicious," or "questionable," even to a typical patron. The normal reaction to such locations would be uncertainty, if not fear, as to whether one should be in this part of town or in this neck of the woods. Some relief may be derived from a mixture of vehicles in the parking lot, ranging from the very expensive to the ordinary or dilapidated.

3. A building or facility itself may be of dubious nature, with a run-down exterior, messy woodpile, smokers, and parts scattered around (Johnson & Staten, 1988). The interior should represent a mixture of plain and gaudy, including numerous religious posters, pictures of Jesus and Dr. Martin Luther King, autographed photos of Elvis and other famous and not-so-famous patrons, and calendars on the walls (see Johnson & Staten, 1988, p. 15). This is to be opposed to the brightly lit, spic-and-span atmosphere of the mainstream eatery. The restroom may only minimally meet health department standards, and may even have a portapotty out back, as in the case of Wild Horse Bar-B-Que near Sallisaw, Oklahoma. The furnishings are "odd," perhaps reminiscent of the 1950s era. Soot from the smoker may be visible on the ceiling, fan blades, and other places routinely inaccessible to cleaning. Thus, patrons are left to wonder about health department regulations.

    Some establishments have actually had trouble with the health department. The

New Zion Missionary Baptist Church's Barbeque (Huntsville, Texas) was forced to move indoors when it first opened sixteen years ago (Koidin, 1996, p. E-6).

4. The staff of a rib joint, and especially the proprietor, may seem of a dubious, shady, deviant nature. Such staff may treat patrons, especially first-time patrons, with what appears as indifference.

5. "Regulars" of the rib joint are disdainful of newcomers, especially if these newcomers seem ill at ease or if the novice is "dressed up." Exceptions are made for the more formal dress of the lunch crowd.

6. Service may be either buffet style or at the table. Some barbeque restaurants provide service in cafeteria or buffet style; that is, the customers queue up, place the food and drink order, pay, then wait until the tray is filled before being seated. In contrasting style, and consistent with many restaurants, the customer is seated, a waiter or waitress takes the food and drink order, and once prepared, brings it to the table. Unless there is a salad or soup bar, it is unnecessary for the customer to leave the table until the meal is completed, when it is time to pay and depart.

PHENOMENOLOGY OF THE MEAL AND OF EATING OUT

Eating in General

As Visser (1991) informs us, eating has meaning far beyond satisfying a physiological need. Symbols and meaning pervade meals, whether they occur in homes with family and friends or in restaurants. One who permits others to eat with one's self, allowing them to observe what and how one eats, is admitting these others into a personal or private space, admitting them to what Goffman (1959) terms the "back stage" of one's self where one is supposedly, authentically what one is. Presumably, as one concentrates on the mechanics of eating and on enjoying the food, one is too preoccupied to maintain a false front. Thus, what one eats and one's manners while eating should be reliable indicators of one's personality.

According to Schutz and Luckmann (1973), socialization into a society provides one with "recipes" for dealing with the situations encountered in life. The recipe is a set of instructions for what one is to expect and on how one is to behave—what to do, when, where, and so on. One could argue that our society has standardized the eating-out experience to such an extent that there are standard recipes for what one is to expect in dining out, and the recipes' attendant rules for the patron's behavior in the eatery are widely shared and well known. For eating out, there are two recipes from which to select, either the one appropriate for fast-food eateries, such as McDonald's, or the one appropriate for the more upscale restaurant, such as Steak & Ale. In either case, the patron knows in advance certain rules of etiquette. In the fast-food eatery, emphasis is on a standardized, highly predictable, immediately provided fare which is quickly consumed in a carnivalized atmosphere (Ritzer, 1996). One's order is quickly provided, one quickly consumes it, one quickly buses one's waste, and one quickly leaves. It is also worthy of note that fast-food eateries tend to cater to children; by contrast, ribs are considered "adult" food. In the upscale restaurant, the principles are essentially the same as in the fast-food eatery; however, the upscale restaurant places more emphasis on and expects more in the way of social decorum or dressing up and minding one's table manners.

Most notable as part of the socialized recipes for eating are contemporary table manners with elaborate rules requiring the use of plates, spoons, forks, and other implements, in order to prevent touching food with hands. Visser states "One of the most spectacular triumphs of human 'culture' over 'nature' is our own determination when eating to avoid touching food with anything but metal implements" (1991, p. 167).

Furthermore, diners are expected to use napkins to clean both fingers and the mouth. According to Visser, "licking fingers is either sternly forbidden or allowed only if certain constraints are applied" (1991, p. 176). With exceptions for children, those who violate such rules are considered "polluted," subject to sanctions, including public disgust and embarrassment (Visser, 1991, pp. 299–303).

The Rib Joint Experience

The eating of meat from the ribs of various animals in restaurants that feature such food both delights and intrigues us. Why is this, since the rib is far from a preferred cut of meat? To the extent that health matters are relevant and to the extent that we are talking about pork ribs, ribs are not for the seriously health-conscious person. Furthermore, ribs are bony and require other than acceptable table manners to extract the meat from the bone. Eating ribs is a greasy and messy enterprise.

Undoubtedly, the attraction of barbeque combines the effect of fire on the meat, the darkening effect of smoke and sometimes burning from direct flames or burning sauce, the smoke and sauce flavoring the meat, and the meat made tender and easily removed from the bone. It may well incorporate a unique style of preparation, dependent on the experience, ability and passion of the pit-boss. Even with a desire for consistency in outcome, unpredictability from one time to the next may reign supreme. Further, there are elements of mystery in that ingredients of the sauces are matters of extreme secrecy. Patrons will inevitably speculate regarding unique ingredients, while certain ones—tomato, mustard, vinegar, and/or honey—may be readily apparent.

The recipes for everyday eating fail the patron of a rib joint, especially the novice, as a rib joint is neither a fast-food eatery nor an upscale restaurant, even when the restaurant may be an upscale one such as Rosie's. In this new—we suggest "deviant"—situation, the novice must abandon the old recipes for eating out and create or learn a new one. In this, one can expect the novice to be uncomfortable and probably not to enjoy the first experience in a rib joint. Even some enlightened whites feel out of place in a rib joint surrounded by blacks. Not unlike Becker's (1953) novice who learns to enjoy marijuana only with practice, the novice in a rib joint must learn to enjoy the experience, with backyard barbeque experiences serving as only partial preparation for the joint experience.

In the ideal type rib joint, there is often no menu to be leisurely examined and reviewed. The sometimes impatient waiter/waitress recites a jargon-filled menu that must typically be explained and repeated so that one simply can be sure of what one is hearing. The novice either blindly selects something or is assured by a regular ribber or waiter/waitress to "trust me" on a particular order. In other joints, the menu is posted on the wall, with little in the way of item description or explanation.

Absent are menu items for children; unless they eat ribs, they are out of place. The ideal rib joint is not prepared to serve children and either serves them regular meals, allows children to eat off their parents' plates, or improvises on the spot. Rib eating is for "adults."

There is no fast food in a rib joint. The food arrives as dictated by the desire of the proprietor or by the dictates of cooking the ribs, which "takes as long as it takes" (Wells, 1991, p. xxi). Furthermore, when the ribs run out, nothing else can substitute, since there are no other entrée items on the menu.

Dining with others is a social occasion which, as with all social occasions, is an experience to be given significance by the participants. Ordinarily, when dining, one goes to great lengths to put on social airs so as to impress others with one's accomplishments. Dress is formal. And, great emphasis is placed on "good manners." In many eating situations, there is an established hierarchy of persons, enforced subtly but rigidly in terms of who is served first, served the better portions, and whose opinions of the meal are most important. In short, dining is an occasion in which to create and demonstrate invidious comparisons among people in terms of respectability (Veblen, 1899). In such a situation, the interests of diners seems to be other than the food itself. Alternatively, especially in fast-food eateries, dining becomes a safe and routinized activity with no special meaning beyond merely providing sustenance.

None of this is true in ribbing. First, the basics of fire-cooked meat brings to mind something of a dangerous experience, as wryly noted by Rita Rudner in her observation that men do not "cook." They barbecue. "Men will cook as long as danger's involved" (Carter, 1992, p. 4). Second, a rib meal is anything but routinized and fast, as indicated elsewhere. Further, in its very essence, a rib meal is antisnob, antiyuppie, antihierarchical. Traditionally, a meal wholly or primarily of meat is a sign of egalitarianism among the select few who together partake of the meal (Visser, 1991). Such a meal meant a time of celebration, a special occasion. The rib meal, consisting of the basics of fire-cooked meat, is interpreted by many ribbers as a return to "primal. Basic" (Kansas City Barbeque Society, 1989, p. 3), a return to times before status hierarchies became institutionalized and the practice of eating became cluttered with "manners" and a seemingly endless variety of equipment.

Ribbing is an "earthy" experience. It is difficult if not impossible to pretend to be better than others with food in one's hand, grease and sauce on one's mouth and hands, wearing a bib, and/or a napkin stuck in the neck of one's shirt.

The rib joint's fare itself is messy. And, even with the improvements in pork quality, it is in opposition to the current "health food" craze which emphasizes small and infrequent helpings of low-fat, well-cooked meat. The meal in a rib joint emphasizes the meat, not the vegetables or desserts (Visser, 1991); indeed, it is permissible to have beverage and ribs only. Dreamland serves pop or beer, white bread, and ribs—that is all. Further, ribs are fatty—which is to be eaten (Visser, 1991)—and juicy.

It is difficult to have what most etiquette books would consider to be "bad table manners" in a rib joint. One is expected to have a "dirty-fingers, greasy mouth, crunchy-bone experience" (Friedland, 1984, p. 13). In a rib joint, one eats with one's hands; puts one's elbows on the table; wears a bib or even places a napkin in one's shirt or uses many paper towels as napkins (from a paper towel roll prominently displayed on the table); gets one's face smeared, passes food from one person to another and/or from one plate to another; smacks one's mouth; exclaims loudly about how good the food is; licks one's fingers and lips so as not to miss a drop of meat, juice, and sauce; and freely and openly uses toothpicks. As one eats, one begins to stack the gnawed-bare bones in a pile on the table, clearly as a trophy of one's accomplishments. In short, one must unlearn "good table manners." Neither Julia Child nor Emily Post—both of whom would heartily disdain rib table manners—are likely to show up for a meal at a rib joint.

Given the above, it should be easy to understand that one does not "dress up" for a rib joint. Dress frequently serves to quickly identify the novice and also further to give the regulars a perhaps "shady" look. Coats and ties, white clothing, numerous rings, necklaces, bracelets are inappropriate—they get in the way of eating. Caps and hats are correct—and they *are* to be worn at the table!

Part of the meaning of ribbing is counter to modern society; it is a rebellious act. Further, it is an act imbued with a "we against the world" attitude, or at least a "we against the 'straights,'" that is to say against those who do not "do ribs." In doing ribs, one is among other things thumbing one's nose at mainstream society. Ribbers see themselves as independent from mainstream customs, free from the need to be well thought of. Lastly, there develops among ribbers an ethnocentrism, an aloofness toward the outside world, to those who put on airs, and toward those who eschew ribs. Ribbers are smug in their knowledge that they understand what truly fine food and good eating are. Simultaneously, ribbers pity and ridicule those not initiated to ribs.

THE RIB JOINT PROPRIETOR

There are few true "individualists" any longer, but the rib joint proprietor may qualify. Typically the proprietor is something of a reprobate, someone who has chosen to avoid or leave the mainstream of typical employment and working for someone else, having chosen to enter one of the most failure prone of businesses, the food-services business. Further, he is in a business little known and little appreciated by the society at large, as evidenced by the small number of rib joints in the United States—6,412 of them according to the Restaurant Consulting Group

(Johnson & Staten, 1988). To open a rib joint would seem like "risky business" indeed. However, success in the common sense seems not to be the major motivating force. While not opposed to financial success, most rib joint proprietors appear to be motivated more by a desire to get out of the mainstream and by the desire to provide a good meal for their patrons. These proprietors are interested in maintaining their "good name" (Fink, 1992). Many, like Holman of the "Wild Horse Bar-B-Que" joint, refuse to do what would be necessary for fame and fortune, choosing instead to serve friends and to enjoy oneself (Fink, 1992). In this, most rib joint proprietors have a demeanor that seems to say "take me as I am—I am not changing; if I cannot make it as I am, I will do something else."

A shady character, the proprietor is often shrouded in mystery, rumor and myth, perhaps more so to occasional patrons and to even the addicts than to the regular patrons, many of whom might be drawn from the neighborhood or from among acquaintances who may know what he is really like. Stories, told and retold, abound about his dealings. Exactly how much truth there is to these stories is uncertain. It is likely there is some embellishment, not altogether to the displeasure of the proprietor. It is also unlikely that such stories and others about the character—present and past—of the proprietor will keep the patrons away, if the ribs are worth eating.

The proprietor is more often a "he" than a "she." Red's of Orlando, Florida, is a notable female exception (Johnson & Staten, 1988, pp. 37, 38). Feedie Smith, who ran a place for a while called Feedie's Barbeque, was at one time married to Leo of Leo's in Oklahoma City (Nachod, 1993). Several Kansas City places have female owners, managers, pit-bosses, or co-owners with their husbands. "Amazing Grace" Harris is the pit master for the Grand Emporium. Marty's Bar-B-Q is owned by Jean Tamburello, a woman.

He is usually black, but may be of poor white Southern stock, or even an immigrant. Abe, of Abe's in Clarksdale, Mississippi, a Lebanese, began barbequing in 1924 (Johnson & Staten, 1988, pp. 64, 65). Werner, of Werner's Specialty Foods in Kansas City, is a German immigrant (Powers, 1992, p. 89).

At best a marginal person, the proprietor has the ability to interact with and serve those of varying socioeconomic and ethnic backgrounds, and to make the dining experience an enjoyable one, to which many return. Usually serving as owner, manager, cashier, waiter, and cook (or pit-boss), the proprietor presents himself to the customer in active, multiple, and unique ways.

He has a certain confidence and air that most other restaurateurs do not have. One rule intimately known by ribbers is "call first." Rib joints are notorious for opening and closing at odd hours (Biskupic, 1985). In many joints, the proprietor prepares a certain number of slabs of ribs per day—when those are sold, the doors are closed. Often the owner will close the joint for a month or so while on vacation, fully expecting the clientele to return when he is ready to get back to work. McClard's of Hot Springs, closes for about three weeks from before New Year's to the middle of January. Slick (of Slick's of Muskogee, Oklahoma) will close on the spur of the moment, if he "just feels like it," often on Saturday at the peak of business. Roy's of Chickasha, Oklahoma, regularly closes at 7:00 p.m., even on Fridays and Saturdays, just as most restaurants are beginning their evening rushes. Ken's Restaurant (Amber, Oklahoma) is open "only four hours a day, three days a week." (Speer, 1993, p. 19).

The rib joint proprietor possesses a passion, a vision, a method, and a secret. The passion is for ribs—real barbeque. His vision is to serve up the best ribs there are, and on a regular basis. The method he has perfected over time, combining particular woods, a certain type of smoker, the application of a marinade, a rub and/or sauce, particular cuts of meat, involves slow cooking with periods of doing nothing interspersed with the attention and care of a perfectionist. Sauces, sometimes invented by the pit-boss, and at other times inherited from family members or friends, represent a crowning achievement. Unique sauces, such as Arthur Bryant's in Kansas City, Dreamland's in Tuscaloosa, Gridley's in Memphis, and Craig's in Devalls Bluff, Arkansas, have certain ingredients as carefully guarded secrets. Unique dry rubs—Angelo's in Fort Worth and the Iron Works in Austin—maintain ingredients as mysterious. Once the ribs are pulled from the smoker, pronounced ready, with sauce available, the work of the proprietor has been accomplished.

When the rib joint proprietor dies (or for some reason closes the operation), the continuation of the joint is not at all certain. Sauce secrets may be taken to the grave. Children or other employees may have neither the skill, experience, or passion possessed by the proprietor. Food quality may not be consistent with that of the founder. Or, there may be conflict among spouses, children, other relatives, and others over ownership, control, and management of the joint, as in the case of the Wild Horse Bar-B-Que (Fink, 1993). These factors seem to explain the tenuous life of the rib joint.

RIB JOINT PATRONS

Ritzer (1996, pp. 177–179) delineates three types of people based on their attitudes and behavior toward "McDonaldization." The typology is derived from Weber's concerns about the consequences of rationalization and, as applied to eateries, is adapted here to help distinguish the patrons of rib joints. The first type refers to those who view the consequences of rationalization as constituting a "velvet cage" connoting that these patrons like McDonald's and welcome it. The second view the consequences as a "rubber cage" with both advantages and disadvantages from which they occasionally and temporarily seek escape. The third group shares with Weber the belief that the disadvantages are more numerous and are similar to an ever-expanding "iron cage" from which ultimately there may be no escape. The velvet cagers always eat at the McDonald's of the modern world, the rubber cagers eat there during the work week and when pressed for time, and the iron cagers never eat there and are fearful that McDonald's will soon be the only type of eatery available.

The velvet cagers would of their volition never select a rib joint. Such persons, when found in rib joints, arrive reluctantly, in the company of others who persuaded them against their "better judgment," and are unlikely to return again.

These people are not likely to order ribs, unless there is nothing else on the menu; if they have ribs, they may attempt to cut the meat from the bone and consume the meat with a fork. These patrons are noticeably uncomfortable and consider rib joints as barbaric and archaic. They are people who do not want eating and dining to be an adventure.

Patrons who are in the rubber cage category are like "weekend warriors," looking for an alternative to the ho-hum routine of the week and who are discontent with certain features of the fast-food eateries. They are willing to risk some uncertainty in finding alternatives—on occasion. While frequenting "barbeque restaurants," these patrons may also wander into a rib joint by accident but are adventurous enough to brave the deviant (or is it, in their eyes, "cute"?) aspects of the joint to stay and try the main dish. Such patrons will even follow the local custom of throwing good table manners to the winds and dine in appropriate rib fashion; in short, they enjoy themselves. Such rubber cagers may return on more than one occasion and bring others with them. However, these people view ribbing as a sometime thing to do when one has time and as only one of numerous alternatives to fast-food eateries. Lastly, rib joint patrons of this second type do not qualify as the ideal type patron in that they remain attached to the highly rationalized fast-food eateries and do not internalize an image of themselves as being first and foremost rib connoisseurs.

It should be noted that the rubber cagers are both boon and bane to the rib joint proprietor. On the one hand, they constitute a healthy portion of the joint's clientele, help to popularize particular joints, and introduce first timers who may eventually become aficionados. On the other hand, these patrons tend truly not to understand the culture and significance of rib joints and from time to time contaminate the joint with culture from the outside world; examples would be for these patrons, who have dined in the joint on occasion, to believe that the proprietor is indebted to them, to expect that they can make special requests, or for them to be in a hurry. Further, by popularizing the joint, the rubber cagers may serve, unintentionally, to destroy the joint by making it too successful.

The third type of patrons are those who view the McDonald's of the world as anathema—pure disaster. As patrons of rib joints, these people do so by choice—indeed, the rib joint is the first thought when eating out occurs. These regulars view themselves as "ribbers" or "rib addicts" and thoroughly delight in the ambiance, decor, food, and manners (or lack thereof) of the joint. These people also differ from the previous type in that for the true rib joint patron, eating here is not a sometime affair to be done when one happens to think about it or when one has enough time. The true patron *always* thinks first of ribs and makes time for them. These patrons are like "sojourners" who "pine for the old days" (Tsai & Palmer, 1977) and view themselves as out of touch with the modern, as alienated from modern food culture. They do not necessarily romanticize the past, but they prefer it when it comes to dining. Further, these patrons view the velvet cagers with disdain and the rubber cagers with wariness. True patrons may even attempt to discourage the first timers or velvet cagers from staying or returning. The wariness toward the rubber cagers is because of the possibility that they may overpopularize the joint, or make it so successful that the joint and proprietor become upscale.

Although the rib addict will eat elsewhere and does enjoy other types of food, he thinks first of the rib joint when time to eat and will not stay away for long. The authors know of one aficionado who recently consumed five barbeque meals at five different rib joints—all in the same day! Another characteristic of the addict is that he and/or she is as if on a search for the Holy Grail, an impossible search for the perfect meal; the rib addict, no matter how many rib meals consumed, believes the perfect rib meal has yet to be barbequed. Johnson and Staten ate in 689 barbeque establishments looking for the perfect barbeque meal (1988, p. 18). The true addict is further distinguished from other eaters as someone who truly enjoys food and concentrates on the details of the meals; this is someone who does not eat just for sustenance, but eats because of the pleasure it brings. In this, the addict is attentive of his company because the ideal rib meal includes equally appreciative partners. Ribbing means joy and freedom from the everyday world. Egerton refers to finding "ecstasy in ribs," an allusion to what is achieved from religious zealousness (1987, p. 149). And, for the addict, ribbing is a self-satisfying and secret protest action against modernity and conventionality. Lastly, the true rib addict views his kind as standard bearers for an honorable and endangered way of life.

THE FUTURE OF THE RIB JOINT

In sum, the rib joint and a rib meal are anachronisms. The very nature of the rib joint makes it unlikely that ribbing will catch on as has Mexican and Italian dining. Franchises, drive-in windows, faster service, and so on, may all find their way into fringes of the rib culture. Barbeque establishments may be located in malls. However, the uniqueness of the food, the proprietor, and the patrons guarantees restricted popularity and limited expansion.

Table manners that permit one to touch the meat with his or her hands are unlikely ever to be made appropriate in most other restaurants. While table rules have been changed in the past, requiring for example the use of the fork, there is no reason to believe that the use of one's hands in the eating of steak would ever be acceptable in a Steak and Ale. (Rules do permit touching chips or tacos in Mexican restaurants, and bread in other restaurants, but, of course, not meat.) Furthermore, it is questionable as to whether eating food high in fat content, such as pork, will be acceptable, especially in the context of the health kick we are now experiencing. Also, it is unlikely that the proprietor of the rib joint would conform to the extent that the rib joint becomes a conventional restaurant. One reason someone becomes a rib joint proprietor is because of being unable to conform to the role of proprietor of a regular restaurant.

The evolution of the rituals in dining seem increasingly to emphasize a style involving attention to neatness and the use of numerous utensils and vessels, all the antithesis of the ideal rib joint and rib meal. And, the subculture of the rib joint will be resisted to the extent that there appears to be a permanent swing toward increased health consciousness in the population. The rib meal hardly qualifies as "health food," and as a mainstay of a diet would surely cause most health professionals to scream. There is also the possibility that animal rights activists could discover the rib joint as a target, attacking the rib meal in defense of the pigs, steers, and sheep.

The steady pace of modernization with its emphasis on speed, efficiency, impersonalization, and processing is another source of concern for the rib joint subculture. The very success of some rib joints has caused some proprietors and some business people (ever attentive to making a buck) from outside the subculture to attempt "rationalizing" the rib meal and to make of it the next "McDonald's." Were the rib joint given too much attention, were it to be mass marketed and mainstreamed, the rib joint as described here would die. In this light, the true rib addict must view "guides to good barbeque joints" and the currently popular barbeque cookoffs ambivalently: recognition of what the addict knew all along as a good thing, but something which brings too much of Madison Avenue into the process. As many aficionados have declared, too much fame for a rib joint is not a good thing. The same concern often follows television or newspaper publicity.

But, it is our prediction that the rib joint will persist. We further predict that the rib joint will remain outside the mainstream food culture. There may be cycles of increasing and decreasing popularity for barbeque "restaurants," but the rib joint will remain a subculture phenomenon as somewhat deviant, as something that raises eyebrows in the mainstream polite society.

A major factor in the perpetuation of the rib joint is the modernization process and its tendency to "McDonaldize" everything it touches. Rib joints are out-of-step anachronisms, throw backs to other times, like the "mom and pop" corner stores with their more personalized and less mechanized, less standardized services. To the extent there is a backlash to the modern, whether this backlash is for only the weekend experiment or as a way of life, rib joints will find a niche in the effort to correct for the alienating effects of modernity. To the extent that poor, yet entrepreneurial men and women are produced in this culture, the rib joint will persist.

Further, as we understand them, rib joints constitute a subculture the members of which have a strong sense of personal identification with its components, which includes a geographical or regional factor. To be a true rib addict is to some extent to identify with the South; to be a Southerner is to know about rib joints and to be more likely than non-Southerners to be appreciative of ribs. As Southerners are always having identity crises (King, 1975) and must therefore devote more attention than others to who they are by defining their uniqueness, we believe Southerners, blacks and whites together, will include room for keeping the rib joint alive as part of what sets them apart from "Yankees" (everyone not from the South). Long live the rib joint!

REFERENCES

Averill, E. (1991, November 9). Wood is the word for best barbecue, say winners. *Tulsa World*, p. C2.

Bass, S. J. (1995, Spring). 'How 'bout a hand for the hog': The enduring nature of the swine as a cultural symbol in the south. *Southern Cultures*, *1*(3), 301–320.

Becker, H. S. (1953). Becoming a marihuana user. *American Journal of Sociology*, *59*, 235–242.

Biskupic, J. (1985, February 3). Pigging out at the pitts during barbecue binge turns up state's finest. *Daily Oklahoma*, pp. 1A, 13A.

Booth, W. (1993, January 25-31). A southerner? Don't bet your grits on it. *The Washington Post National Weekly Edition*, p. 12.

The Bushes go home: A guide to life after Washington. (1993, January 25). *Newsweek*, p. 6.

Carlton, M. (1993). Seeking a president's roots. *Southern Living*, *28*(5), 42, 43.

Carter, C. (1992, November 29). But I didn't know if I'd be good. *Parade Magazine*, *29*, 4–5.

Davis, H. (1989). *Great grilling*. New York: Weidenfeld and Nicholson.

Denzin, N. (1970). Rules of conduct and the study of deviant behavior: Some notes on the social relationship. In J. Douglas, (Ed.), *Deviance and respectability* (pp. 120–159). New York: Basic.

Egerton, J. (1987). *Southern food: At home, on the road, in history*. New York: Knopf.

Fink, J. (1992, October 10). Sun sets on wild horse: Famed sallisaw barbecue joint closes doors. *Tulsa World*, pp. A-11, A–26.

Fink, J. (1993, April 14). Family feud means more "q." *Tulsa World*, pp. C1, C2.

Fisher, M. (1991). *Best barbeque recipes*. Phoenix, AZ: Golden West.

Friedland, S. R. (1984). *Ribs: Over 80 all-American and international recipes for ribs and fixings*. New York: Harmony.

Goffman, E. (1959). *The presentation of self in everyday life*. Garden City, NY: Doubleday.

Hatch requests ribs for last meal. (1996, August 5). *Daily Oklahoman*, p. 7.

Johnson, G, & Staten, V. (1988). *Real barbecue*. New York: Harper & Row.

Kansas City Barbeque Society. (1989). *The passion of barbeque*. Kansas City, MO: Pig Out.

King, F. (1975). *Southern ladies and gentlemen*. New York: Bantam.

Koidin, M. (1996, July 13). Divine barbeque puts Texas a little closer to heaven. *Tulsa World*, p. E–6.

Kurian, K. (1990, June 24). Brain food. *Dallas Life Magazine*, 21, 22.

Nachod, N. (1990, November 21). Yankee proves ingenuity by serving up some fine southern-style, ribs, fixin's. *Oklahoma Gazette*, pp. 17, 18.

Nachod, N. (1993, February 25). Barbecue lovers flocking to Feedie's despite confusion of quick relocation. *Oklahoma Gazette*, p. 14.

National live stock and meat board and national pork board. (1991). *Focus on Pork* (revised). Chicago: National live stock and meat board and national pork board.

Oklahoma Gazette 12th annual best of Oklahoma City. (1996, August 22). *Oklahoma Gazette*, pp. 20–39.

Pope, T. (1991). *Barbecue on my mind*. Atlanta, GA: Cherokee.

Powers, R. (1992). *BBQ pocket guide*. Kansas City, MO: Pig Out.

Reed, J. (1990). *Whistling dixie*. Columbia, MO: University of Missouri Press.

Ritzer, G. (1992). *Sociological theory* (3rd ed.). New York: McGraw-Hill.

Ritzer, G. (1996). *The McDonaldization of society: An investigation into the changing character of contemporary social life* (Rev. ed.). Thousand Oaks, CA: Pine Forge.

Schutz, A., & Luckmann, T. (1973). *The structure of the life world.* Evanston, IL: Northwestern University Press.

Sokolov, R. (1991). *Why we eat what we eat.* New York: Summit.

Solomon, C. (1990). *Gourmet grilling.* New York: Perigee.

Speer, B. (1993, September/October). Mystic spareribs. *Oklahoma Today*, pp. 19, 20.

Tsai, Y., & Palmer, C. E. (1977). Modern 'sojourners' in an American city: A case study of a group of illegal Chinese immigrant restaurant workers. In H. P. Chalfant, E. Curry, & C. E. Palmer, (Eds.), *Sociological stuff* (pp. 106–116), Dubuque, IA: Kendall/Hunt.

Veblen, T. (1899). *The theory of the leisure class: An economic study of institutions.* New York: The Macmillan.

Visser, M. (1991). *The rituals of dinner: The origins, evolution, eccentricities, and meaning of table manners.* New York: Penguin.

Weber, M. (1947). *The theory of social and economic organization.* (A. M. Henderson, & T. Parsons, Trans.) New York: Free Press (Original work published prior to 1920).

Wells, C. (1991). *Barbeque great Memphis style: Great restaurants; great recipes; great personalities.* Kansas City, MO: Pig Out.

Whyte, W. (1973). The social structure of the restaurant. In A. Birenbaum, & E. Sagarin (Eds.), *People in places: The sociology of the familiar* (pp. 244–256). New York: Praeger.

6

Old Wine in New Bottles: Critical Limitations of the McDonaldization Thesis—The Case of Hospitality Services

Roy C. Wood

The main theme of this essay is that the so-called "McDonaldization" thesis of Ritzer (1993; 1996) has caused unwarranted academic excitedness and, far from celebrating and embracing Ritzer's nostrums, caution and restraint should be exercised in the interpretation and application of his ideas. In seeking to maintain this position throughout what follows, there will be no extensive rehearsal or deconstruction of Ritzer's analysis: familiarity with the claims and arguments of *The McDonaldization of Society* and its antecedents in the work of Weber is assumed. Rather, the approach taken here has two dimensions. The first of these is an attempt to place Ritzer's work in a specific analogous context and in so doing to demonstrate that the novelty value of his arguments have been exaggerated and are seriously flawed. This context is supplied by particular reference to the relatively contemporaneous work of Harry Braverman, whose book *Labor and Monopoly Capital* (1974) has thus far demonstrated itself to be extensively influential in academic debates about rationalisation. The second dimension to the approach taken in this essay is to relate the foregoing concerns to a specific case—namely the hospitality industry. Since the very term "McDonaldization" emanates, as it were, from this source, and constitutes the phenotype of Ritzer's model of analysis, this seems an especially salient empirical locus to expand upon in any effort to evaluate the likely durability—and indeed utility—of McDonaldization as a concept and framework for analysis. The main purpose in pursuing these lines of enquiry is to offer some justification for the view that Ritzer's thesis is primarily of illustrative rather than analytic use in understanding processes of social and economic rationalisation and to suggest that Ritzer's McDonaldization thesis represents little more than "old wine in new bottles."

THE FRUIT ON THE VINE

As Weber amply demonstrates, the rationalisation of social life, its fragmentation and reconstitution in diverse forms, has been a major concern of social science from the very first. In contemporary social science and the humanities, explicit concerns about rationalisation as a process of modernity have found—somewhat insubstantial—form in the obsessive and increasingly abstract debates about postmodernism and postmodernity where any idea of reality (except, of course, the reality of texts on postmodernism) is rejected and where many traditional concerns of social scientific research—class, poverty, gender inequality—are flatly denied, or consigned to the status of circulating ciphers in a meta-universe that not even a drug-crazed genius could conceptualise on one of their wilder trips (see Hassard and Parker, 1993, a particularly helpful sceptical collection of essays with more than a passing relevance to the topic of "McDonaldization"; Lash and Urry, 1994; Wood, 1994a). Although—and certainly from a UK perspective—it may seem that of late, scholars of the postmodern have had it all their own way, this is to obscure the work of writers who, with a certain irony in some cases, have pursued in the most general sense Merton's prescriptions for "theories of the middle range"—conceptual schema that fuse overt but precisely defined theorising with a certain amount of empirical groundedness.

One such case is the Marxist Harry Braverman whose world view is not particularly Mertonian in outlook. Braverman is nevertheless responsible for one of the most stimulating works of social science of the last thirty years. Consider the following. In 1974, Braverman published *Labor and Monopoly Capital* (henceforth *LMC*), a succinct restatement of many of the arguments of Marx's *Das Kapital* wrought around a variety of forms of empirical evidence concerned primarily with the labor process in industrial production. Not only was *LMC* succinct, but it was accessible, intelligible to almost any generally well-educated layperson. *LMC* was also populist in tone and style: it made Marx and Marxism appear attractive while at the same time tapping into a central concern of the *zeitgeist* of many advanced Western industrial nations, namely the degradation of work, and of workers, and the relegation of the latter to the status of relative automata. With no stake in capitalism other than the need to sell their labour power to ensure subsistence, workers face a lifetime of soulless employment, pawns in a capitalist system predicated on dubious morality and certain exploitation. The labor process, subject to the Taylorist excesses of scientific management, and especially the separation of conception from execution in work, with the latter the province of most manual laborers, represents for Braverman the engine of rationalisation in the modern workplace. Although Braverman focuses principally upon manual labor in the manufacturing sector, his arguments are clearly intended to have a wider application, and he gives some indications of the extent to which the capitalist labor process has affected the nonmanual work of managers and supervisors to a similar extent to that of "ordinary" workers, as well as some interesting and underrated discussions of the degradation of service work, of which more later.

Now consider *The McDonaldization of Society* (henceforth *TMS*). Appearing nearly twenty years after *LMC*, *TMS* offers a vigorous restatement and a very particular interpretation of another classical sociologist's views, this time Weber on rationalisation. Again, the main arguments of the book are intertwined with different forms of empirical evidence concerned with rationalisation in both the fields of production and consumption. *TMS* is succinctly written and the author's declared aim is, indeed, to make his work accessible to the intelligent layperson. *TMS* is populist in tone and style, again tapping into generalised concerns about the reduction of "culture" and experience to the lowest common denominator, processes over which the majority have little control or little desire for control because the structure and tempo of advanced capitalist societies lends a virtuousness to rationalisation in terms of the (positive) values attached to efficiency, quantifiability, predictability, and control—the four horsemen of the McDonaldization apocalypse.

To generalise the implied similarities between the work of Braverman and Ritzer, it can be said that both

- fuse scholarship and contemporary social preoccupations with a moral concern for their subject matter: both works represent a form of social scientific—and particularly sociological—analysis that has become increasingly unfashionable as sociology has become ever more professionalized and preoccupied with internal theoretical debates;

- have a clear vision of their respective theses and a desire to communicate this vision beyond the academic community, a strategy which makes for immensely readable texts;

- draw on the work of classical sociologists as a form of analytical justification for interpreting the recent past and present; and

- explore a tension between production and consumption in capitalist societies, the forms that each take, and the influence they have upon human experience.

In the following discussion, these issues will be elaborated with a particular emphasis upon the last, which is at the nub of the present comparison and constitutes the locus around which some empirical debate has begun to stir.

THE PRESSING OF THE GRAPE

In the relative emphasis given to production and consumption, Braverman is undoubtedly the one who lends greatest weight to the former: his remarks on consumption are cursory, relative to his main narrative. For a parallel consideration of contemporary consumption in this Marxist context, one is thrown back on the work of the "Frankfurt" school of Adorno and Horkheimer. If anything, the situation with Ritzer is the reverse, he is less single-minded in respect of the focus on production. Outside of his summary of Weberian rationality, Ritzer touches on Taylorization, Fordism and Post-Fordism and even, in a nod to the current mainstream of sociological endeavour, postmodernism. However, his main focus is consumption rather than production, or more precisely, the effects of production on consumption. Certainly there are many references to different aspects of production in Ritzer's work but they tend to be highly generalised just as Braverman's remarks on consumption show a more relaxed grip than in his analysis of the productive relations of capitalism.

Why is all this important? The answer lies in the intensity of each author's narrative, an intensity that largely derives from the aforementioned moral dimension to each writer's work and which, despite different starting points, *leads them to the same conclusions*. In both instances, the morality is a negative morality: Braverman clearly loathes capitalism in the same way Ritzer despises McDonaldization (despite an almost seemingly self-serving mission to promote the idea of McDonaldization's ubiquity, much of the latter's book is determined to warn off its readership, Ritzer even suggesting examples of how this might be— and in certain cases is—achieved). Both writers are routinely pessimistic about the possibility of resistance to rationalisation and both invoke what Braverman alone pursues as "habituation," that is, the incorporation of challenges to the prevailing hegemony within the capitalist system, hence neutering resistance. Thus are Braverman's and Ritzer's narratives driven. From separate starting points they arrive at similar analytic destinations: production and consumption under capitalism have been degraded, as have producers and consumers. In this light it is difficult to see why we should accord Ritzer's work any privileged status.

Contemporary sociological debates have eschewed the (always) erroneous view that Weber's approach to the study of society is in inimical opposition to that of Marx: differences in the emphasis both writers place on different social processes does not disguise a striking measure of agreement on many issues. Furthermore, if Braverman plunders Marx in an effort to provide a systematic contemporary account of the relevance of his thought for modern society, the degree of Ritzer's inspiration by Weber is, to put it kindly, defined by a lightness of touch. If Ritzer's treatment of the chosen elements of Weber to theoretically inform his own work is a little lightweight, then so is his aforementioned treatment of topics such as Fordism, post-Fordism and postmodernism. It is difficult to lend the seriousness required of the investigative scholar to Ritzer's thesis when on a single page of his book he claims that (a) Fordism has not been entirely eclipsed by post-Fordism; and (b) that Fordism has, in fact, been transformed into McDonaldization (1996, p. 152). In contrast, Braverman's treatment of *his* classical source is never less than serious, even po-faced. It is in this that the greatest irony resides, for some two-and-a-half decades after the publication of *Labor and Monopoly Capital* the judgement on Braverman is that whatever profundities emanate from his work, there are many more claims and assertions that if not simply superficial, do not bear close critical scrutiny.

Of course, Braverman has not been around to defend himself either against critics or the self-appointed acolytes that have, like moths to a flame, claimed him for their own (Braverman died in 1976). Ritzer has yet to enjoy (*sic*) any seriously sustained critique of his work (this book is meant to be a start: somewhat self-referentially, in writing this piece the memory of Andrew Zimbalist's 1976 edited work, broadly supportive of Braverman's thesis, sprung to mind: readers may draw what parallels they will). However, the leading UK higher education newspaper got round to reviewing Ritzer in August 1996. The reviewer, Gilling, was somewhat less flattering than the account given above. At the heart of his review, Gilling (1996, p. 24) writes:

This book is too simplistic and sloppy to have much educational value. It is certainly not sociology and it would certainly not teach students how to reason. When something does not fit Ritzer's theoretical scheme, he fails to mention it and redescribes it.

In the colloquial language of many a Hollywood western, this is fighting talk. However, Gilling's statement contains at least one serious point—the tendency to sins of omission by morally committed writers (note here that in observing thus, no claim is made as to the intentionality or otherwise of authors' motives: in this, a strictly poststructuralist attitude has been struck in respect of texts!). To assert that despite apparently different starting points, both Braverman and Ritzer arrive at similar conclusions, and to compound this by stating that in respect of the latter at least, we should be unfazed by his claims, it is necessary to enunciate an appropriate critique. Fortunately, the template for such a critique in respect of Ritzer's work is already with us in the key issues that have resolved from the Braverman debate. Any brief consideration of the broad consensus attached to the latter instantly illuminates the parallel applicability to Ritzer through simple transliteration. The focus here will be on three such critical issues (see S. Wood, 1982, for one of the best early and detailed collections of responses to Braverman; and R. C. Wood, 1992, for a less sophisticated rehearsal of these in the context of the hospitality industry).

First, then, Braverman has been accused of historical inadequacy in his analysis, specifically in respect of the privileged role he affords the idea of a halcyon era of employment dominated by craft skill in the preindustrial period. Many researchers have demonstrated that this is an exaggerated view. By extrapolation, the moral drive of Ritzer's thesis leads him to make the same error. McDonaldization is contrasted, in both past and present, with an ideal of historical non-McDonaldized production, though interestingly, this standard tends to be largely implicit and unelaborated. Put another way, Ritzer tells us how horrible and dehumanising McDonaldization is, without offering any details of the historical precedents against which this judgement is constructed. The past is thus an implicit explanatory resource in Ritzer's work, it is his *deus ex machina*. We can go further than this, however, and extend the original criticism of Braverman to Ritzer in another way in respect of consumption rather than production. Specifically, a thematic concern in Ritzer's work is with the consequences of McDonaldization for consumption: McDonaldization, he argues, creates health and environmental hazards, dehumanises consumers and has adverse effects on the quality of human relationships. Though perhaps unintentionally, Ritzer sails very close to suggesting that these effects are *uniquely* associated with consumption in its McDonaldized form, reflecting the same careless historicism of which Braverman is accused. However, even a casual understanding of any of the main strands of contemporary sociological thought reveal that it is not only neo-Marxist analysis that adumbrates many of the characteristics that Ritzer attributes to McDonaldization specifically (Bocock, 1993).

A second and third criticism levelled against Braverman, both equally applicable to Ritzer, is that the former attributes too much importance to the role of scientific management, Taylorism, in the rationalisation and degradation of work, and is reluctant to accept the possibility of counter-tendencies to deskilling. More precisely, scientific management is afforded the status of a steamroller, resistant to attempts to undermine its application as demonstrated by its widespread adoption in the world of work. In the McDonaldization context, it has been argued that Ritzer similarly imbues the process of rationalisation with an unjustifiable omnipotence and that product differentiation and mass customisation are manifestly contradictory processes which undermine McDonaldized production and service (Lyon, Taylor, & Smith, 1994, 1995). One objection to this aspect of the McDonaldization thesis is the level of *consumer* resistance to processes of rationalisation. Just as Braverman is accused of treating workers as (effectively) cultural dopes, unwilling and unable to resist the mighty historic god engine of Taylorisation, then Ritzer also treats consumers as incapable of discriminant behaviour: we are all—or at least the majority of us are—seduced by McDonaldization.

This, of course, raises a fascinating philosophical point. If it is the case that the majority of consumers are so seduced by McDonaldization, can the process be regarded as sufficiently generalisable to be a "social fact"? Certainly, Ritzer's view parallels Braverman's in this respect: for Braverman, as we have already noted, resistance to the Taylorisation of the labor process in capitalist production is overcome by incorporating, as it were, the opposition within the mainstream. Thus the arguments of writers like Lyon, Taylor, and Smith (1994; 1995) about resistance to McDonaldization in the form of product differentiation and mass customisation do not rest easily with Ritzer's thesis, for the logic of the latter's conclusion is that such resistance too must give way to McDonaldization. There is, however, a clear difficulty with the customisation/differentiation argument in this context. It is that, for writers like Taylor and colleagues (and within this ambit we can reasonably include not only the core management writers from whom Taylor and colleagues derive their intellectual impetus, but their fellow travellers also) product differentiation and mass customisation are producer-led phenomena. It may well be that McDonald's (or any other fast-food business) offers customers the "choice" of chicken, vegeburgers, or any number of a myriad of products, but this alters little the fact that such product differentiation/customisation is offered on the provider's terms—it is a choice supplied on the basis of McDonaldized processes.

Several of the issues arising from Ritzer's thesis require more detailed consideration in the context of the chosen exemplar—that is, consumer provision in the commercial hospitality industry. Before advancing to this task, it is appropriate to take stock of the argument so far. In essence, the perspective rendered here is a sceptical one that can see little theoretical justification for pressing Ritzer's analysis as comprising novel social-theoretical or empirical insights into the nature of production and consumption in advanced capitalist societies. In drawing on Braverman's work and its critical reception, the intention has been to show parallels in the treatment of rationalisation and the degradation of consumption/labor. By extension, several of the key criticisms levelled against Braverman can be seen to apply at least at a superficial level to the claims of Ritzer. The advantage of utilising Braverman as a comparitor lies in the disciplinary inheritance of sociology—both Braverman and Ritzer may be assumed up to a point to share a common intellectual heritage. However, both before and since Braverman's work, the issues of rationalisation and degradation have occupied scholars in a range of disciplines. Thus in the 1970s, Levitt (1972) opened debate with others on the "industrialisation of service," a debate that has had a profound influence on emergent specialist literature and conceptualisation in the field of services management. Parallel considerations have been paramount in other strands of Marxist thought (notably the Frankfurt school); in social anthropology (Douglas and Isherwood's 1974 *The World of Goods* recently reissued is a case in point); and in the historical analysis of consumption (see Preteceille & Terrail, 1985, for an interesting collection of papers). Even in marketing itself, doubts have been raised about the underlying ideologies of that discipline in terms of its assumptions about consumer sovereignty and choice (Brown, 1995, offers a brilliant if ultimately hopeful critique of such ideology). Nor has hospitality studies as a field of enquiry ignored these issues. For example, in the specific context of the fast-food industry, Burgermeister (1988) too draws an explicit analogy between Weber's model of bureaucracy and fast-food restaurants. He specifically argues that the fast-food restaurant fits the ideal type classical mechanistic organisation because there exists

a. tight division of labour and specialisation of tasks;

b. positions broken down by production and service;

c. a form of communication, the content of which comprises mainly orders and instructions;

d. a concentration of decision-making at the apex of the organisation;

e. a stress on obedience; and

f. an attachment of status and prestige to functions in the firm.

Where does this leave us? The key point, now well laboured, is that Ritzer's work is hardly novel on the subject of work rationalisation or indeed, as we shall see, to debates about employment and consumption in the hospitality industry. Perhaps the more pressing issue, however, is, "Is Ritzer wrong?" This may seem a strange question to pose at this juncture. By analogy with Braverman, certain weaknesses have been identified as characterising Ritzer's work, but, just as Braverman has attracted substantial and substantive critique, then so to do even his harshest critics concede that there is some truth in his observations. Given its conceptual origins in the field of commercial hospitality services, McDonald-ization deserves at least the beginnings of a similar treatment even if different conclusions are drawn. In pursuing this goal it should prove possible to both confirm the analysis proffered thus far and identify those areas worthy of further consideration.

A LITTLE FERMENTATION

Nobody doubts that McDonald's is a growing company, an ambitious company striving for global ubiquity. According to the international weekly *The Economist* (1996) in May of that year, Lithuania became the ninety-fifth country to be "McDonaldized." At that time there were some 18,700 outlets worldwide serving 33 million people daily. McDonald's reported that in 1996 and 1997 they intended to open around 3,200 new restaurants (compared to 1,787 in 1994 and 2,430 in 1995) of which around two-thirds would be outside of the United States. This fact is significant. If Ritzer is correct, then McDonald's have colonised their country of origin, but as of 1996, fewer than 40 percent—in fact 38 percent—of the chain's units were outside of the United States. Furthermore, a decade earlier, in 1985, some 22 percent of the units were located overseas, accounting for $2.2 billion (20 percent of total sales) and 18 percent of operating profit: by 1995 these figures were $14 billion (47 percent of total sales) and 54 percent of operating profit.

This is an impressive record, but the spread of McDonald's outside of the United States should not be exaggerated either in quantity or effect. Ritzer, of course, uses McDonald's as template for describing more widespread processes of rationalisation. In the discussion that follows, the purpose is to demonstrate that, in fact, McDonald's is barely an adequate template for analysing the commercial hospitality industry. In so doing the earlier themes will be revisited in this highly localised illustrative context. To frame the discussion, I shall examine Ritzer's specific "hospitality" conceptualisation of McDonaldization under two of the headings recognisable from his own book: "the process of rationalisation"; and "the irrationality of rationality."

THE PROCESS OF RATIONALISATION

As noted earlier, the four horsemen of the rationalisation apocalypse are efficiency, calculability, predictability, and control. Table 1 shows the major "gripes" Ritzer attributes to each of these in the specific context of the fast-food restaurant. Running throughout all of these is Ritzer's concern with the degradation of production and consumption. The veracity of this model lies in whether or not it represents an accurate description of fast-food culture. If we apply what might be termed the "Braverman test" (that is, the three principal criticisms of Braverman's thesis examined in the previous section) then it seems reasonable to assert that

- the fast-food restaurant constitutes a relatively recent form of catering service production that historically represents at least a partial break from traditional modes of food-service operations because of the extent to which technology governs the production of the service exchange;

- the application of technology in the fast-food context has not been unproblematic in respect of resistance to its application: resistance has come from both employees and consumers; and

- this second theme is reflected in the existence of countertendencies to deskilling that exist both within the fast-food sector and elsewhere in hospitality markets.

Table 1
Ritzer's Taxonomy of the Ills of McDonaldization

Efficiency

- The restaurant cookery process is streamlined and denuded of gastronomic content

- Product ranges are simplified and consumer choice restricted

- Customers are required to put certain labour inputs into the hospitality process (e.g., self-service)

Calculability

- Quantity rather than quality becomes the by-word of consumption

- Predictability and stability are valorised over creativity and experimentation

Predictability

- Employees are subjected to regularised behaviors

- Brands are established and replicated across cultural and geographical boundaries with little regard for either

- The drive for higher levels of productivity and associated standardisation delimits diversity

Control

- Taylorised control leads to excessive and dehumanising constraints on employee behaviour

- Social and technical controls are placed on consumers, controlling their experiences and expectations of the fast-food restaurant in such a manner as to dehumanise their experience.

If we summarise the above crudely, we can say that on the first count there are some grounds for accepting the view that relative to previous systems of production and service in commercial hospitality, the fast-food restaurant does represent a clear break with tradition, though this does not completely invalidate the criticism of Braverman (and by extension Ritzer) that they compare contemporary provision with an idealised and empirically unspecified model from the past. Thus, the Weberian rationality of the fast-food restaurant does not begin with Ray Kroc. Indeed, the process of rationalisation in food-service production has clearly been established as part of the Escoffierian revolution of the nineteenth century (Mennell, 1985; Saunders, 1981) which comprised two elements, namely (a) a clearly defined and widely adopted division of labour among chefs and cooks in commercial kitchens according to culinary specialisation; and (b) the evolution of printed matter for use in commercial cookery—recipe books and the like—that supported and reinforced the Escoffierian model of kitchen and restaurant organisation. In many respects, the Escoffierian model of the organisation of commercial food production and service refined and rationalised the multilayered and hierarchical system of domestic servitude prevalent among both European and U.S. élites (although the U.S. case was somewhat distorted by the legacy of slavery). Its effectiveness and durability as a system is supported by a variety of historical sources. For example, Hayner (1936), in perhaps the first serious academic commentary on the hotel industry, recorded instances of the impersonality of the U.S. commercial hospitality product that he saw as emanating from mechanistic technologies and work practices. A similar phenomenon was bemoaned in the period 1870–1930 by many other commentators (see Wood, 1994b; 1995 for reviews) and in the food-service industry. Whyte's (1948) pioneering study of the Chicago restaurant trade finds that leader of the human relations movement simultaneously criticising the effects of Taylorism in the industry while advocating technological and heavily rationalised means of overcoming work-flow problems in the sector. In short, therefore, we find that while the fast-food restaurant represents a distinctive, modern, form of production and service, the origins of this form lie in processes of rationalisation that can be traced back to an earlier phase of industrialisation.

If we turn quickly to the second and third issues identified at the top of this discussion, we find that the application of technology to food production and service has not only been highly problematic but has been resisted on several fronts, not least in Bravermanian-style employee resistance to deskilling. The extent of deskilling in hospitality services has been systematically reviewed elsewhere (Wood, 1992, 1997). In general, certain subsectors of the industry have seen substantial elements of deskilling, and this applies especially to the profession of cookery. Here, deskilling has been engendered by the application of various technologies, including advances in food-preservation techniques, that allow restaurant units merely to regenerate gastronomic items. Both in cookery and elsewhere in commercial hospitality services, however, the extent of deskilling is difficult to establish to any precise degree. Conceptually, it is immediately problematic to discuss the extent of deskilling in an industry where the majority of occupational categories have been anyway labelled semi- or unskilled. Indeed, this appears to be precisely the point at the heart of Braverman's own limited excursion into the world of services, which he sees as little different to that of manufacturing in terms of the extent to which work has been degraded. The work of chefs and other restaurant workers is not unlike that of manufacturing employees in that it takes the form of tangible products: "restaurant labor, which cooks, prepares, assembles, serves, cleans dishes and utensils, etc., carries on tangible production just as much as labor employed in any other manufacturing process" (Braverman, 1974, p. 360).

More than this, the analysis can be extended beyond the "obvious" categories of those involved in production and service of meals to workers in accommodation services (Braverman, 1974, p. 361):

Chambermaids are classed as service workers, but their labors are not always different, in principle from those of many manufacturing workers, in that they take shape in a tangible result. When . . . chambermaids . . . make beds they do an assembly operation which is not different from many factory assembly operations . . . the result is a tangible and vendible commodity.

Here, then, we have Braverman's inflexible view of the deskilling and degradation of work. It is a view which, as already noted, permits of no possibility of resistance. Ignoring for the sake of expedience the substantial research that shows many of the technological innovations and work practices identified by Braverman to have been welcomed by employees in the hospitality industry precisely because of the manner in which they invest work practices with control and meaning, there is evidence from even within the fast-food sector that employees both positively and negatively resist attempts to constrain their work behaviors. Negative resistance comes in traditional forms, including "voting with the feet," that is, leaving a particular employment or employment in hospitality generally (one figure quoted for annual staff turnover in British McDonald's outlets is 200 percent, (*The Economist*, 1995, p. 75), although this has to be set in the context of the composition of the workforce, which consists mainly of young people, arguably more prone to transitory employment: in 1995 64 percent of McDonald's employees were aged sixteen to twenty (Vallely, 1995, p. 13). What might be termed "positive" resistance, where workers stay within their job situation but try and adapt the situation to their own needs through developing compensating mechanisms, is well documented in the hospitality industry case (see Wood, 1992, chap. 3–5). It is worth adding, as Lyon, Taylor, and Smith (1995, pp. 119–120) note, that in addressing the issue of deskilling in the fast-food sector, it is important to recognise that McDonald's did not invent poor working conditions in the hospitality industry and there is no *a priori* reason for assuming that, in nonindustrialised production and service systems working conditions are any better than in a fast-food joint. Ritzer engages in a sleight of hand in promoting the concept of McDonaldization, a form of populist prestidigitation that obscures the historical inadequacy of his analysis while at the same time distracting his audience's gaze from the fact that the fast-food restaurant, far from "inventing" the modern ills Ritzer identifies, is merely the latest extension of widespread processes of rationalisation with more complex social-historical origins.

Analysis of resistance to deskilling and rationalisation cast in a Bravermanian mould is, of course, not the only response to the issues raised by Ritzer in the hospitality industry context. Another strand of response is well articulated by Lyon, Taylor, and Smith (1994; 1995) and Taylor, Lyon, and Smith (1997) and is relevant here. The core of the argument advanced by Taylor and his coauthors is that (a) competition between fast-food operators is at the level of both product differentiation and the differentiation of production and service methods and styles; (b) much so-called standardisation in both McDonald's and other fast-food operations is in fact ameliorated by customisation according to perceived local variations in the cultural acceptability of fast-food concepts (thus in the salubrious North London suburb of Hampstead where local residents, including many famous thespians, artists, and writers, opposed the opening of a McDonald's unit, the unit is now decorated with commissioned artworks depicting local scenes); and (c) fast-food constitutes only one sector of the food-service industry and many other styles of operation exist to serve varying consumer needs.

Elsewhere, I have taken issue with points (a) and (b) above, and with due deference to Taylor and his colleagues I see no reason to alter my position here (Wood, 1994c). In essence, it seems to me that Taylor's team adopt too loose a definition of terms like "product differentiation" and "customisation." Adapting menus to incorporate vegetarian foods and local specialities are merely examples of the methods by which organisations like McDonald's seek to incorporate opposition and conflict in a manner intended to pacify and neutralise hostility to their activities. At the same time, it does not seem acceptable to me to uncritically accept Ritzer's view that processes of product differentiation and customisation are invariably cynical McDonaldized processes of "sneakerisation" designed to contain and constrain consumer choice.

In this context, Taylor and his colleagues offer a useful vector away from the sterility of Ritzer's analysis and back to more generalised and substantive empirical concerns (Lyon, et al. 1995). This relates to the diverse ways in which, in the hospitality sector at least, consumer needs and wants can be met by varying systems. There are problems with this position if it is pressed naively, and arguments about mass customisation have their dangers. This is because such approaches underrate the capacity of powerful capitalist interests to mould consumer taste and choice, or even deflect these tastes so as to remove effective choice (to play on an example proffered by Taylor et al. we can refer to this as the Henry Ford syndrome—you can have any colour you like so long as it's black).

Nevertheless, consumers can and do resist the Taylorisation/McDonaldization of the marketplace, albeit this is rarely construed by consumers themselves as resistance. At one level, catering facilities are, as a substantial body of research literature suggests, judged in terms of fitness to purpose (Clark & Wood, 1996; Wood, 1995)—that is, consumers select restaurant types and styles, and actual restaurants, according to the nature of local supply (restaurant markets are essentially local markets and their "supply" therefore finite) and the particular nature of the motivation to dine out (i.e., convenience, celebration, family occasion, and so on). In this sense, consumer choice is constrained by what operators are prepared to provide—and where—but thereafter individual elements and preferences come into play. For the most part, these choices are a complex mix of *individual* preferences and selections. At a second level, we see resistance to McDonaldization on the part of operators themselves, though again, such resistance is not always directly experienced as such. In most Western economies, the hospitality industry is characterised by many small firms catering to highly localised consumer needs. As noted above, these needs are demonstrably calculated by consumers according to measurable criteria, and it is precisely because of this that, despite their growth in numbers, fast-food restaurants have been unable to establish a culinary hegemony. They are but one kind of service in a range of services and consumers express preferences according to particular requirements. The important point is that over any period of time, consumers may make multiple selections as their requirements change. In the UK, for example, a young child's birthday may be celebrated at McDonald's but a mature adult's birthday will almost always be celebrated elsewhere. More significant yet is what might be termed proactive resistance to the encroachment of McDonaldized dining. Again, the evidence here is fairly well established (although, problematically, often ignored by sociologists of all inclinations, and certainly by industrial sociologists: for some observations on the failure of cross-fertilisation in sociological specialisms related to food and eating, see Beardsworth & Keil, 1997; Wood, 1995). An array of directed forces opposes McDonaldization in the sphere of public dining. A key motivation of chefs, patrons, and others in establishing fine-dining style restaurants is an aversion to manufactured dining experiences (Finkelstein, 1989; Wood, 1991). Food writers (cooks, restaurant reviewers, critics) consistently oppose the perceived implementation of McDonaldized dining (Fattorini, 1994; Mennell, 1985; Wood, 1996). The general public regularly engage in opposing planning applications from fast-food restaurants (Tansey & Worsley, 1995). If the latter is a form of direct action, then so are the efforts of the U.S. "Pure Food Campaign" to issue customers of McDonald's with alternative till receipts itemising the environmental and social costs of their practices, and the activities of the two environmental campaigners who have been engaged by McDonald's in a libel trial that has extended over twenty-four months in London's High Court (Silverstone, 1995). The likely long-term outcome of processes of rationalisation is far from certain as Ritzer suggests. Within the limitations of current critiques of processes of rationalisation, it is simply not possible to sustain such a view, and Ritzer, again like Braverman, falls prey to the conceits of the classical sociologist, to assumptions about the inevitability of social and economic processes that history has revealed to be far from inevitable.

THE IRRATIONALITY OF RATIONALITY

Under this heading, Ritzer discusses what he sees to be the negative aspects of rationalisation/McDonaldization, focusing on the claim that rational systems are unreasonable systems both because they dehumanise people and are intrinsically inefficient. Some of his key objections relative to fast food *per se* (but also generalised to other areas) include the following:

- *Queuing.* Queuing is a necessary feature of the "rational" system of food production applied by organisations like McDonald's but in fact is a symptom of the inefficiency of the system—"fast" food is not all that fast if people have to queue.

- *Customer input.* Rational systems cannot be wholly efficient if they require customers to engage in part of the production/service process by self-serving some or all foods themselves as in the case, for example, of salad bars in certain types of restaurant.

- *Opportunity cost.* Can rational systems ever be truly and intrinsically efficient? The process of packing the family into the car, driving to McDonald's, loading up food, and returning home (Ritzer, 1996, p. 123) in many cases must be less efficient than preparing a meal at home.

- *Productivity.* Rationalised systems are usually low in productivity, often being labor intensive—another type of inefficiency.

- *Product development.* McDonaldized organisations, including fast-food restaurants, peddle familiar products and have a poor track record of product and service innovation.

- *Public health.* The content of most fast food is of an order that, consumed in large quantities over time can lead to serious health problems throughout the populace; more immediate are problems of food poisoning linked to intensive food-production systems.

- *The environment.* In terms of the resources utilised for packaging (trees) and the subsequent output of near-indestructible Styrofoam garbage, the fast-food industry may be regarded as environmentally damaging.

- *Employment.* Employment in rationalised systems is dehumanising and degrading, mechanical, and devoid of the scope for initiative and creativity, workers have little stake in rationalised organisations and labor turnover is especially high in the likes of fast-food restaurants leading to inefficiency because of the costs incurred in hiring and training replacements.

- *Dehumanisation of Customers.* Largely as a result of being engaged in scripted interactions and the uniformity imposed by the fast-food concept: contact between participants in the service exchange are minimised, and regular customers rarely get the opportunity to develop a relationship with staff because the latter move on so quickly.

Further examples of Ritzer's thesis could be culled from his discussion of the irrationality of rationality but the exercise would be a limited one. In the listing above we see the closest Ritzer gets to empirical illustration of his arguments. This empiricism rarely, however, goes beyond rhetoric and, at best, constitutes little more than engaging sophistry. To clarify this charge, we can respond to each of the above items in turn.

- *Queuing.* Ritzer's charge here borders on the bizarre. Queuing may be an intrinsic element of many "rational" systems of production and service, but it is neither caused by nor unique to such systems. Is waiting at a bus stop a symptom of the irrationality or inefficiency of the road transport system? Is queuing at an airport departure gate an instance of the irrationality of aviation inefficiency, or, rather, the most efficient way of ensuring security, safety, and order?

- *Customer input.* The involvement of consumers in the production and service process is not always a *defining* feature of rationalised systems. In the hospitality industry, there is a view that by simple critical engagement with the restaurant, consumers are committing themselves by definition to acts of mutual exchange (Finkelstein, 1989). Self-service elements in food-service systems in their contemporary form have evolved from the nineteenth-century idea of the "grande buffet" and have been employed by hospitality organisations from the 1940s onwards as a means of both product differentiation and reassurance of the customer as to product quality (in the UK the phenomenon was at its height in the 1970s "carvery" restaurant which for the most part involved self-selection of only a main course: the number of waiting staff required by the operator was hardly diminished by this process as employees were still required to service other elements of the meal experience).

- *Opportunity cost.* Ritzer's example in this instance is an intriguing one. The pattern of pre- and postpurchase behaviour he suggests is a clever intellectual conceit which may perhaps be relevant to the U.S. context without necessarily being capable of generalisation. In the UK for example, the idea of an entire family going by car to McDonald's and returning home with the food is a pattern of behaviour that at best applies only to a significant minority. Consumption at fast-food restaurants is usually integrated to other activities, notably shopping. Food consumption is frequently off the premises. Indeed, one of the fastest growing sectors of the UK fast-food industry in the 1990s has been home deliveries, in which field pizza restaurants have fared the best in terms of market share. The suspicion here must be that Ritzer is generalising an ethnocentric viewpoint, and, if this is true, then clearly such a viewpoint is flawed.

- *Productivity.* Ritzer clearly has the fast-food and wider hospitality sectors in mind when making this point. It is problematic because in relatively nonrationalised systems of hospitality production and service productivity has always been low. This was as true of the hotels observed by Hayner (1936) and the restaurants studied by Whyte (1948) considered earlier. Productivity is not simply a function of systems, however, but of organisational *culture*, and the way in which such culture enables what is organisationally possible. In hotels and restaurants, for example, low productivity is as much a factor of the lack of flexibility in labor utilisation and the pursuit of low-wage policies as it is of any overarching system of provision (Wood, 1997).

- *Product development.* Ritzer's comments here constitute a routine critique of rationalised systems. It is a fruitful area for debate, but, as was noted earlier in the context of claims by writers like Lyon, Taylor, and Smith (1994), it is beset by definitional problems. In this sense, any discussion is likely to be largely semantic as to what is meant by product development and innovation. A more effective approach to the issue is to ask why product and service development and innovation should both be valorised as intrinsically worthy activities. In this way, any debate can be oriented in terms of the ideological motivations underpinning such claims.

- *Public health.* Allegations about the (poor) health value of fast-food have tended to focus for the purposes of exemplification on the kinds of products proffered by McDonald's and similar restaurants. Again, however, any debate about the health disadvantages of "burger culture" is prone to critique in terms of the ideological content of the arguments deployed, including the arguments of nutritionists and food scientists. To accuse the purveyors of "burger culture" of purposely undermining public health is a grossly distorted simplification of a complex issue that embraces individual choice and freedom, the wider nature of the food system and accuracy of scientific knowledge in the field of nutrition (Gofton, 1996) and the frequent and casual articulation of the public health accusation against fast food is naive and even intellectually insulting.

- *The Environment.* The case for environmental damage resulting from McDonaldized food production and service is a sturdier one, but again we can note that this issue, with that of pollution more generally, is a global one and not confined solely to such systems. At the local environmental level in terms of physical surroundings, it is possible to note actual *improvements* as a result of the presence of fast-food operations. In the UK for example, citizens' objections to planned fast-food developments have heightened operators' sense of the need to ensure sponsorship of street cleaning and maintenance programmes, albeit at a fairly basic level. Again, there are dangers in unqualified advocacy of the environmental damage argument which verge on the irritatingly naive.

- *Employment.* It is worth briefly emphasising the point here that in the hospitality industry, high labour turnover has been a feature of *all* systems, in most periods, since the onset of industrialisation. It is not unique to McDonaldized systems, nor is the nature and organisation of work itself. Furthermore, as was suggested earlier, workers in the industry have devised many ways of "bucking" the system which may not alter the objective fact of fast-food work as degrading and dehumanising but allows for the development of compensatory strategies and mechanisms which to a degree alleviate the negative aspects of employment.

- *Dehumanisation of Customers.* From the point of view of the hospitality industry, this is possibly the most interesting aspect of the rationalisation debate. As part of the wider intellectual debate on modernism and postmodernism it must be said, of course, that the argument is a persuasive one, whether cast in the postmodernist mould of dedifferentiation and circulating multiple meaning(lessness) or in more conventional terms such as alienation and anomie. The area of greatest concern lies in the extent to which capitalist organisations, in the manner described by the Frankfurt school, seek to reinvent social relationships that have been disrupted by processes of capitalist development. In the hospitality industry these have been all too evident processes for many years now, as has been noted elsewhere (Wood, 1994a). More recently, attempts to emphasise the "hospitality" dimensions of the hospitality industry have adopted new forms. At the level of the employee, these focus on empowerment and customer care. At the level of the consumer, the emphasis is on concepts such as "added value" (tangible or intangible advantages that form additional benefits to the basic product or service purchased) and "delighting the customer" (i.e., exceeding their expectations). In this sense, what appears to be happening is that far from dehumanising the customer, there are attempts to rehumanise the whole process of hospitality provision, although according to very specific and ideological concepts of customer wants and needs. Ritzer's easy assertions about the dehumanising of consumers do not bear close critical scrutiny. Rather, the issue is one to be established empirically, and not in the field of hospitality services alone.

To conclude this section, it is worth returning to Gilling's (1996) critique of Ritzer. One of the most interesting aspects of Ritzer's list of charges against McDonaldization in the context of the irrationality of rationality (especially in the items from "product development" through to "dehumanising the customer" listed above) is the extent to which they touch on genuinely interesting and fundamental concerns in sociology and philosophy, concerns that deserve and require profound reflection and detailed examination but which in Ritzer's work (and that of many similarly inclined sociologists) are treated as hyperbolic resources for deft conceptual promotion at the cost of hard analysis. The result is a worrying superficiality based on convenient and unproved assumptions. As Gilling (1996, p. 24) puts it: "From a less preconceived and deterministic view of society, Ritzer would be able to ask more interesting questions." As it is, Ritzer's charges concerning the irrationality of rationality amount to little more than a peculiar kind of sociologically populist babbling that avoids engagement with the truly pressing issues arising from the crisis of modernism.

FROM THE CHATEAU TO THE SUPERMARKET SHELF: A FINAL TASTING

In this essay I have attempted to show that Ritzer's McDonaldization thesis is far less exciting and original than might be implied by some of the responses to it. By analogy with a parallel academic work by Braverman, an effort has been made to offer some insight into how a critique of Ritzer might be constructed at a conceptual level. By reference to Ritzer's "source" industry—the hospitality industry—I have elaborated the basis of a more empirical critique of McDonaldization, albeit in a rather localised instance. Ritzer's thesis belongs to a long tradition of doom-laden sociological scenarios that rely for their impetus on a narrow reading of some "classical" writer, in this case Weber, and proceed to extrapolate such a reading in one or both of two directions: to the empirical nether world of the present (where attractive assertions that resonate with current social concerns can ultimately be revealed to be far from exhaustive in analysis); and to the future where putative trends are, periodically, constructed on the basis of selective *post hoc* interpretations of past events and phenomena. In this way is Ritzer able, with considerable chutzpah, to rewrite a century of sociological debate on rationalisation as "McDonaldization."

Ritzer's book is an accessible and likeable tract which, according to the back cover of its revised edition has been adopted at some 200 colleges in the United States. In an amusing and presumably unintentional aside, one of the endorsements in the same place alludes to the usefulness of Ritzer's book in terms of it preparing students for "more difficult and challenging work." This seems to me to imply a pleasing epithet (or perhaps epitaph!) for *The McDonaldization of Society* which in itself might be perceived as belonging to the very process of which it writes, a point that Ritzer in the preface to the revised edition seems at least to partially appreciate. Modern sociological research and writing is beset by many problems including a preoccupation with the interior landscape of the discipline, a literary obtuseness which on more occasions than not renders sociological writing almost incomprehensible, and a tendency to valorise the socially trivial over the socially substantive. In this respect, at least, Ritzer deserves credit for addressing a substantive issue with some lucidity. It is regrettable that in so doing, the mission to popularise the topic sees the topic itself submerged in a morass of pseudopopulist illustration, of variable conceptual and empirical substance. Ritzer misses the opportunity to advance in a well-ploughed furrow, preferring instead to repackage and rebrand that which has gone before. In this respect, the process of McDonaldization is indeed very much evident in *The McDonaldization of Society* which is, perhaps, not simply an old wine in a new bottle, but a *vin de pays* masquerading as a great vintage.

REFERENCES

Beardsworth, A., & Keil, T. (1997). *Sociology on the menu: An invitation to the sociology of food and society*. London: Routledge.

Big Mac's folly. (1995, July 1). *Economist, 75*.

Bocock, R. (1993). *Consumption*. London: Routledge.

Braverman, H. (1974). *Labor and monopoly capital*. New York: Monthly Review.

Brown, S. (1995). *Postmodern marketing*. London: Routledge.

Burgermeister, J. (1988). Communications in fast food organisations. *Hospitality Education and Research Journal, 12*(3), 52–54.

Clark, M., & Wood, R. C. (1996, November). Consumer loyalty in the restaurant industry: A preliminary exploration of the issues. Paper presented at the IAHMS Autumn Symposium, Leeuwarden, Netherlands.

Douglas, M., & Isherwood, B. (1974). *The world of goods*. Harmondsworth, UK: Penguin.

Fattorini, J. E. (1994). Food journalism: A medium for conflict. *British Food Journal, 96*(10), 24–28.

Finkelstein, J. (1989). *Dining out: a sociology of modern manners*. Oxford, UK: Polity.

Gilling, A. (1996, August 16). Review of G. Ritzer *The McDonaldization of society* (Rev. ed.). *The Times Higher Education Supplement*, 24.

Gofton, L. (1996). Bread to biotechnology: Cultural aspects of food ethics. In B. Mepham (Ed.), *Food ethics* (pp. 120–37). London: Routledge.

Hassard, J., & Parker, M. (Eds.). (1993). *Postmodernism and organizations*. London: Sage.

Hayner, N. (1936). *Hotel life*. Chapel Hill, NC: University of North Carolina Press.

Lash, S., & Urry, J. (1994). *Economies of signs and space*. London: Sage.

Levitt, T. (1972). Production line approach to service. In R. P. Olsen, & D. D. Wyckoff (Eds.), *The management of service operations* (pp. 345–353). Boston: Allyn and Bacon.

Lyon, P., Taylor, S., & Smith, S. (1994). McDonaldization: A reply to Ritzer's thesis. *International Journal of Hospitality Management, 13*(2), 95–99.

Lyon, P., Taylor, S., & Smith, S. (1995). Is Big Mac the big threat?: A rejoinder to Silverstone and Wood. *International Journal of Hospitality Management, 14*(2), 119–122.

Macworld. (1996, June 29). *Economist*, 77-78.

Mennell, S. (1985). *All manners of food: Eating and taste in England and France from the Middle Ages to the present*. Oxford, UK: Blackwell.

Preteceille, E., & Terrail, J. P. (1985). *Capitalism, consumption and needs*. Oxford, UK: Blackwell.

Ritzer, G. (1993). *The McDonaldization of society*, Thousand Oaks, CA: Pine Forge.

Ritzer, G. (1996). *The McDonaldization of society* (Rev. ed.). Thousand Oaks, CA: Pine Forge.

Saunders, K. (1981). *Social stigma of occupations*. Farnborough, UK: Gower.

Silverstone, R. (1995). A response to Lyon, Taylor and Smith: The Ritzer debate continued. *International Journal of Hospitality Management, 14*(2), 111–115.

Tansey, G., & Worsley, T. (1995). *The food system: A guide*. London: Earthscan.

Taylor, S., Lyon, P., & Smith, S. (1997) Consumer choice in the future: An illusion or the next marketing revolution? In M. Alfino, J. Caputo, & R. Wynyard, (Eds.). *McDonaldization revisited: Critical essays on consumer culture*. Westport, CT: Greenwood.

Vallely, P. (1995, June 10). The Big Mac. *Independent, 13*.

Whyte, W. F. (1948). *Human relations in the restaurant industry*. New York: McGraw-Hill.

Wood, R. C. (1991). The shock of the new: A sociology of nouvelle cuisine. *Journal of Consumer Studies and Home Economics, 15*(4), 327–338.

Wood, R. C. (1992). *Working in hotels and catering*. London: Routledge.

Wood, R. C. (1994a). Extended review of S. Lash and J. Urry. *Economies of signs and space: Postmodernism and organizations, work, employment and society, 8*(3), pp. 459–463.

Wood, R. C. (1994b). Hotel culture and social control. *Annals of Tourism Research, 21*(1), 65–80.

Wood, R. C. (1994c). Misunderstanding and misinterpreting McDonaldization: A comment on Lyon, Taylor and Smith. *International Journal of Hospitality Management, 13*(4), 293–295.

Wood, R. C. (1995). *The sociology of the meal*. Edinburgh, Scotland: Edinburgh University Press.

Wood, R. C. (1996). Talking to themselves: Food commentators, food snobbery and market reality. *British Food Journal, 98*(10), 7–13.

Wood, R. C. (1997). *Working in hotels and catering* (2nd ed.). London: International Thomson Business Press.

Wood, S. (Ed.). (1982). *The degradation of work? Skill, deskilling and the labour process*. London: Hutchinson.

Zimbalist, A. (Ed.). (1976). *Case studies on the labor process*. New York: Monthly Review.

7

McDonaldization and Consumer Choice in the Future: An Illusion or the Next Marketing Revolution?

Stephen Taylor, Sheena Smith, and Phil Lyon

INTRODUCTION

Has product and service standardization reached the point where we are starved of choice? George Ritzer's book *The McDonaldization of Society* (Ritzer, 1993) suggests that industrial societies create and promote powerful rationalizing forces that *inter alia* give us bland products, routinized production, and deskilled workers. Ritzer uses the McDonaldization thesis explicitly and as a metaphor. The process can, he claims, be observed not just in the diminished diversity of restaurants but in the organization of services for the provision of, for example, hotel accommodation, hypermarkets, education, and medical treatment. In earlier critiques (Lyon, Taylor, & Smith, 1994, 1995; Taylor & Lyon, 1995), we drew attention to certain general problems with the model and here we extend our thoughts by looking at the validity of its application not only to fast food but also to hotel accommodation. The application does not stop here, of course, and neither do the possibilities for some measure of criticism.

MCDONALDIZATION: STANDARDIZING PRODUCTS AND SERVICES

For Ritzer, the neologism of McDonaldization refers to standardized production systems delivering a standardized product/service. This is epitomized by McDonald's itself where "the customs of food consumption embedded in traditional eating houses are pared away to a new minimalism of finger food, fast-moving queues and do-it-yourself table-clearing" (Lyon, Taylor, & Smith, 1994, p. 96). However, comment on the transposition of mass production principles from the factory to the service environment is not new. Classic contributions advocating the "industrialization of service" have been made by Levitt (1972, 1976) who argued that such a move would radically improve the quality of many services. Indeed, his first contribution (Levitt, 1972), *"Production-line approach to service,"* drew extensively on the activities of McDonald's. In more recent times, some concern has been raised about the extent to which service industrialization can negatively impact upon service quality (Teboul, 1988). This concern about the negative implications has been considerably extended in Ritzer's work, particularly in relation to the spread across different kinds of operation within the service sector so that McDonaldization is becoming increasingly prevalent across sectors of American society as well as in many other societies throughout the world.

While acknowledging that the term *McDonaldization* does perhaps suggest something about changes in product range and service provision, our contention is that Ritzer's thesis is overstated. We have some difficulty in accepting a number of the points that he makes. The first is that the process is inexorable. He claims that "we confront a future of accelerating McDonaldization" (Ritzer, 1993, p. 158). For Ritzer this process is the vanguard to the advent of an increasingly rational world. His point is starkly made, but, as argued later in this essay, there are grounds for believing that the process could never run its course in this way. Ever-increasing rationalization seldom works out the way intended because of the complexity of human needs and the markets that serve them.

Second, Ritzer argues that the process is "bad" because it eliminates alternatives. Directly and metaphorically, "diversity, which many people crave, is being reduced or eliminated by the fast-food restaurant" (Ritzer, 1993, p. 138). Lower levels of consumer choice within a market sector and even within a restaurant are predicted. Overlooked in this gloomy prognosis is the possibility that the fast-food restaurant is actually providing a product/service that customers want. Millions of people use them (MSI, 1991; McDonald's, 1994), and unless one believes that there are no alternatives or that people are brainwashed to the point where "the craving for diversity is being supplanted by the desire for uniformity and predictability" (Ritzer, 1993, p. 139), they cannot all be wrong about the advantages. Perhaps also there is a touch of élitism here. For as we have previously noted, Miller (1987) has "observed that the denunciation of the inauthenticity of contemporary consumer culture—long a staple of élitist critics of modernism—has typically resided upon fanciful notions of preindustrial or postcapitalist society" (Lyon, Taylor, & Smith, 1995, p. 121). The evidence we suggest speaks for itself—it cannot be doubted that fast-food restaurants have extended the prospect of "eating out" to the masses and have contributed to a possibly emergent trend where domestic eating assumes the status of a weekend/special occasion event (Blair, 1994).

Third, Ritzer argues that any fast-food menu/service innovation is superficial, even illusory, because the production system remains the same. We feel this is too dismissive and that the changes are more substantial in their impact. McDonald's restaurants today have an average menu containing thirty-three items, some 25 percent up on 1980. McDonald's is also test-marketing a new Golden Arches Cafe and a McDonald's Express concept (Crawford-Welch, 1994). All this amounts to something a little more than a burger bar. Ritzer appropriately draws our attention to problems associated with the "industrialization of service" (Levitt, 1972) but, in our view, vastly overstates the case. He also fails to see that such systems—portrayed as profoundly limiting—can also potentially give rise to better consumer choice.

THE TERMINAL DECLINE OF CONSUMER CHOICE?

Before we take Ritzer's line and become too readily critical of McDonald-ization, it is worth remembering that the consumer society we have today was borne upon the back of the rise of mass production. This system enabled manufacturers to mass produce a huge range of goods at an acceptable quality and price thus, initially at least, rapidly expanding consumer choice. However, at the heart of this system there exists a self-reinforcing cycle (Pine, 1993) that leads to an increasing output of standardized products which, in turn, result in increasingly homogenized markets, thus ultimately constraining consumer choice:

In the world of mass production, consumers accepted standard goods; their acceptance facilitated the extension of the market and the reduction of prices, through increasing economies of scale; and the growing gap between the price of mass-produced goods and that of customised goods further encouraged the clustering of demand around homogeneous products. (Piore & Sabel, 1984, pp. 190–191)

For most of this century this industrial system has been in objective, economic terms, extremely successful. The rise in the standard of living in industrialized countries can be largely attributed to the wealth creation associated with the mass-production approach. From the original Model T through to the automatic washing machine and color television, the masses have seen their lives transformed in the course of one generation. Moreover, such is the dynamic strength of this industrial system that it has been increasingly adopted by service businesses. The "industrialization of service" as exemplified by McDonald's and the motel/budget hotel sector have equally brought many advantages to the consumer. Relatively low prices are only one aspect of their attraction. The effect is also to iron out traveler uncertainty. Some "adventures" with unknown accommodation could take on a nightmare quality, and, as Ritzer himself notes, "many travelers preferred the predictable Holiday Inn" (Ritzer, 1993, p. 85) rather than risk trying the local, nonbranded alternative. The reality is that a franchised product offers the customer reliability: they know what they should expect and are more likely to have that expectation met. If travelers want something different—either for sustenance or accommodation—then there are both copyist rivals and "real" alternatives that will exploit that demand. Despite Ritzer's gloom, there is competition and, as demonstrated below, even the market leaders cannot afford to be static.

THE DECLINE OF BIG MAC?

If the fast-food industry is the archetypal example of limited choice, for many people, it is also a representation of all that is bad in mass production (see Silverstone, 1995, for a recent example). Does this industry's success, in financial terms, result through the narrowing of consumer choice and the obliterating of alternatives? It is worth remembering that the genesis of McDonald's at the hands of its founder Ray Kroc in the 1950s was in response to an unsatisfied consumer demand for simple food at a low-cost and consistent quality in a clean and safe environment. The fact that Kroc was able to develop a restaurant concept capable of delivering this quality, service, cleanliness, and value—what McDonald's refer to as QSC & V—provides evidence to the power of the marketing concept if nothing else. McDonald's in the 1980s and 1990s, however, provide an example of another aspect of marketing, namely that as one satisfies the current demands of consumers, one effectively raises their future expectations. What was extraordinary yesterday is passé today. In the United Kingdom, McDonald's was rudely reminded of this fact:

Customers . . . told McDonald's they were loud, brash, American, successful, complacent, uncaring, insensitive, disciplinarian, insincere, suspicious and arrogant. . . . We thought we knew about service. Get the order into the customer's hands in 60 seconds—that was service. Not according to our customers. They wanted warmth, helpfulness, time to think, friendliness and advice. . . . we had failed to see . . . that our customers were now veterans in the quick-service market and their expectations have gone through the roof. What was revolutionary in the seventies was ghastly in the caring nineties. (Donkin, 1994, p. 9)

In the United States, McDonald's has had to confront the limitations of mass production much sooner than elsewhere. In the United States during the late 1970s and early 1980s price competition had become fierce and McDonald's core market was saturated. Its traditional price/value relationship became eroded as a result of rising costs, and it was facing shifting demographics and rapidly changing eating habits.[1] The message was clear—mass production for homogeneous markets belongs to a past era. It was clear that a new paradigm was demanded—that of mass customization.

MASS CUSTOMIZATION: REDISCOVERING CUSTOMER CHOICE?

The decline in the effectiveness of the mass production paradigm finds today's successful companies dancing to a new tune in this "age of diversity" (McKenna, 1988). As we will demonstrate here, the new paradigm of mass customization is rapidly replacing mass production and providing consumers with an increased level of choice at affordable prices, a combination hitherto impossible. To understand why this is now possible, it is necessary to understand the nature of mass production and how this new alternative of mass customization differs. In this section we outline these differences and explain why, in the final analysis, mass production, and therefore McDonaldization, must ultimately fail.

With mass customization we see the focus shifting away from the standardized outputs of mass production and towards the creation of

variety and customization through flexibility[2] and *quick responsiveness.*[3] This is the controlling focus of . . . mass customization . . . [which shares] . . . the goal of developing, producing, marketing and delivering affordable goods and services with enough variety and customization *that nearly everyone finds exactly what they want.* (italics in original, Pine, 1993, p. 44)

Thus there is a critical shift is away from the Fordist approach—as adopted by McDonald's—of inducing sales volume through lowering unit costs (which in turn increases demand/sales volume which leads to lower unit costs, and so on) and towards a stimulation of sales through a better matching of output with customer needs and wants. Ultimately this becomes another self-reinforcing cycle (Pine, 1993). Meeting customer demands leads to higher profits which, in turn, facilitates the organization's ability to increase its customization capability which, in turn, stimulates further market fragmentation.[4]

Mass customization, as the originator of the phrase, Stan Davis (1987), acknowledged, is an oxymoron—the combining of apparently contradictory concepts. In the "good old days" things were very straightforward: low unit costs required high volumes, thus standardization; customization was driven by low volumes and high unit costs. The recent advancements in technology and the advanced management approaches it underpins, allow us to realize the "impossibility" of customized outputs on a mass basis. Mass customization—which is really the combination of two Japanese systems: the adaptable marketing system (AMS) and the flexible manufacturing system (FMS) or lean production—is ultimately an umbrella for a large number of other elements within the firm (Yasumuro, 1993). These include, for example, new business "strategies" such as kanban, kaizen, total quality management, empowerment, internal marketing, supply chain management, electronic data interchange, information technology-linked network organizations,[5] and business process re-engineering. Mass customization is the product of the interplay and mutual reinforcement of many such elements.

As Davis comments in the preface to Pine (1993), at the core of this enlightenment is a shift away from the mechanistic "parts/whole" interpretation of the universe as exemplified by Newton. Simply, when applied to business, the argument is that the organization is the sum of its parts. An alternative approach—and one that any hospitality professional intuitively embraces—is that the parts (e.g., the employee) are the whole (the organization) from the perspective of the customer. In short, the customer perceives the organization in holistic terms. The intellectual challenge is thus to perceive that "mass" is to "whole" what "customization" is to "parts."

The certainties of the past are fast disappearing. We are, it would appear, now in an era of paradoxes.[6] To a large extent this can be seen to be largely due to—as Davis points out—our enslavement by false dichotomies, for example, strategy versus operations, cost versus quality, centralization versus decentralization. Science has confronted this issue and its solution to the existence of seemingly irreconcilable differences (e.g., light consists of waves *and* particles) is to "embrace interpretations that accept contradictions without trying to resolve them. Quantum mechanics does that in physics, mass customizing does that in business" (Davis in Pine, 1993, p. xi).

Managers have known for sometime that all was not well. The old recipe and its associated certainties was failing to deliver what it had previously done so successfully in the past. Why was mass production failing? Two key reasons identified by Pine (1993) are

1. The limits to the process itself resulting from input stability. For example, how low can labor costs go and how high its productivity?
2. The required market homogeneity no longer exists. Markets have become fragmented.

Additional factors include the maturing and, ultimately, saturation of many markets (mass production needs growth markets); technological shocks in the form of new products that have led to the obsolescence of many products; process technology is experiencing such shocks too (e.g., lean production). The stable demand required by the mass-production process is vanishing. The time of Ford, Taylor, Gilbreth, and more recent adherents of rationalism such as Kroc has passed. The 1980s saw companies and indeed whole industries begin to play a new game, with new rules (Barker, 1988).

Just how different is this new game of mass customization to mass production? The key differences are highlighted in Table 1. A critical aspect, and arguably one that really lies at the core of the difference between the two paradigms, is *the reversal of the importance of products and processes*. In mass production the product is developed first, and then, in turn, the focus shifts towards the process which will produce the product. Here the process becomes permanently coupled to the product. The most graphic illustration of this in practice was Ford's Model T. In 1927, in the face of a huge slump in demand (not least because Alfred Sloan and General Motors had begun to provide consumers with a choice in both vehicle type and color), Ford had to cease production and spend the next one and a half years retooling his factory for a new product—the Model A (McNamee, 1985).

With mass customization it is the processes which are created first—not the products—and these remain permanently decoupled from the products. Whereas mass production essentially lowers costs through economies of *scale* (quantity), mass customization utilizes economies of *scope* (variety) as its main lever upon costs. There are clear echoes in this with the cybernetists' law of requisite variety which states that market fragmentation necessitates flexibility in production and increased diversity of output (Ashby, 1956). Many of the recent advances in management previously alluded to—for example, kanban, lean production, compression of the new product development process and so on—are the means by which this can be achieved.

Table 1
Mass Customization Contrasted with Mass Production

Dimension	Mass Production	Mass Customization
Focus	Efficiency through stability and control	Variety and customization through flexibility and quick responsiveness
Goal	Developing, producing, Marketing and delivering goods and services at prices low enough that nearly everyone can afford them	Developing, producing, marketing and delivering affordable goods and services with enough variety and customization that nearly everyone finds exactly what they want
Key Features	Stable demand	Fragmented demand
	Large, homogeneous markets	Heterogeneous niches
	Low-cost, consistent quality, standardized goods and services	Low-cost, high-quality, customized goods and services
	Long product development cycles	Short product development cycles
	Long product life cycles	Short product life cycles

Source: B. J. Pine, (1993), *Mass Customization: The New Frontier in Business Competition.* Boston: Harvard Business School Press.

BIG MAC MEANS CHOICE?

The extensive standardization of McDonald's, vilified by Ritzer, has experienced the same discontinuities as other mass producers. Here too there has been extreme pressure for change. Archrival Burger King, having failed to beat McDonald's at its own game, changed the rules and embraced the principles of mass customization—"Have It Your Way!" and "Sometimes You've Gotta Break the Rules!" Here the focus is upon the "hamburgers and fries," but this was simply a foretaste of a much more significant shift.

The fast-food industry became increasingly competitive during the 1980s. Companies such as Pizza Hut, Domino's, Kentucky Fried Chicken, and Taco Bell all moved towards variety in their output and began to exert significant pressure upon McDonald's. Once again, just as had been the case in the 1950s with Ray Kroc, it was a recognition of changing consumer demands that catalyzed this shift:

[This] emphasis on new product development and introduction in the hospitality industry was, in essence, a response by corporations to the plurality of the marketplace and the diverse price/value needs of multiple market segments. In today's hospitality industry there is no such thing as a mass market. Mass markets are a vestige of the past. (Crawford-Welch, 1994, p. 169)

The competitive response first saw the introduction of a special breakfast menu (Egg McMuffin), then in the latter part of the 1980s, output variety mushroomed throughout the industry. In the 1990s, in the United States at least, the McDonald's offer has expanded to include "pizza, chicken fajitas, breakfast burritos, submarine sandwiches, spaghetti and meatballs, bone-in chicken, a grilled chicken sandwich, carrot and celery sticks, fresh-ground coffee and even bottled water" (Scarpa, 1991). Indeed, the total number of existing menu items or new products currently being test marketed is estimated at over 150 (Pine, 1993).

To achieve this radical expansion in its output variety has required that McDonald's underwent a paradigm shift that demanded shorter development and production cycles,[7] flexibility, autonomy, process innovations, and the adoption of a true customer focus (Pine, 1993). The process of new product development is now undertaken at both a headquarters level and at an individual unit level. Franchisees can innovate to ensure a closer fit with their own unique customer environment (Scarpa, 1991). Now, even at McDonald's, customers can "have it their way." The shift towards variety has not been without difficulties; McDonald's initially encountered stiff internal resistance from their own operations staff who felt

It was a big mistake. Our stores are small. They didn't have space for the new equipment that was needed. It [the menu item] was really popular with our customers, but started to mess up the rest of our operation. . . . Marketing people are often very creative but should concentrate more on being total businessmen. Operations people tend to rate marketing folks on how well they understand the operation. (Langeard, Bateson, Lovelock, & Eiglier, 1981, p. 89)

This highlights the organizational reality of embracing mass customization, operations personnel adhere to the old ways which believe in the "absolutism of scale economy" where efficiency is prized above all else (Yasumuro, 1993). The need for the operations and marketing functions to cooperate in the delivery of strategically effective outputs (i.e., customer orientated) while maintaining optimum efficiency is one of the key challenges of the new paradigm. However, while Schlesinger and Heskett (1991) assert that market fragmentation faced by service organizations like McDonald's cannot be tackled within the confines of "production-line thinking," others, such as Yasumuro (1993), looking at McDonald's from a consumer durables manufacturing perspective, see cause for optimism inherent in their traditional approach:

Somewhat contrary to commonsense, the success factor of McDonald's hamburgers is not their "uniformity," but their "variety." McDonald's created variety through the combination of standardized materials. (Yasumuro, 1993, p. 215)

HOTELS: ACCOMMODATING THE MASS-CUSTOMIZATION CONCEPT?

Ritzer's proposition can be extended to motel/budget hotel chains as a clear example of the McDonaldization process. Here, as elsewhere in the thesis, rationality and predictability supplant the unpredictable or even the quirky. Ritzer's description (Ritzer, 1993, p. 83) of the "delights" of staying in motels prior to the advent of the "McDonaldized" chains of franchised motels would seem to many hotel users as perverse at best. Many of us can see little or no virtue in having to endure a "Fawlty Towers" type experience while resident in a motel. After all, we find Basil Fawlty—the character played by British actor John Cleese—and his antics funny because we have all experienced something of the *awful* reality on which—in extreme form—it is based. In this section, we suggest that recent advances in the hotel accommodation sector are beginning to move beyond the standardization phase to incorporate some real progress towards increased consumer choice.

The application of mass customization to McDonald's and fast food more generally is perhaps fairly obvious given its clear foundations in scientific management and mass production. What about hotel accommodation? Since the 1950s we have seen the steady rise of the hotel chain—more markedly in the huge geographic expanses of the United States with the birth of the motel, stimulated by the explosion in road-based travel. In the United Kingdom, hotel chains have had less of an impact because of slightly different demand characteristics, for example, the initial emphasis being more upon overseas tourism than business usage. But even in the United Kingdom we have recently seen a dramatic increase in the number of "lodges"—motel-type operations on or near major roadways. Large operators such as Whitbread plc are estimated to be opening two new lodges a month in the United Kingdom, while Forte plc, the United Kingdom pioneer of the concept, now operates over a hundred lodges and claims an occupancy rate of 95 percent during the summer months. It is worth noting, however, that the United Kingdom hotel industry continues to be dominated by smaller independent and more craft-oriented outlets—small private hotels and bed-and-breakfast establishments. How long this may continue is open to debate. Recent expert opinion predicts that up to 18,000 "Fawlty Towers" rooms in the United Kingdom will be replaced by 10,000 rooms in chain-operated budget hotels (Slattery, & Feehely, 1995).

Today's hotels are increasingly becoming what Skinner (1974) termed *focused factories.*

A factory that focuses on a narrow product mix for a particular market niche will out-perform the conventional plant, which attempts a broader mission . . . the focused factory is manageable and controllable. Its problems are demanding but limited in scope. (Skinner, 1974, pp. 114, 116)

The relevance of the application of this concept to the service sector— with some minor caveats—has been argued by Dierdonck and Brandt, who state: "There is little doubt that the concept of the focused factory applies equally well, or even more, to service industries. The better managed companies in the service industries are precisely characterized by a high degree of focus" (1988, p. 34). In the past, hotels tried to serve an impossibly varied range of needs and customer types with the same offer. At best, this resulted in the needs of one or two dominant customer groups being serviced at the expense of other customer groups. At worst, it could result in no single group's needs being satisfied. This situation coupled with the explosion of demographic "norms" (Donaldson & Taylor, 1996) has led to radical changes in the hotel sector. Most major hotel chains now operate across a broad range of market segments (see Table 2) and meet a diverse range of product, service, and price needs.

Table 2
Example of Product Segmentation in Hotel Industry

Market Segment	Holiday Inn	Marriott	Forte
First class	Crowne Plaza	Marriott	Exclusive Collection
Middle Market: full service limited service	Holiday Inn Garden Court	n/a Courtyard	Crest Posthouse
Economy/Budget[8]	Express	Fairfield Inn	Travelodge

Sources: Adapted from Pannell Kerr Forster Associates. (1990). *Hotel Product Segmentation in Europe,* London: PKFA; and J. Connell. (1992). *Case Study, Forte Hotels Rebranding Exercise 1991,* Glasgow: Queen's College.

This fragmentation in demand and increasing competition has led to an increased emphasis being given to the practice of branding both macroproducts (e.g., hotels) and microproducts/services within these. For example, Forte plc in addition to the hotel brands shown in Table 2 also have a range of products/services available *across* the hotel brands such as *Venue Guarantee* (aimed at business meeting planners), *Business Guarantee* (aimed at business travelers), *Leisure Breaks* (aimed at couples and families), and *Incentive Guarantee* (aimed at incentive travel organizers) (Connell, 1992). As with Forte's hotel brands, these service brands consist of certain core elements which ensure standardization on key quality dimensions, but they also have a number of more flexible elements attached to enable the final offer to be customized to meet the needs of the customer and the capabilities of the hotel unit involved. The latter dimension, in turn, being driven by the core elements of the actual hotel brand.

Mass customization of hotel services, at its most basic, involves the room size and type (e.g., single, double, smoking, nonsmoking), proximity to main services, fire exits, and so on. Guests could be asked what they prefer from the available alternatives. Advances in technology mean that guests can now customize their in-room video entertainment and the guest room environment through individual temperature controls (Pine, 1993). In the 1980s some United Kingdom business hotels began to introduce "hotels within hotels" with the creation of concierge floors which provided extra service levels and facilities at an extra cost. This, however, was simply the beginning of a much more radical shift towards the creation of a range of standardized products (Skinner's focused factories) where the workforce and their equipment became fully dedicated towards a particular customer segment. Thus Forte caters *(sic)* for the needs of the upscale business and leisure traveler with their *Forte Crest* brand (the really upscale traveler can visit one of *Forte's Exclusive Collection* which includes the *George V* in Paris), the business traveler on a more limited budget needs are served through the *Forte Posthouse* brand, while the economy traveler has their needs catered for by the *Travelodge* brand.

To obtain a glimpse of the future, however, we need to look at the activities of the hotel organization widely acknowledged as being the most innovative and marketing-orientated firm in the industry—the Marriott Corporation. A classic example of Marriott's approach (and of Skinner's focused factory concept in practice) is its development of the *Courtyard by Marriott* brand which has had a significant impact on the North American lodging market. Its success with consumers resulted in many hospitality firms replicating the concept in much the same way as many have replicated McDonald's successful formula (see Wind, Green, Shifflet, and Scarborough, 1989, for a discussion of the development of the *Courtyard by Marriott* brand). More generally, through the use of technology, Marriott is mass customizing its users' experience using a customer database, what it calls its "Guest Recognition System." This is a guest history system which enables the company to store and retrieve guest preferences as to the type of room, eating and drinking habits, and any special requirements while in residence. Radically, this information is not limited to just front-desk personnel but is available to all guest-contact staff. Hotel firms have adopted many of the practices of their airline cousins in an effort to establish customer (i.e., brand) loyalty. The most obvious manifestation of this is the frequent-traveler programs which not only reward loyalty but enable the capturing of valuable guest data to facilitate (consummate?) the relationship. With the advent of the "smartcard," the potential for increased levels of mass customization takes another leap forward. The individuality of guests can be stored on a silicon chip awaiting capture by the hotel's computer. The subsequent data interface facilitates the efficient matching of guest wants and needs with available facilities of the hotel in its role as service provider. All this leaves the hotel's staff free to interact with guests to ensure the fine tuning of the service provision in a way that technology is yet (never?) to replicate.

Our discussion above highlights that the mass providers of hotel accommodation are increasingly recognizing the individual needs of their guests. While Ritzer might prefer that our needs for overnight accommodation be serviced by "local" providers, he misses the point of why the franchised chain has been so successful over the last two decades or so. For many of us, the experience of an overnight stay, away from the comforts of home, induces a feeling of insecurity resulting from the lack of control we have over the alien environment of a strange hotel. Regular travelers frequently attempt to reduce their anxiety and regain *some* control by electing to stay in the familiar surroundings of a Holiday Inn or similar. For the unseasoned traveler the attraction of the "McDonaldized" offer, as opposed to the local "Bates Motel" alternative, is likely to be measurably greater. Thus, the demise of many of the lodging alternatives to the franchised offer is as much a product of consumer choice as producer (i.e., market) power. To suggest that these standardized accommodations dehumanize us is to ignore the reality of the human condition—our basic need for warmth, shelter, food, and security. We would argue that it is the ability of the "McDonaldized" lodging chains to *reliably* deliver on these critical dimensions that has led to their rise and to the decline of the frequently "colorful" alternatives.

CONCLUSION

In this essay we have explored not only the manifest fast-food dimension to Ritzer's thesis but its application to hotel accommodation. Obviously, the metaphor is such that we could also question the application of the McDonaldization thesis to a wide range of consumer situations. Ritzer has argued that the future for customer choice looks increasingly bleak. The McDonaldization of society will mean that future choices will be—at best—merely variations within a theme and—at worst—illusory. From this perspective, a certain future of increasing McDonaldization looks decidedly depressing. However, we have argued that this is an unnecessarily depressing portrayal of the future. The perspective we have developed in this essay is considerably more optimistic. Our view is that Ritzer has exaggerated a half truth. There are other trends operating within society that suggest there is the potential that technology ends up offering more choice rather than constraining it to narrow limits à la McDonald's menu.

Drawing loosely upon the analogy developed by Wood elsewhere in this book, Ritzer is looking at his metaphorical bottle of wine and, like the pessimist, complains that it is half empty and getting emptier! We, on the other hand, prefer to see this same bottle as being half full and *perhaps* getting fuller. As such, we would accuse Ritzer of *petitio elenchis*, when the actual outcome is far from certain. Moreover, there is evidence, as we have presented here, that we may confront a very different future from that suggested by the "*McDonaldization of Society*" thesis. In this essay we have highlighted the increasingly apparent failure of mass production to deliver the outcomes desired by society. This, in turn, has translated into a failure to deliver the economic benefits demanded by producers within the capitalist system. The response to this has been a paradigm shift whereby mass customization is rapidly replacing mass production's "low-cost, standardized output" focus with one which offers low cost products and services with a dramatically increased emphasis upon the needs of individual consumers. In the final analysis, if society can meet our needs as *individual consumers*, do the means (i.e., processes) by which this is achieved really matter?

NOTES

1. For example, the healthy eating trend led to lower fat products such as McDonald's *McLean Burger* and Kentucky Fried Chicken's *Lite 'n Crispy* skinless fried chicken. However, the United States consumer has rejected McDonald's low fat burger and this has now been withdrawn.

2. The term flexibility and its operationalization can be problematic. See Upton (1994).

3. There is a paradox here in being able to tailor output yet retain the responsiveness associated with a standardized output. For tactics of how to resolve this, see McCutcheon, Raturi, and Meredith (1994).

4. For a discussion of market fragmentation and, in particular, psychographic fragmentation, see Mueller-Heumann (1992).

5. The development and deployment of American Airline's *SABRE* system is an excellent illustration of this. See Hopper (1990).

6. This was one of the key findings of a report produced by the Naisbitt Group on behalf of McCann-Erickson Ltd. (Restall, 1987).

7. The launch of McDonald's *McLean Burger* is a case in point. Although the development process took three years and cost $2 million, the test marketing prior to full launch was an incredibly short four months. McDonald's historically utilized a very protracted roll-out process for new product launches (Crawford-Welch, 1994, p. 206). As indicated in note 1 above, this product has not been successful. The transition from mass production to mass customization is not a simple one and requires fundamental changes in an organization's systems and its culture.

8. This category can be further subdivided to include lower, middle, and upper with respect to facilities and pricing (Pannell, Kerr, and Forster Associates, 1990).

REFERENCES

Ashby, W. (1956). *An introduction to cybernetics.* New York: John Wiley.

Barker, J. (1988). *Discovering the future: The business of paradigms.* London: Pergamon.

Blair, K. (1994, October). Appetite for bigger slice of pizza sales. *The Scotsman, 18.*

Connell, J. (1992). *Case study: Forte hotels rebranding exercise 1991.* Glasgow, Scotland: Queen's College.

Crawford-Welch, S. (1994). Product development in the hospitality industry. In R. Teare, J. Mazanec, S. Crawford-Welch, & S. Calver, (Eds.), *Marketing in hospitality and tourism: A consumer focus.* London: Cassell.

Davis, S. (1987). *Future perfect.* Reading, MA: Addison-Wesley.

Dierdonck, R., & Brandt, G. (1988, January 6-7). Focused factory in service industries. In R. Johnson (Ed.), *The management of service operations: Proceedings of the Operations Management Association (UK) Annual International Conference* (pp. 33–49), Bedford, England: IFS Publications.

Donaldson, S., & Taylor S. (1996). The mature market segment in hospitality: Grey clouds or a silver lining? *Proceedings of the Fifth Annual Council of Hospitality Management Education Research Conference* (pp. 144–162). Nottingham: Nottingham Trent University.

Donkin, R. (1994, October 28). No relish for cheese and pickle sandwich. *Financial Times,* p. 9.

Hopper, M. (1990, May/June). Rattling SABRE —New ways to compete on information. *Harvard Business Review,* 118–125.

Langeard, E., Bateson, J., Lovelock, C., & Eiglier, P. (1981), *Services marketing: New insights from consumers and managers.* Cambridge, MA: Marketing Science Institute.

Levitt, T. (1972, September/October). Production-line approach to service. *Harvard Business* Review, 41–52.

Levitt, T. (1976, September/October). The industrialization of service. *Harvard Business Review,* 63–74.

Lyon, P., Taylor, S., & Smith, S. (1994). McDonaldization: A reply to Ritzer's thesis. *International Journal of Hospitality Management,* 13(2), 95–99.

Lyon, P., Taylor, S., & Smith, S. (1995). Is Big Mac the big threat?: A rejoinder to Silverstone and Wood. *International Journal of Hospitality Management, 14*(2), 119–122.

McCutcheon, D., Raturi, A. S., & Meredith, J. R. (1994). The customization-responsiveness squeeze. *Sloan Management Review, 35*(2), 75–84.

McDonald's. (1994, September 30). *The Times* (Supplement), 1-8.

McKenna, R. (1988, September/October). Marketing in an age of diversity. *Harvard Business Review,* 88–94.

McNamee, P. (1985). *Tools and techniques for strategic management.* London: Pergamon.

Miller, D. (1987). *Material culture and mass consumption.* Oxford, UK: Blackwell.

MSI. (1991). *Databrief: Fast food UK.* Marketing Strategies for Industry.

Mueller-Heumann, G. (1992). Market and technology shifts in the 1990s: Market fragmentation and mass customization. *Journal of Marketing Management, 8*(4), 303–314.

Pannell, Kerr, and Forster Associates (1990, August). Hotel Product Segmentation in Europe. London: Pannell, Kerr, and Forster Associates.

Pine, B. J. (1993). *Mass customization: The new frontier in business competition.* Boston, MA: Harvard Business School Press.

Piore, M., & Sabel, C. (1984). *The second industrial divide: Possibilities for prosperity.* New York: Basic Books.

Restall, C. (1987). Leisure futures: A summary of a recent study commissioned by McCann-Erickson Ltd. from the Naisbitt Group. *Journal of Marketing Management,* 3(1), 1–11.

Ritzer, G. (1993). *The McDonaldization of society: An investigation into the changing character of contemporary social life.* Newbury Park, CA: Pine Forge Press.

Scarpa, J. (1991, July 1). McDonald's menu mission. *Restaurant Business,* 110-117.

Schlesinger, L. A., and Heskett, J. L. (1991, September/October). The service-driven service company. *Harvard Business Review,* 71–81.

Silverstone, R. (1995). A response to Lyon, Taylor and Smith: The Ritzer debate continued. *International Journal of Hospitality Management, 14*(2), 111–115.

Skinner, W. (1974, May/June). The focused factory. *Harvard Business Review,* 113–121.

Slattery, P., & Feehely, G. (1995). *Kleinwort Benson securities: Quoted hotel companies UK. Ninth Annual Review.* London: KBS.

Taylor, S., & Lyon, P. (1995). Paradigm lost: The rise and fall of McDonaldization. *International Journal of Contemporary Hospitality Management, 7*(2/3), 64–68.

Teboul, J. (1988, January 6-7). De-industrialize service for quality. In R. Johnson (Ed.), *The management of service operations: Proceedings of the Operations Management Association (UK) Annual International Conference* (pp. 131–138). Bedford: UK: IFS Publications.

Upton, D. (1994). The management of manufacturing flexibility. *California Management Review, 36*(2), 72–89.

Wind, J., Green, P. E., Shifflet, D., & Scarborough, M., (1989, January/February). Courtyard by Marriott: Designing a hotel facility with consumer-based marketing models. *Interfaces*, *19*(1), 25–47.

Yasumuro, K. (1993). Conceptualizing an adaptable marketing system: The end of mass marketing. In R. Tedlow, & G. Jones (Eds.), *The rise and fall of mass marketing* (pp. 205–235). London and New York: Routledge.

8

The McCommodification of Society: Rationalization and Critical Theory

Thomas M. Jeannot

INTRODUCTION

The power of George Ritzer's *The McDonaldization of Society* consists in its unrelenting presentation of concrete examples from virtually every domain of social life: work and leisure, education and health care, mass media and family life, culture and politics. It is hard to think of a better cultural icon to dramatize Weber's theme than McDonald's, the ubiquitous emblem of a consumer ethos whose world is fashioned from fast food, cars, television commercials, and malls. Ritzer appeals to McDonaldization in order to illustrate how deeply the instrumental values of efficiency, calculability, predictability, and control are anchored in the lifeworld. All right, then, we denizens of the North Atlantic cultures live in a McDonaldized society.

But from the Marxist perspective from which this essay takes its bearings, a further question arises concerning the role of McDonaldization in the dynamics of capitalist accumulation. Ritzer acknowledges that among the forces driving McDonaldization, it is "impelled by material interests, especially economic goals and aspirations," and preeminently profitability (Ritzer, 1993, pp. 147–48). However, this is not the principal theme of his work, nor does his Weberian account of "material interests" spontaneously glide into a Marxist conceptual framework, which regards capitalism as the global context within which contemporary socioeconomic, political, and cultural processes should be explained and evaluated. In the note in which he addresses this question, Ritzer writes that his analysis "resembles Marx's critique of capitalism," but that "this book is . . . premised far more on the theories of Max Weber" (Ritzer, 1993, p. 191). Still, if the linkage cannot be simply assumed, it can be argued for. The point of appropriating Ritzer's account of McDonaldization into a Marxist framework, then, is twofold: first, because it enriches the Marxian critique of consumer culture; and second, so I will argue, because the pathological phenomenon of McDonaldization can be adequately grasped only by placing it within its capitalist context. (As to why we should think of McDonaldization as pathological in the first place, in this essay I take Ritzer's evidence that we live in Weber's "iron cage" for granted.)

The relations between Marx and Weber, the histories of their respective receptions, and the implications each theoretical perspective holds for the other are notoriously complex and subject to wildly divergent interpretations.[1] Fortunately, Habermas has written *The Theory of Communicative Action* (*TCA*), which advances the work the Hungarian Marxist Georg Lukács began of integrating Weber's theory into Western Marxism (Lukács, 1971, pp. 83–222). Despite Habermas's description of himself as "the last Marxist," his version of critical theory is neo-Marxist at best; on the other hand, it provides a bridge from Weber to Marx, and therefore a *tertium quid* in terms of which McDonaldization can be understood. Accordingly, first, I will undertake a partial review of *TCA*, with the aim of linking Ritzer's gloss on Weber's thesis of rationalization with Habermas's presentations of reification and colonization; then I will move from Habermas's account to Marx's concept of commodification. These complementary ways of conceptualizing social reality converge on McDonaldization, a peculiarly American dialectical image of the one-sidedly rationalized, reified, colonized, and commodified lifeworld at the center of late capitalism.

RATIONALIZATION AND THE THEORY OF COMMUNICATIVE ACTION

Needless to say, Habermas's monumental two-volume work is too dense and rich to admit of any facile summary. My intention in characterizing it here is simply to retrieve the notion of a "colonization of the lifeworld" he presents in the penultimate section of the second volume (Habermas, 1987, 2:332–373). Habermas's thesis of colonization goes together with the familiar critical-theoretic theme of reification, which Lukács first introduced as an interpretive lens on Marx in *History and Class-Consciousness* (Lukács, 1971), originally written in 1922. Weber's thesis of rationalization, in turn, is integral to the development of both ideas.

Habermas holds that (1) the lifeworld is colonized, (2) by the autonomous subsystems of economy and state administration, (3) which are anchored in lifeworld institutions, (4) through the "de-linguistified" media of money and power, when (5) they displace, subvert, stand in for, or otherwise obstruct linguistically mediated interactions oriented to reaching understanding. "When stripped of their ideological veils, the imperatives of autonomous subsystems make their way into the lifeworld from the outside—like colonial masters coming into a tribal society—and force a process of assimilation upon it" (1987, 2:355).

"Colonization" is to Habermas what the "totally administered society" was to Horkheimer and Adorno, and what the "iron cage" of Weber's most widely

project, in part because Habermas is the leading second-generation Frankfurt school theorist, and therefore heir to the "convergences . . . between Weber's rationalization thesis and the critique of instrumental reason along the lines of the Marx-Lukács tradition" (1:345). This heritage is crucial, of course, for historically situating Habermas's intellectual horizons, themes, and preoccupations. Within critical theory, his major innovation is his achievement of a paradigm shift from an exhausted "philosophy of consciousness" to the "theory of communication"—"a communications-theoretic turn" from an egologically structured, subject-centered reason to a communicatively structured, intersubjective reason (1984, 1:386, 397).

But Habermas's central theme—his mission, we might say—has a deeper historical grounding than Lukács's reception of Weber and its aftermath. He is intent upon retrieving the "philosophical intentions unfolded from Kant through Marx," that is, the great period of classical German philosophy, in the epoch politically initiated by Frederick the Great, when the German states were just beginning to catch up with modernity. In other words, the theme of modernity (or more narrowly, bearing in mind his significant reference to Kant, the theme of the "enlightenment project") is the predominating theme in his thought.

A complex network of outlooks today has arrayed itself *against modernity*, ranging from Alasdair MacIntyre to Richard Rorty, and from the rearguard of the American Catholic Philosophical Association to Jean-François Lyotard. If they cross a common axis, it can be designated by a formulation in Alasdair MacIntyre's widely read book, *After Virtue*: "The Failure of the Enlightenment Project" (MacIntyre, 1981, pp. 49–75). As against this trend, Habermas is decisively *for modernity*, for the enlightenment project, and for the "philosophical intentions unfolded from Kant through Marx." These intentions are directed to the creation of a society based on the twin ideals of reason and freedom. In its deepest intentions, in other words, the enlightenment project is a project of liberation. Linking this emancipatory interest back to its late eighteenth-century point of departure, Habermas's position is that rationalization—the principal element in his theory of modernity—is a positive, progressive accomplishment. Obviously, this evaluation is quite different from Weber's, on the one hand, and Adorno and Horkheimer's on the other. The problem is not that modernity has exhausted itself in the "polar night of icy darkness and hardness" (Ritzer, 1993, p. 188); the problem is rather that it has only partially begun to realize its promise. The problem, then, is not that society has become too rational, but that we have yet to become a rational society. With Weber, Habermas regards modernization and rationalization as correlative processes. They follow on the heels of a progressive "disenchantment," the breakdown of traditional societies and the power of traditionary forces to secure the ongoing material and symbolic reproduction of social life. With respect to symbolic reproduction in particular, the process of secularization robs religious and metaphysical worldviews of their cohesive force as bonds of solidarity, with profound implications for culture, society, and personality. Obviously, there are great losses brought on by disenchantment: the fragmentation of consciousness, a loss of meaning, and the dark prospect of an iron cage or a totally administered society—the loss of freedom—to the extent that the lifeworldly domains of culture, society, and personality lack the communicative resources to check and resist colonization. This brings us to a consideration of the colonizing powers.

The possibility of colonization is conditioned by the internal dynamics of the rationalization process itself. If premodern societies are "organic," rationalization brings in its wake the differentiation of an organic whole (on the symbolic level, a religious-metaphysical unity) into the separate domains of science, morality, and art, of which there is no clearer reflection than the architectonic of Kant's critical philosophy, developed in the last decades of the eighteenth century.

Moreover, as crucially for Habermas as for Weber, rationalization also gives rise to the further differentiation of morality from legality. This differentiation was basic to Weber's understanding of the Protestant, inner-worldly vocational ethic, the rational-methodic conduct of life, and their joint role in the development of capitalism.[2] The differentiation *within* the lifeworld of morality and law is the condition, as Habermas sees it, for the further differentiation of autonomous subsystems *from out of* the lifeworld. Based on this differentiation, he establishes a "rough and ready" boundary between the subsystems of economy and state administration, on the one hand, and the spheres of private and public life on the other (1987, 2:310). On the one hand, the capitalist economy and state administration need to be *anchored in* the lifeworldly domain of society, and the formal rationality of law serves just this purpose. On the other hand, once law is severed from morality, economic and administrative subsystems can begin to function as autonomous spheres "neutralized against the lifeworld" (1987, 2:309). Here is where Habermas finds Weber's account of bureaucratic rationality, in capitalist enterprises as well as public and political administration, most trenchant: "action within organization falls *under the premises* of formally regulated domains of action. Because the latter are ethically neutralized by their legal form of organization, *communicative action forfeits its validity basis in the interior of organizations*" (1987, 2:310). Then they become self-regulating systems, and it becomes possible for delinguistified steering media to displace communicative action altogether, and to "*disempower* its validity basis" (1987, 2:311). To cut to the chase, this is Habermas's explanation of how it has come to pass that our lives are ruled by money and power.

But of all writers, Habermas is exceedingly careful not to leap to so rhetorical a conclusion. Aside from his methodological and systematic rigor, he wants reasoned grounds for social hope, against the iron cage and the pessimism of his critical-theoretic predecessors; nor can his last line be, as it is for Ritzer, to quote Dylan Thomas's advice only to "Rage, rage against the dying of the light" (Ritzer, 1993, p. 188).[3] He is not ready to concede that "the tendencies toward bureaucratization described by Weber will ever reach the Orwellian state in which all integrative operations have been converted . . . over to systemic mechanisms" (Habermas, 1987, 2:312). However, if Habermas is correct that our social world has not been *entirely* colonized by money and power, and if McDonaldization is *not* all that is left, then he needs to explain why the iron cage is not necessarily the final destination of rationalization, since he agrees with Weber that the process that threatens us with it is irreversible. Habermas comes to terms with the potentially radical privatization of substantive values that follows from Weber's ambivalent values pluralism, his separation of facts from values, and his decisionism essentially by challenging Weber's ambiguous foreshortening, truncation, and one-sided presentation of the rationalization process. Although he scrupulously avoids a reductive reading of Weber, appreciating the complexity and density of his thought, in the last analysis it is the Weber of the iron cage who finally misconceives the positive potentials of rationalization and the emancipatory project of the Enlightenment.

We might say schematically that in Weber there is too much "Nietzsche" and not enough "Kant." On the one hand, this is the "'Parsonized' Weber" of his positivist epigones; on the other, it is the darkly prophetic Weber who heralds the triumph of Adorno and Horkheimer's "instrumental reason" and Marcuse's technocratic domination and one-dimensionality. The thesis of the "loss of meaning" shines through in the former; the thesis of the "loss of freedom" (the "iron cage," the "totally administered society") shines through in the latter.

The reasoned grounds of Habermas's social hope, therefore, in contrast to an impotent rage against inevitable night, consist not in betraying or abandoning the Enlightenment project, but in steadfastly mobilizing the as yet unvanquished social forces and resources that still hold out the prospect of realizing its emancipatory promise; of overcoming the contradiction implicit in the one-sided, partial, and selective rationalization that underwrites the logic of colonization—the encroachment of cognitive-instrumental rationality, and of instrumental and strategic action, into domains irreducible to them, domains of moral-practical and of aesthetic-expressive rationality, which also symbolically structure the lifeworld through the as yet only partially and incompletely developed potentials of communicative action.

With an eye on these potentials, Habermas concludes *TCA* by calling for the reconceptualization and renewal of the interdisciplinary work of the Institute for Social Research that initiated critical theory (Habermas, 1987, 2:378). The theory of communicative action, as opposed to a "philosophy of history," is the conceptual framework within which Habermas aims to preserve the emancipatory interest of a critical theory of society, the deepest intention of which still belongs to the *Aufklärung*.

The "philosophy of history" projected a teleology that Nietzsche already knew to be doomed, but to which Lukács still pinned his hopes in the victory of the proletariat. Once the disenchanted thinkers of the Institute for Social Research found themselves compelled to abandon that hope, but still thinking within the "philosophy of history," Weber's "rosy blush" of a "laughing Enlightenment" (Weber, 1958, p. 182) turned into Adorno and Horkheimer's bleak scowl. The Hegelian idealism of a realized totality that Lukács still positively valorized became the nightmare of totalitarianism.[4] As against this historical chapter, which he deems to be closed for good, Habermas believes he has found a way to renew "the philosophical intentions unfolded from Kant through Marx" in his "communications-theoretic turn," which is no longer a philosophy of history and which projects no assured victories. The ideal of a socially achieved *Vernunft*, the restoration on the higher plane of reason of the lost religious-metaphysical unity of a premodern worldview, must be forsaken. On the other hand, the quest for meaning, freedom, social integration, and vital human solidarity remains as a latent cognitive potential of communicative action, operative in the "countermovements" against colonization harbored in the lifeworld. These countermovements are based on "a nonreified communicative everyday practice" among citizens, as opposed to "expert cultures" (1987, 2:398). The potential unity of a "nonreified communicative everyday practice" is the (fallibilistic, not guaranteed) goal toward which we can still struggle to emancipate ourselves from fragmentation, cultural impoverishment, and the loss of meaning and freedom.

In his "Backward Glance" before drawing *TCA* to a close, Habermas recalls the optimism of the Enlightenment project by briefly returning to the figure of Condorcet (whom he had considered at some length early in volume one; see Habermas, 1987, 2:326; 1984, 1:145–51). Condorcet wore Weber's "rosy blush" because he was convinced that the cognitive potentials, not only of science, but of morality and art as well, could be unleashed and developed to secure a reign of justice and happiness for humankind. If anything is clear, however, it is clear that Condorcet's "extravagant expectation" has not come to pass (1987, 2:326). Hence we find ourselves at the crossroads briefly discussed above.

Habermas agrees that the bloom is off the rose of Enlightenment, but also that "now, as then, there is a difference of opinion as to whether we should hold fast to the intentions of the Enlightenment, in however refracted a form, or should give up the project of modernity as lost" (1987, 2:326–27). As we have seen, he stands for holding fast. But what has yet to be explained is why we should think that his diagnosis of the times is more cogent than Weber's disenchanted one, or what founds his chastened hope if not the teleological guarantees of a philosophy of history.

The forces of colonization that threaten the lifeworld at the end of our century, so well exemplified by Ritzer's presentation of McDonaldization, have generated the social pathologies of "two interlocking, mutually reinforcing tendencies: *systemically induced reification*"—which Habermas defines as "a pathological de-formation of the communicative infrastructure of the lifeworld" (1987, 2:375)—"and *cultural impoverishment*" (2:327). Ritzer's documentation of McDonaldization in scores of concrete examples furnishes a wealth of empirical ballast to give depth and weight to Habermas's neo-Weberian diagnoses of fragmentary consciousness, the loss of meaning, and the loss of freedom.

Still, Habermas locates powerful resources from within the lifeworld that can serve both as defensive and offensive countermeasures. In that connection, what "social theory can accomplish . . . resembles the focusing power of a magnifying glass" to bring the lifeworldly sources of social hope and liberation into clear view (1987, 2:383). From Habermas's perspective, this is just the critical-theoretic opportunity that Weber's theorizing misses. Weber had brought the *pathologies* of the lifeworld into clear view, but his diagnosis "does not explain . . . why pathologies of this kind appear in the first place" (1987, 2:327).[5] Habermas criticizes the limits of Weberian explanation in a two-stage argument (relying on "an explanation of the Marxian type" [1987, 2:328]).

First, as we have already seen, Weber finally explains rationalization in the one-sided, partial, and selective way that invites Lukács to reformulate it as "reification" in *History and Class-Consciousness*. "But this does not explain why modernization follows a highly selective pattern," why *specifically* the cognitive-instrumental action orientation should have been so thoroughly rationalized, while the rational potentials "for moral-practical will formation, expressive self-presentation, and aesthetic satisfaction [do] not get utilized" (1987, 2:328). To answer *this* question, Habermas argues, we would have to "investigate the drive mechanism behind the autonomized expansion of the economic system and its governmental complement," and here is where Weber fails (1987, 2:328).

An adequate explanation would point us in the direction Marx takes in *Capital*. Instead of developing the logic of capitalist valorization processes, however, Weber focuses (as Habermas argues at great length in volume one, 1984, pp. 157–271) on the differentiation of cultural value spheres within Occidental rationalism, the religious and ethical sources of capitalism, the spread of instrumental orientations, and the rationalization of law, in which "questions concerning the institutional embodiment of moral-practical rationality are not only shoved aside but directly turned into their opposite" (1984, 1:267).

Second, if capitalist rationalization is therefore a house divided against itself, then Weber settles into his "paradox of societal rationalization" by adopting a disposition both critical and apologetic (1987, 2:330). The loss of meaning and freedom, pathological deformations that led the earlier critical theorists to run "rationalization" and "reification" together, would seem in Weber's analysis to be the price of admission to modernity. This is what Ritzer identifies as the paradoxical "irrationality of rationality" (Ritzer, 1993, pp. 121–146). Habermas proposes another way.

Modernized societies are characterized by "stubborn systemic disequilibria" that can lead to "crises," and that certainly "call forth *pathologies* in the lifeworld" (1987, 2:385). The pathological deformations inevitably lead to conflict, first, with respect to "a center composed of strata *directly* involved in the production process and in maintaining capitalist growth as the basis of the welfare-state compromise," and second, with respect to "a periphery composed of a variegated array of groups that are lumped together," bound by their shared "critique of growth" (1987, 2:392–393).

The new social movements—for example, peace, civil rights, feminism, environmentalism—are sites of struggle against colonization, and so Habermas turns principally to them as the spaces wherein the best opportunities to complete the modern project presently lie, with the potential of emerging "counterinstitutions" that could "set limits to the inner dynamics of the economic and political-administrative action systems" (1987, 2:396). Significantly, he warns against equating the *functionalist rationality* of systems with the *communicative rationality* of cultural modernity (1987, 2:396).

Once again, we find Habermas arguing that the pathologies of modern capitalist society are not the result of modernization *per se* but of "modernity at variance with itself"; not rationalization *per se*, but the domination of "functionalist" over "communicative" rationality; and not systemic complexity *per se*, but the untapped cognitive potentials of a lifeworld that has yet to achieve the promise it still holds of enlightened emancipation. For all its ubiquity, neither is McDonaldization the last word.

In summary, then, despite his consideration of alternatives (the "velvet cage," the "rubber cage"), Ritzer finally agrees with Weber's own thesis that the cage is fashioned from iron (Ritzer, 1993, p. 162). Nevertheless, he wants to maintain a "niche" for hope (1993, pp. 187–188), which he carves out mainly by proposing individual alternative "lifestyles" such as his own as a tenured university professor (1993, pp. 178-181). From the perspective of this essay, however, this response to the iron cage, aside from its anemia, is deeply problematic. If the Weberian treatment of rationalization is correct, then the pessimistic resignation of Adorno and Horkheimer seems to be the more thoughtful response. On the other hand, if Habermas's critique of Weber has merit, then we can search out grounds for social hope from other quarters. Here is where Marx comes in.

HABERMAS AND MARX

Habermas's modernist rationalism situates him along with Marx, Weber, Harvey, and Ritzer within the horizons of a "critical modernism" rather than "postmodernism." Postmodern themes are developed elsewhere in this collection, whereas I propose to criticize Habermas on different grounds, and then only with the bare sketch of an argument. Habermas's rationalist perspective offers one solution to the problem Ritzer raises concerning the "irrationality of rationality," certainly a better one than capitulating to irrationalism. Ritzer himself proposes a "reason" distinct from Weberian "rationalization," which he connects with the theme of "dehumanization" (Ritzer, 1993, pp. 121, 130–146).

Marx too argues that capitalist rationalization and modernization are dehumanizing and irrational, and he grounds his argument in his theory of value and the "commodity form." Meanwhile, although Habermas explicitly links both his thesis of colonization and his critique of Weber to a missing premise in

Weber's argument that he has to turn to Marx in order to retrieve, he must finally be read as rejecting Marxism—certainly in its "classical" form, and also as a "philosophy of history," but most decisively in his critique of Marx's theory of value. This is where I believe he deserves to be challenged.

When Habermas first opens his "Backward Glance," he reviews the difficulties he had discerned in Weber's social theory as he had reconstructed it in volume one. Then, architectonically, he asserts that "Weber's explanatory strategy can be rid of these and similar and difficulties if we assume that":

(p) the emergence of modern, to begin with capitalist, societies required the institutional embodiment and motivational anchoring of postconventional moral and legal representations; but (q) capitalist modernization follows a pattern such that cognitive-instrumental rationality surges beyond the bounds of the economy and state into other, communicatively structured areas of life and achieves dominance there at the expense of moral-political and aesthetic-practical rationality; and (r) this produces disturbances in the symbolic reproduction of the lifeworld. (1987, 2:304–305)

In terms of this argumentative scheme, *p, q, and r*, Habermas schematically proposes that Weber advances the propositions *p* and *r*, but that he fails to develop *q*. However, *q* is the decisive proposition required to explain why the societal rationalization processes that constitute modernity take the peculiarly and selectively *capitalist* form they achieve in Western and westernizing societies. This fundamental deficiency in Weber's explanation can be rectified only by linking *p* to *r* through *q*; or in other words, by turning to Marx.

Habermas's retrieval and appropriation of Marx is fundamentally a matter of discovering the *causal mechanism* to which his Weber had paid insufficient attention. But "the *causal explanation* of the transition to the modern age could succeed only with the discovery of the conditions *sufficient* for utilizing—however selectively—the available cognitive potential, so as to bring about the *characteristic* institutional innovations" (1987, 2:316). Furthermore, an adequate causal explanation of specifically capitalist institutions must be sought on the level of "system" rather than "social" integration: for it is *in capitalism* that the "system" is first "uncoupled" from the "lifeworld"; *in capitalism* that it then develops as an interlocking network of autonomous economic and administrative processes, the autonomy of which Habermas explains by way of the "language-independent steering media" of money and power; and *in capitalism* therefore that the particular pathologies of a systemically colonized lifeworld (which we may now also call "McDonaldization") specifically appear.

Habermas therefore finds it necessary to incorporate Weberian theory into an explanatory framework that focuses, not on "Occidental rationalism" in general, but on the logic of capitalist accumulation in particular. "The loss of freedom that Weber attributed to bureaucratization can no longer be explained by a shift from purposive rationality that is grounded value rationally to purposive rationality without roots" (1987, 2:318).

The transition from a "purposive rationality that is grounded value rationally" to a "purposive rationality without roots" is, in brief, Weber's "dissolution" of the Protestant ethic of "worldly asceticism . . . into pure utilitarianism" (Weber, 1958, p. 183), the triumph of the "formal rationality" of bureaucracy, technique, and instrumental values, yielding "this nullity" of "specialists without spirit, sensualists without heart" (p. 182), over the "substantive rationality" of humane, choiceworthy, and spiritually satisfying ends.

As compelling and illuminating as this diagnosis is, however, Habermas requires us to undertake a fundamental shift of emphasis in order to grasp the deeper causal roots of our *almost* thoroughly technicized social world. The "pertinent phenomena" must instead be accounted for as *"effects of the uncoupling of system and lifeworld"* (1987, 2:318). For Ritzer, the "paradox of societal rationalization" is the "irrationality of rationality," a pathological grammar of dehumanization that is nothing less than the "McDonaldization of society." McDonaldization, the tyranny of the instrumental values of efficiency, calculability, predictability, and control over our personal and corporate lives, is explained by Weberian theory. Habermas accepts this Weberian account, but he argues that it is incomplete in virtue of its failure to locate its basic causality.

If the problem were only that plural domains of value clash in the way they shape action orientations, then Ritzer's list of alternative action orientations, fixated on the level of "individual responses" (along the lines of "watch as little television as possible," Ritzer, 1993, p. 185), might be adequate to redress it (1993, pp. 182–187). From both a Habermasian and a Marxist perspective, however, the insufficiency of Ritzer's "practical guide" is that his "nonrational-ized"—not to say irrational—"alternatives" (p. 182) miss the systemic forest for the lifeworldly trees.

In other words, alternative action orientations presented on the level of individual responses can have no serious impact on the logic of systemic imperatives that both materially and symbolically structure our personal lives. If the pathological effects of McDonaldization can be reversed at all, then they must be reversed systemically. Or: the iron cage is not only a values orientation, but also a colonizing system of institutionalized values that lie beyond the capacity of merely private persons to substantially affect. Moreover, the problem is both more intractable and more vicious than a question of "bad taste," as Ritzer's list might otherwise lead us to think.

Anyone who finds this critique of the limitations of Weberian social theory persuasive will naturally turn to Marx, as Habermas does. In particular, Habermas emphasizes Marx's model "for the process of real abstraction" based on the "transformation of concrete work activities into abstract labor power that can be sold as a commodity" (1987, 2:322). As Habermas understands it, the exchange between wage-labor and capital is "a specific case" (1987, 2:342) of the more general process through which the complementary and interlinked autonomous subsystems of economy and state are abstracted or "uncoupled" from the lifeworld (hence, "real abstraction").

Which explanatory model we accept, a broadly Weberian or a broadly Marxian one, will have decisive implications for practice. As Habermas sees it, for Weber, only a Nietzschean "heroic nihilism" could be "adequate for legitimating a type of domination based on value skepticism" (1987, 2:324). Some of us *may be* "heroic nihilists," but most of us, for reasons that need not condemn us, *will be* the conformity-oriented herd animals of whom Nietzsche was often contemptuous (though from Aristotle's perspective, only because a human being is a *zoon politikon*) (Aristotle, 1985, 1097610). But furthermore, from the standpoint of this essay, "heroic nihilism" is really only the ineffectuality of Thomas's "rage," against which Alfred E. Newman's slogan, "What? Me worry?," the pop song's "Don't worry, be happy," and the beer commercial's "Why ask why?," seem to offer the more sagacious advice. On the other hand, Habermas's turn from Weber to Marx opens onto the horizon of another kind of practice.

[Weber's] difficulties disappear if we connect the phenomena he described critically with our revised version of the bureaucratization thesis, and attribute them to a colonization of the lifeworld by system imperatives that drive moral-practical elements out of private and political-public spheres of life. (1987, 2:324)

From this perspective, informed by Marx, the terms and conditions of practical struggle are better directed against just those "system imperatives that drive moral-practical elements out." A well-placed political rage against the system should therefore take the place of a misplaced, privatized, futile rage against "dying light."

From this more political-economic Marxian point of view (focused on "systems"), as opposed to a more culturalist, Weberian point of view (focused on "lifestyles"), Habermas's "radical reformism" is on behalf of radical democracy: "Between capitalism and democracy there is an *indissoluble* tension; in them two opposed principles of societal integration compete for primacy" (1987, 2:345). The critique of Habermas toward which I am headed, however, is to the effect that Habermas's conception of democracy is not nearly radical enough, mainly because he has abandoned class analysis. To make this case, we have to return both to Habermas's use and also his critique of Marx in *TCA*.

In the penultimate section of volume two of *TCA*, on "Marx and the Thesis of Internal Colonization," Habermas comes first to praise Marx, then, in effect, to bury him. First, to understand what Habermas appreciates about Marx's theoretical approach, we have to recall what he thinks he himself has accomplished for social theory: namely, a way to understand society *both* as "lifeworld" *and* as "system," and of social processes *both* as processes of "social integration" *and* as processes of "system integration."

A one-sided focus on the "lifeworld" filters out processes of material reproduction that are "not intended by [participants] and are usually not even perceived within the horizon of everyday practice" (Habermas, 1987, 2:150). This blind spot is the limitation and weakness of "the hermeneutic idealism of interpretive sociology" (1987, 2:151). On the other hand, an equally one-sided systems-theoretic approach suffers from an equal and opposite limitation and weakness, for "unlike structural patterns in biology, the structural patterns of action systems . . . have to be gotten at hermeneutically, that is, from the internal perspective of participants" (1987, 2:151). Accordingly, the best social theory will avoid either limitation by treating *both* "system" *and* "lifeworld," as well as the complex relations between them.

Therefore, Habermas writes that the "Marxian approach owes its theoretical superiority . . . to an ingenious coup de main: the analysis of the commodity form" (1987, 2:334). He condenses Marx's theoretical achievement by naming it "the process of *real abstraction,*" which Marx himself had analyzed as "the transformation of concrete into abstract labor power [,] a process in which communal and individual life become reified" (1987, 2:336). Ritzer's account of the rationalization of work under the headings of Fordism and Taylorism, in which McDonaldized workers essentially trade in their humanity for the machinelike status they assume in a workplace organized by instrumental values—an analysis whose *locus classicus* is Marx's own account of the machine in the *Grundrisse*—is obviously and easily assimilable to "the process of real abstraction," which is no mere obsolete phenomenon of the mid-nineteenth century (Marx, 1973, pp. 690–704; Ritzer, 1993, pp. 24–27, 60–61, 97, 131–132, 153–155, 168–171).

In short, Habermas praises Marx for discriminating and then relating "the two analytic levels of 'system' and 'lifeworld'" (1987, 2:338). However, next he develops several fundamental criticisms of Marx, including a "decisive . . . weakness": "the overgeneralization of a specific case of the subsumption of the lifeworld under the system" (1987, 2:342). What Marx allegedly "overgeneralizes" is the relation between wage-labor and capital that the value theory of *Capital* aims to explain. Marxists, as opposed to the wide range of views that are inspired in one way or another by Marx, still take this relation as fundamental.

Habermas's critique of Marx entails the conclusion that Marx's "critique of political economy has been unable to produce a satisfactory account of late capitalism" (1987, 2:343). In effect, Habermas (who is only repeating longstanding criticisms of Marxism and Marxian value theory) claims that Marx's theoretical explanation is economistic and reductive, and that it explains social relations by way of a falsely totalizing logic.

Our estimate of the merit of Habermas's critique of Marx very much depends on whether we should agree with his basic view regarding the success of the welfare state compromise (1987, 2:347–349). Since in my view, McDonaldization cannot be properly understood without linking it to the logic of value and the "commodity form," a brief development of this observation is in order. With the success of the welfare state compromise, Habermas holds that the economic crisis tendencies Marx identified have been mooted and that class conflict has been "pacified" (1987, 2:348). Hence, his political emphasis shifts from economic classes to social movements, and his interest shifts to "a new type of reification effect" that "arises in class-unspecific ways," having to do mainly with problems of legitimacy and mass loyalty that come into play in the symbolic reproduction of the lifeworld, rather than in the class-specific problematics of its material reproduction (1987, 2:349–350).

First, however, as Habermas would agree, it is an empirical question whether the welfare state compromise has achieved a "new equilibrium," solved its distribution problems, and "render[ed] class antagonism . . . innocuous" (Habermas, 1987, 2:350). But as John F. Sitton has recently pointed out, although Habermas's "analysis of social conflict is predicated on the idea that the welfare state will survive," he himself "provides much evidence that the welfare state compromise is crumbling" (1996, p. 194).

Moreover, inasmuch as Habermas's theory displaces class into the domain of system integration, he renders it invisible in the lifeworld. This is only partly an empirical, but also a conceptual question. The touchstone for Habermas's sense of the social world, at least while he was writing *TCA*, seems to have been the prosperous West Germany of the late 1970s, when the successes of the welfare state compromise would have been easy to affirm, making it possible to imagine a picture of social life in which the overwhelming majority is a "middle class" to whom the rhetoric of class conflict would have seemed anachronistic.

Not to construct an *ad hominem* argument, but one's images of social reality inevitably affect one's conceptualization of it. In a rising tide of capitalist prosperity, when dentists live next door to auto workers in the suburbs, class may well have a lifeworldly invisibility. But on this point, Habermas can be reminded of his own critique of the "hermeneutic idealism of interpretive sociology." And in any case, as the dynamics of capitalist growth start crashing into intractable structural barriers (which I think is already the case even for the domestic economies of the North Atlantic states), fault lines in the welfare state compromise come into clear view, as the lifeworld residents of South Central Los Angeles and dozens of other American cities can testify. Then also, if class relations and class antagonisms had been invisible to perhaps even most participants, we would have to adopt Peirce's method of the ostrich not to see them at work.

Finally, and most importantly, as Sitton again points out, "the central factor for analyzing the prospects of the welfare state will be how global capitalism develops" (1996, p. 195). Habermas's unit of social analysis is apparently the individual nation-state, or the cluster of such states in the North Atlantic. But the "dynamic of capitalism is global" (Sitton, 1996, p. 200). Summarizing the world-system theory of Immanuel Wallerstein, Sitton pertinently remarks that it "forces us to consider the degree to which the alleged eclipse of the importance of class structure and class identity in advanced capitalism may be merely a provincial, Eurocentric viewpoint" (1996, p. 200).

Indeed, in the New World Order that has emerged after the collapse of the Warsaw Pact and the Soviet Union, two considerations are obivous. First, now that—for us—we are no longer held spellbound by the cold war, a long overdue realignment of our thinking from a north/south perspective is warranted. Second, what we ought to be thinking about is the rapidly emerging global integration of a single-world capitalist economy dominated by transnational corporations. Marx's "free-trader Vulgaris" is no longer the individual capitalist entrepreneur, but the impersonal, bureaucratized, for-profit transnational corporation, with assets larger than the gross domestic products of several nation-states.

As against these desiderations, Sitton writes:

Habermas's theory largely disregards economic global considerations because his social theory is based on the domestic compromise that produced the welfare state. The idea, for example, that the welfare state was only possible because these countries stand at the pinnacle of an international division of labor does not come into view at all. This leaves the puzzle of why only a few nations in the world have been able to construct such successful (for the moment) welfare states. (1996, p. 195)

Although Sitton believes that world-system theory has its own problems, he rightly comments that "it is a more persuasive approach than that of categorizing global capitalist pressures as somehow avoidable" (1996, p. 195).

After raising other difficulties for Habermas's social theory, Sitton concludes by offering three challenges. First, "Systems theory cannot sufficiently specify the dynamic and endogenous problems of either a capitalist economy or the interventionist welfare state" (1996, p. 198). Second, "'Cultural revolution' has never been enough" (1996, p. 198). "Finally, the welfare state's displacement of economic problems into the political and normative spheres must be reconsidered in the context of the globalization of capitalism" (1996, p. 198).

Accordingly, Sitton concludes that

We need to supplement Habermas's analysis of systemic colonization of the lifeworld with the historical effects of real colonization of nations and the continuing national lifeworld reactions against such colonization. We also need to observe the dynamic of contemporary capitalism from the perspective of those parts of the system where material progress has never been assured, to say the least. (1996, p. 199)

In short, globally and in "those parts of the system where material progress has never been assured," "colonization" is not simply a metaphor.

That is, "colonization" is metaphorical only to the extent that the social conflicts that a critical theory of society needs to explain concern the *symbolic* reproduction of the lifeworld. Habermas has more or less assumed that its *material* reproduction has been (more or less) adequately provisioned by the autonomous subsystems whose differentiation from out of the lifeworld he deems a progressive and irreversible accomplishment of modernity. But this assumption is also what led him to conclude that class structure has been displaced and class conflict pacified. Among other criticisms that can be made, this one has the greatest bearing on his "decisive" objection to Marx, that Marx had "overgeneralized" his "specific case" of the relation between wage-labor and capital. If class analysis is still indispensable, however, then we have good reason to reconsider the value theory Marx originally presented in order to explain class antagonisms.

Perhaps the best way to make our way back to Marx in the context of this essay is to return to the scene of Marxism's first serious encounter with Weberian social theory in the work of Lukács. Douglas Kellner capably summarizes Lukács's use of Weber in his essay on "Critical Theory, Max Weber, and the Dialectics of Domination" (1985, pp. 90–95). Here, I will supplement Kellner's summary by developing the sense in which Lukács's concept of rationalization as reification is directly tied to Marx.

In a nutshell, Lukács's specific achievement was to have linked Weber's account of bureaucratic rationality and the rationalization process to Marx's presentation of "The Fetishism of the Commodity and Its Secret" (Marx, 1976, pp. 163–77). The "commodity form" originates in the process of production itself, it mediates the elementary processes of production and exchange that structure the capitalist form of life, and it extends across a vast network of social relations. In the famous section on the commodity fetish, Marx argues that the commodity has a "mystical" character (Marx, 1976, p. 164) that "transforms every product of labour into a social hieroglyphic. Later on, men [sic] try to decipher the hieroglyphic, to get behind the secret of their own social product" (1976, p. 167). But why is there a "secret" to be deciphered in the first place? Marx answers this way:

the labour of private individuals manifests itself as an element of the total labour of society only through the relations which the act of exchange establishes between the products, and, through their mediation, between the producers. To the producers, therefore, the social relations between their private labours appear as what they are, i.e., they do not appear as direct social relations between persons in their work, but rather as material [dinglich] relations between persons and social relations between things. (pp. 165–166)

An alternative term to express this reduction of social relations to a dehumanized, thing-like status is "reification," the term Lukács employs and then links to Weberian rationalization in his essay "Reification and the Consciousness of the Proletariat" (Lukács, 1971, pp. 83–222).

Kellner (1985) condenses Lukács's critical point:

For Lukács, rationalization is therefore a product of capitalist production processes which transform individuals into subjects of exploitation and administration, reduce them to abstract labor exchanged for a wage, replace qualitative aspects of people and their products with quantitative exchange values, and mystify capitalist exploitation through a veil of reification and fetishism. (p. 92)

Where is the error of this account? Habermas may be right to reject Lukács's "philosophy of history," his romanticization of the proletariat (and its Stalinist aftermath), and his Hegelian "totality-thinking" that projects the telos of history as a restored "subject-object identity." But disencumbered of these theses and taken only as an account of the dehumanizing effects of the capitalist mode of production, Lukács's critique seems unimpeachable.

Therefore, taking Lukács's affiliation of rationalization with reification and commodity fetishism as a starting point, we can go on to ask why the theme of "privatization," so fundamental to the well-known passage just quoted from *Capital,* as well as to Marxism itself, is so muted a theme in *TCA.* Inasmuch as the answer is linked to Habermas's qualified, ambivalent endorsement of the welfare state, it is also linked to his sense that class conflict has been "institutionalized," "tamed," "normalized," "pacified," and "neutralized."[6] For Marx, "privatization" refers (1) to the private monopolization of the means of production in the hands of a class of capitalist owners and their class allies; and (2) to privatized, atomized, or mutually isolated workers who do not own such means, and who are therefore compelled to alienate their capacity to work in exchange for a wage. Furthermore, workers are also compelled to compete with one another for whatever work is made available to meet the accumulation requirements of capital. Finally, when these mutually private parties meet in the exchange between wage-labor and capital, the *social* process of *private* production commences. This process is the basic descriptive feature of the morphology of capitalism. The welfare states of the North Atlantic societies and parts of the Pacific Rim may have ameliorated some of the deleterious consequences of this relation on the basis of a post-World War II prosperity, but they have not reversed its underlying logic.

In the processes of production and exchange, as Marx argues, social relations are not transparent but veiled, or mystified. They appear as material [*dinglich*] relations between persons and social relations between things. Again, in Marx's account, this is because *capitalist* social relations are mediated by the "commodity form," the generalized form of which is the "money form." In turn, money is the material carrier of "value," the long-term maximization of which is the immanent *raison d'être* of both production and exchange. "Value," in turn, is the abstract, ghostly principle by which the entire social process of production and exchange is fundamentally organized—the "real abstraction" that Habermas had identified with the autonomous subsystems of money and power.

Habermas essentially affirms the systemic imperatives of those subsystems, on the basis of their instrumental capacities to steer the differentiated complexity of modernized societies: the "rationalities" of the market and of state administration may be mixed blessings, but they are blessings nevertheless, necessary as means to preserve the achievements of modernization. What he fears are their colonizing potentials. For him, then, the challenge society confronts is to confine the functionality of those imperatives successfully to their own interlocking domains of instrumental action and material reproduction, and to successfully resist their encroachment on other domains.

The Marxist rejoinder can only be that the "real abstraction" of value, materially carried by the commodity form and the money form, is inherently totalitarian in its objective, governed only by the imperative of its own "ceaseless augmentation" (Marx, 1976, p. 254). According to its own logic, it will not be contained. Capital, or "self-valorizing value":

becomes transformed into an automatic subject. . . . [Value] is here the subject of a process in which, while constantly assuming the form in turn of money and commodities, it changes its own magnitude, throws off surplus-value from itself considered as original value, and thus valorizes itself independently. For the movement in the course of which it adds surplus-value is its own movement, its valorization is therefore self-valorization. (p. 255)

The "real abstraction" of value, "transformed into an automatic subject," becomes "self-valorizing," obedient to no other imperatives than its own. And indeed, the "capitalist knows that all commodities, however tattered they may look, or however badly they may smell, are in faith and in truth money, . . . and what is more, a wonderful means for making still more money out of money" (p. 256).

By emphasizing more how the identities of "citizen" and "worker" have been "crystallized" into the "client/consumers" of the goods and services provisioned by the welfare state compromise (Habermas, 1987, 2:348–51)—a theme about which he is not uncritical—Habermas has tended to gloss over a social world that is still composed of capitalist organizations and working people. Therefore, he has also perhaps underestimated how much the old-fashioned value of "making still more money out of money" is still our dominant theme, both within domestic economies and transnationally. Moreover, this is true, not fundamentally because people's value orientations are misguided, but because there is a deep systemic logic to the palpable social fact that money makes the world go 'round. Hence, the McDonaldization of all things cannot be properly understood except also as the "McCommodification" of all things, pervasively and tangibly real, and really directive, both in the autonomous subsystems of economy and administration, and also in the lifeworldly domains of culture, society, and personality.

CONCLUSION

Ritzer's thesis of McDonaldization, which seems more to assess the lifeworldly effects of instrumental rationality than their systemic causes, at least has the singular virtue of showing us how thoroughly anchored McDonaldization is in the lifeworld. Also, I suspect he would agree that the systems are McDonaldized as well; that is, if he would be willing to reconceptualize his thesis in relation to Habermas's distinction between "lifeworld" and "system" in the first place. Habermas's critical evaluation of Weber can be assessed on its own merits; in this essay, however, I undertook the turn to Habermas in order to bring McDonaldization within the orbit of neo-Marxist critical theory. But in that respect, I had an ulterior motive: my real interest was to clear a path from Weber to Marx, so that in the end, I could characterize McDonaldization as McCommodification.

To make my way there, however, I had to develop a Marxist rejoinder (one of several that might have been developed) to Habermas's own critique of Marx. If Habermas's attempt to trump Marx fails, as I think it does, then we can ask again what the Marxist Lukács found in Weberian social theory: namely, an intimate connection between Weber's concept of rationalization and Marx's concept of the commodity form. The term that links them is "reification." Whatever other weaknesses we may identify in Lukács's theory, the descriptive power of his explanation of "rationalization as reification" is worth preserving.

Marx's theory of value and the commodity form, all too briefly discussed here, explains the Midas-like commodification of all things by uncovering both the logic and the dynamics of "self-valorizing value," a "real abstraction," as Habermas rightly grasps, that emerges on the level of an impersonal, systemic process with totalitarian intent. How an "intent" can be attributed to an "impersonal systemic process" is the subject for another essay. What seems hard to deny, however, is that something like that intent is concretely embodied and ruthlessly prosecuted by the all too real, lifeworldly enterprise of "making still more money out of money." That enterprise, in turn, can be adequately assessed, both with respect to its causes and its effects, only by way of a class analysis.

In global terms, aside from important ecological considerations, dehumanizing effects fall on beneficiaries and casualties alike of submitting, whether voluntarily or by force, to the imperatives of an impersonal system that subordinates all other motives and savages anything that stands in its way. In the prosperous North Atlantic and Pacific Rim societies, we confront the whole range of pathologies that are consequent to a consumer culture created in the image of the commodity form and mandated by the logic of capitalist accumulation and realization. Here, our colonization may be more or less a metaphor. In a larger world too complex to outline now, however, colonization (or neo-imperialism) is too literal a fact. The McDonaldized society is as shallow and vapid as Weber could have expected. Its material effects—globally and ecologically—are perhaps only just now beginning to come home to us.

Finally, then, we can affirm the "irrationality" of the "rationality" Ritzer depicts by concurring with Lukács's assessment that the "fundamental irrationality" belongs to "the capitalist system as a whole" (see Kellner, 1985, p. 92). Lukács, in turn, was only elaborating on Marx in this respect. Aside from the "fundamental contradiction . . . rooted in its basic structuring forms" (Postone, 1993, p. 358), Marx also thought that capitalism is irrational because it is dehumanizing (see Marsh, 1995, pp. 265–289), as Ritzer holds of instrumental rationality when the relentless logic of efficiency, calculability, predictability, and control dominates human affairs.

For Marx, the commodification of all things is irrational for a *moral* reason along with the others he develops: it is a process that reduces human beings to a merely thing-like status. Like Habermas, he too holds fast to the emancipatory hope of the Enlightenment project, that we can build social institutions and achieve a social solidarity that are worthier of our humanity than the tyranny of value. Is this only the naiveté of a Condorcet? Certain Weberians and critical theorists will hasten to answer yes. Only, the instrumental rationality that is yoked to the totalizing logic of value make us prisoners of an iron cage. Is this the best we can do?

NOTES

1. For an excellent collection of essays representing a broad spectrum of perspectives on the Marx-Weber relation, see Antonio & Glassman, (1985).

2. Habermas writes: "At the level of principled moral consciousness, morality is deinstitutionalized to such an extent that it is now anchored only in the personality system as an *internal* control on behavior. Likewise, law develops into an *external* force . . . to such an extent that modern compulsory law, sanctioned by the state, becomes an institution detached from the ethical motivations of the legal person and dependent upon abstract obedience. . . . This development is part of the structural differentiation of the lifeworld. It reflects both the growing independence of the societal component of the lifeworld—the system of institutions—in relation to culture and personality, and the trend toward the growing dependence of legitimate orders on formal procedures for positing and justifying norms" (1987, 2:174).

3. In this respect, I agree with Jane Rinehart's concerns about Ritzer's conclusions and proposals for change in "It May Be Polar Night of Icy Darkness, but Feminists are Building a Fire," included within this collection. Among other things, Ritzer's proposals are far too individualistic and not nearly enough communitarian. In part, this is because, even though Ritzer acknowledges his debt to Marxian theory (Ritzer, 1993, 191), Weber trumps Marx; as I see it, then, his work is too Weberian and not nearly Marxist enough.

4. For an excellent account of the fate of the idea of "totality" in critical theory and Western Marxism, see Jay (1984).

5. Habermas goes on to argue that Weber does not explain "why the differentiation of economic and administrative subsystems of action at all pushes beyond the bounds of what is necessary for the institutionalization of money and power, why the subsystems build up irresistible internal dynamics and systematically undermine domains of action dependent upon social integration [,] why cultural rationalization not only sets free the inner logics of cultural value spheres, but also remains encapsulated in expert cultures; why modern science serves technical progress, capitalist growth, and rational administration, but not the understanding that communicating citizens have of themselves and the world; why, in general, the explosive contents of cultural modernity have been defused" (1987, 2:327–328).

6. Thomas McCarthy, the translator of *TCA*, lists these terms in rapid succession in his "Translator's Introduction" to Habermas, 1984, 1:xxxiii.

REFERENCES

Adorno, T., & Horkheimer, M. (1972). *The dialectic of enlightenment*. (J. Cumming, Trans.). New York: Seabury.

Antonio, R. J., & Glassman, R. M. (Eds.). (1985). *A Weber-Marx dialogue*. Lawrence, KS: University of Kansas Press.

Aristotle. (1985). *Nicomachean ethics*. (T. Irwin, Trans.). Indianapolis, IN: Hackett.

Habermas, J. (1984–1987). *The theory of communicative action: Reason and the rationalization of society* (Vols. 1-2). (T. McCarthy, Trans.). Boston: Beacon.

Harvey, D. (1989). *The condition of postmodernity: An enquiry into the origins of cultural change*. Oxford, UK: Basil Blackwell.

Hegel, G.W.F. (1977). *Philosophy of right*. (T. M. Knox, Trans.). London: Oxford University Press.

Jay, M. (1984). *Marxism and totality: The adventures of a concept from Lukács to Habermas*. Berkeley, CA: University of California Press.

Kellner, D. (1985). Critical theory, Max Weber, and the dialectics of domination. In R. J. Antonio, & R. M. Glassman (Eds.), *A Weber-Marx dialogue* (pp. 89-116). Lawrence, KS: University of Kansas Press.

Lukács, G. (1971). *History and class consciousness: Studies in Marxist dialectics*. (R. Livingstone, Trans.). Cambridge, MA: The MIT Press.

MacIntyre, A. (1981). *After virtue*. Notre Dame, IN: University of Notre Dame Press.

Marsh, J. L. (1995). *Critique, action, and liberation*. Albany, NY: State University of New York Press.

Marx, K. (1973). *Grundrisse: Introduction to the critique of political economy*. (M. Nicolaus, Trans.). New York: Random House.

Marx, K. (1976). *Capital: A critique of political economy* (Vol. 1). (B. Fowkes, Trans.). New York: Random House.

Postone, M. (1993). *Time, labor, and social domination: A reinterpretation of Marx's critical theory*. New York: Cambridge University Press.

Ritzer, G. (1993). *The McDonaldization of society*. Thousand Oaks, CA: Pine Forge.

Sitton, J. F. (1996). *Recent Marxian theory: Class formation and social conflict in contemporary capitalism*. Albany, NY: State University of New York Press.

Weber, M. (1958). *The Protestant ethic and the spirit of capitalism: The relationships between religion and economic and social life in modern culture*. (T. Parsons, Trans.). New York: Charles Scribner's Sons.

9

Missing the Cultural Basis of Irrationality in the McDonaldization of Society

Ngure wa Mwachofi

INTRODUCTION

This essay is a critique of the perspectives taken by George Ritzer in *The McDonaldization of Society*. In the book, Ritzer examined many aspects of life that have been routinized by rational systems; he presented a wide range of examples in which bureaucratic inertia alienates human beings. He accurately identified the sense in which those very rational processes of routinizing contradict the purpose for which they were intended when he observed that "Employees are controlled by the division of labor, which allocates to each office a limited number of well-defined tasks" (Ritzer, 1996, p. 20). Beyond citing Weber's bureaucracy (pp. 17–20, 143–144), Ritzer also discuses the sense in which routinization, predicated on "reason" and intended to create "efficiency," "calculability," "predictability," and "control," presents the dilemma of both good and bad consequences of McDonaldization to society.

While I accept Ritzer's line of argument and description of what Marcuse (1962) dubbed the "dialectic of civilization," Ritzer's analysis would have been more successful if he had gone beyond the *description* of what he has dubbed McDonaldization of society. Ritzer's main drawback is his failure to go beyond Weber; he needed to do a critique of ideology that requires explaining the role of language and culture as key agents that sustain McDonaldization. As observed by Ormiston and Sassower, "language is understood *in a more productive or performative sense [italics added]: language creates the conditions, that is to say the labyrinth of fictions, that make its performance possible; it creates the culture in which it is performed"* (1989, p. 17). My argument is as follows: Since language is not neutral because it performs the role of affirming or negating existing social configurations, focusing on the discursive nature of language is fundamental; doing so would highlight for us the sense in which language produces and reproduces meanings that are at the core of our everyday consciousness; such insights would illuminate the sense in which human beings are alienated by McDonaldization.

Because he does not identify language to be at the core of his social inquiry, Ritzer not only fails to articulate the linguistic origins of rationality, but he remains rather descriptive of the way things are. Ritzer needed to address the ideological nature of rationality in order to explain how and why rational systems become irrational. In other words, to address the discursive nature of rational systems such as McDonaldization, he needed to look into culture and the agents of social change; specifically, it is vital to investigate the sense in which the technological mindset, as an aspect of language, alters our sense of time and space, thereby changing our expectations.

Clearly, we humans engage in contradictory acts; on one hand we have come to desire goods and services in a hurry because, with science as the guarantor of limitless possibilities, we accept the "reality" that "the sky is the limit." On the other hand, we are the same people who, in reaction to negative aspects of rationality, condemn the very science-based processes of providing those goods and services. This is the point that Ritzer does not analyze enough, a critique of reason that would require understanding of the rhetorical nature of reason (Billig, 1991).

To appreciate the rhetorical nature of reason requires a communication perspective. A communication perspective, in the critique of Ritzer's McDonaldization, enables us to examine "motivation" (the ideology) in human beings as well as the ideology of McDonaldization, rationalization of technologies, and other human systems. In short, whereas Ritzer's project, McDonaldization, is about *what* phenomena are like, this communication perspective emphasizes a philosophy of science, *why* phenomena are the way they are. "Explanations" are the primary focus.

In applying a communication perspective, I conceptualize McDonaldization as a ubiquitous phenomenon similar to science and technology that are prevalent in modern culture. Culture, in this case, is conceptualized as ideology. Hall observed that "ideologies are the *frameworks* [italics added] of thinking and calculation about the world—the 'ideas' which people use to figure out how the social world works, what their place is in it and what they *ought* to do" (1985, p. 99). (For more on ideology and rationality, see Aronowitz, 1988; Leiss, 1990; Ormiston & Sassower, 1989; & wa Mwachofi, in press.)

In applying a communication perspective, I conceptualize McDonaldization as an ideology, an example of a dominant human culture. Culture is similarly understood as an ideology; it links with power and domination (Deetz, 1992; Deetz & Mumby, 1985; Hall, 1985; wa Mwachofi, in press; Witten, 1993). Witten sees culture as "a set of capacities for thought and behavior—patterns of interpretation and 'strategies of action'" (1993, p. 99).

By articulating the ideological nature of McDonaldization, it will be possible to explain Ritzer's ambivalence: On one hand, Ritzer acknowledges the positive attributes of McDonaldization (1993, pp. 12, 199—203), but on the other hand he proposes ways to overcome McDonaldization (pp. 199–203). But first let us examine Ritzer and his interpretation of Weber's thesis.

RITZER'S REGURGITATION OF WEBER

With respect to his ambivalence, Ritzer provides a slew of suggestions on how to resist McDonaldization (1996, pp. 199–201 for "actions individuals can take to cope with McDonaldization," and pp. 202–203 for "steps to be taken to prevent children from becoming mindless supporters of McDonaldization"). And yet, at the same time, he observes, "perhaps I am wrong about the irresistibility of McDonaldization" (1996, p. 203). This contradiction suggests the problems of not recognizing the ideological nature of culture and institutions.

Following Weber (1958) who, in *The Protestant Ethic and the Spirit of Capitalism*, recognized the relentless human dilemma inventing solutions that turn out to perpetuate rather than solve problems, many scholars have attempted to articulate Weber's "iron cage" (Deetz, 1992; Green, 1995; Hisao, 1976; Ritzer, 1996). Some of these scholars have extended Weber's thesis by taking a critique of ideology (Deetz, 1992; Hall, 1985). A key weakness, perhaps, in Ritzer's analysis is his regurgitation of Weber's thesis without extending it by going further and accounting for human motivation, human interests, and ideology. The absence of a critique of ideology results in Ritzer's generalized formulations.

Ritzer's proposition that as social actors we fall prey to our own snares because we invent systems which, once accepted, end up controlling us, is well taken. While this is true, the key focus, perhaps, should be an attempt to explain why this is the case. Thus, Ritzer's greatest shortcoming, perhaps, is in his failure to explain to the reader how and why we fall prey to our own snares. He needed to articulate the discursive nature of systems in order to clarify the sense in which rational systems, as ideologies, turn out to be irrational and control us. To state that McDonaldized systems will remain dominant until such a time that society is unable to cope (1996, p. 160) is not enough; there is need for a systematic clarification of the discursive nature of systems. That some members of society already benefit and others suffer from rationality needs investigation.

Weber recognized that systems represent the ideologies of those who put them into place and, consequently, serve primarily the interests of those people rather than all people. For example, in *The Sociology of Religion*, where he wrote about castes, estates, classes, and religion, he observed,

Finally, the glorification of Russian sectarians by the Narodniki combined an anti-rationalist protest against intellectualism with the revolt of a proletarized class of farmers against bureaucratic church that was serving the interests of the ruling classes, thereby surrounding both components of the social struggle with a religious aura. (Weber, 1969, p. 84)

Weber was aware of ideology and, consequently, the conflicts among social actors. Pointing out the sectional interests that were being contested by the various sections, he went on to observe that "what was involved in all cases was very largely a reaction against the development of modern rationalism, of which the cities were regarded as the carriers" (p. 84). But Ritzer only regurgitates these ideas and provides many examples. He lacks the critical theory perspectives that would interrogate the issues further.

Weber did not generalize; he took a "conflict-based" approach (Lehman, 1992). Lehman observes that a conflict-based approach compels the critic to focus "on the evolution of relations of cooperation and conflict in reproducing collective existence" (1992, p. 55). Ritzer's list of the positive changes brought by McDonaldization (1996, p. 12), and his conclusion that McDonald's provides progressive support to minorities and society overall (p. 13) fails to account for any conflict in those social dynamics; it remains descriptive. McDonaldization of society, as a social phenomenon, needs to be conceptualized as an attempt to romanticize social change. The romanticization of social change results in depoliticizing the discussion. A critical theory approach to analysis ought to recognize that systems could support the interests of some sections of people and simultaneously suppress the interests of other people; it also ought to account for the "motives" (ideologies) of the systems.

As Weber observes, it is more accurate to state that systems serve some sections of people positively and they serve some sections of the people negatively; this is particularly the case in dichotomies such as the "poor" versus the "rich," or the "workers" versus the "owners" of businesses that employ the workers. The point about taking a conflict-based approach is crucial to understanding the discursive nature of systems; for example, Ritzer's rationality needs to be conceptualized as an ideology (Aronowitz, 1988; Deetz, 1992; Lehman, 1992). A conflict-based approach is especially critical today because, as Aronowitz observes, "science itself no longer is only a hegemonic ideology of the new social order of capitalism and its industrial stage, but *becomes integrated into the practices and discourses of production*" [italics added] (1988, p. 9). McDonaldization needs to be understood as the most pervasive and powerful myth in our contemporary society because it has become the *central* system of ideas from which the everyday social human transactions revolve. This process, the marking of the *center* versus *periphery* is key to understanding the discursive nature of social configurations and their related aspects—ideology, power, and domination.

To explain the notion of science as a discourse, Aronowitz observes that

The interchangeability of science and technology is, of course, either denied or ignored by most philosophers or scientists, but their growing convergence extends beyond the workplace. As scientific discourse permeates state and civil society, scientific culture spills over beyond the laboratory. *Business dares make no decisions that are not grounded on mathematical calculation that provides projections; legislators enact laws based on "data" generated by scientifically trained experts* [italics added]. (1988, p. 9)

Clearly, when rational systems metaphorically occupy the center, the results of the metaphorical structuration go beyond the metaphorical structuration (Schon, 1988); they are realized in concrete forms that affect myriad facets of our lives as described by Ritzer. In other words, the scientific discourse is a regime in itself; because it reorganizes the culture to conform with its logic, social actors have to conform with the culture.

Once a rational mindset as a culture is understood to be an ideology, it becomes possible to conceptualize McDonaldization as a political enterprise that benefits different social actors while it denies others. Thus, Lehman's highlighting of a "conflict-based approach" to interpretation emphasizes the point that the "antagonisms between opposing social constituencies" are made to "occupy the foreground of analysis" (1992, p. 55) rather than to occupy the background. Lehman goes on to elaborate that a conflict-based approach compels the critic to focus "on the evolution of relations of cooperation and conflict in reproducing collective existence" (1992, p. 55).

Let me provide my own sense of the cultural dimensions of McDonaldization. This requires conceptualizing science and technology as discursive and, therefore, instances of competing ideologies.

THE CULTURAL DIMENSIONS OF MCDONALDIZATION: RATIONALITY AS IDEOLOGY

From the paradox that social actors invent culture and, in turn, culture controls the social actors, systems once put in place exert their own autonomous power. Thus, systems go beyond the social actors that invented them. Ritzer is aware of this point, but he does not pursue it any further.

To explore this paradox, let us consider the example of the traffic light—an invention, a system, that regulates traffic. The traffic light functions well in "regulating" traffic; it provides "order." But to regulate is to require that traffic movement functions only in accord with the code (red for "stop," yellow for "decide to stop or to go," and green for "go"). Through this regulation, motorists' desires are permitted only when they accord with the code. Whenever they desire to go at a time when the lights are red, even if there was no traffic, motorists are constrained. In the same vein, if motorists wished to continue to talk to friends by the road side, once the lights turn green, they would have to abandon their talk, however important the talk may have been to them. This is an example of the rational system constraining social actors.

The system shifts from being a "means" to being an "end" in itself. For example, if I ran a red light at 2:00 a.m. in a small city during a time when there is virtually no traffic, I could very well be prosecuted and found guilty for disobeying the code (the culture). Supposing I presented my argument in the following manner:

Your honor, since the traffic lights were erected to regulate traffic and since there was virtually no traffic to regulate at the time I ran the red light, since it was 2:00 a.m., the regulation did not apply.

Would the judge accept my argument? Most likely, the judge would respond as follows:

> Well, if we make an exception to people who would make your argument, soon we would
> have our court system inundated with these kinds of arguments and the traffic code would
> lose its meaning or purpose.

Such a response tells us that the *means* (the traffic system) does slide into being the *end* in itself. Whereas the original end was to regulate traffic; the judge's interpretation illustrates the dynamics of "making concrete" through "meaning systems." The point that the "traffic code would lose its meaning or purpose" indicates that the very process of asserting meaning is discursive. This is the sense in which the traffic system is culture; it has naturalized and acquired an ideology of its own, beyond what the social actors who put it there intended. What is the reason for the slide from "means" to "end"?

My interpretation is that the slide arises from mathematical modeling; through math, social actors fashion fixed systems to deal with situations that vary endlessly. The very idea of a "system" or "order" implies "fixity." In language terms, once you set a name (e.g., a "table") to an object, you are always bound to use that name in order to talk about the object. Fixing fulfills the role of classification. And systems constitute classification or ordering. Order is rigid. It is inevitable that to make sense of our world we need to classify or to order the phenomena in question; but there is the problem that the classification freezes or gets fixed into such rigid states that it stifles human desires rather than helps to fulfill them. This phenomenon of fixing, which I refer to as ideology, is common in institutions such as organizations, and in all sorts of human-made systems such as McDonaldization.

In his *Democracy in an Age of Corporate Colonization,* Deetz observed that "Both the rising and passing of the concept of organizations as rational instruments for goal accomplishment hide goal and value conflict" (1992, p. 58). Deetz observed this point in reference to the problem of language when it closes the social actors in ways that they find themselves bound rather than freed by the very structures they, initially, saw as liberating. So, what is language?

DISCURSIVITY IN LANGUAGE-AS-CULTURE

In thinking of Witten's conceptualization of culture as "a set of capacities for thought and behavior—patterns of interpretation and 'strategies of action' . . . available to organizational members" (1993, p. 99), language is at the core of it; as argued by Schon, our solutions to problems depend on how we "saw" the problems. Seeing is metaphorical (Richards, 1936).

Regarding language, Mickunas (1973) observes that "[l]anguage . . . must be understood in its broadest sense, ranging from bodily gesture to *social institutions* [italics added], to the most sophisticated meta-linguistic constructs" (p. 180). This view offers the possibility of conceptualizing McDonaldization in a much more complex manner, an institution (a language), rather than the simple polarized version of good versus bad system. The view allows the conceptualization of McDonaldization as a duality—a process and a product—in the same vein as culture. The view enables inquiry to go beyond objectivity-privileging discursive closures because it offers a cultural-theory and a philosophy-of-language-based approach to social inquiry, communication.

If we can conceptualize "language" in a broader sense, to represent all sorts of human systems, verbal, nonverbal, mechanical tools or anything that we use for solving problems (e.g., computer programs and calculators), then we can imagine the infinite possibilities in which we are both helped and at the same time hindered by the languages we put into place. I will return to the issue of language later; for now let me propose that the dichotomies between "science" and "nonscience" issues need to be understood as rhetorical positions rather than objectively verifiable facts (Aronowitz, 1988; Ormiston & Sassower, 1989).

DISCURSIVITY IN LANGUAGE: THE FALSE DICHOTOMIES OF "SCIENCE" VERSUS "NONSCIENCE" ISSUES

In their *Narrative Experiments: The Discursive Authority of Science and Technology*, Ormiston and Sassower present a convincing argument that because issues of science and technology are mediated in culture by social actors through language, science and technology cannot be purified from the media, language, and culture that bring them into existence, even though they are able to slide out of that connection through becoming "grand narratives" (1989, p. 22). The scholars observed that "Fictions, representations, or the narrative of science, for example, are frames or 'posts,' as Jean-François Lyotard remarks, 'through which various kinds of messages pass'" (1989, p. 22). Recognizing the linguistic nature of rationality, Ormiston and Sassower argue against the binary ontology, the scientific and the nonscientific. Ormiston and Sassower observe:

The issues typically associated with scientific investigation and technological innovation can no longer be comprehended as limited to the domains of *science* and *technology*. Instead, they are understood within what we call the *labyrinths* [italics added] of cultural and linguistic usage. Stated in a more direct manner, *there are no issues of science and technology as such.* [italics added] (1982, p. ix)

This quote underscores the need to reflect, rather than simply accept, what rationality means. For too long now we have observed phenomena in isolation of their labyrinthine nature (their interconnections to the various aspects of concrete human experiences such as ideology, power, and class relations). Such is the folly of modernity in which, like Plato's "metaphysical realm," *quantification*, as a method of inquiry assumes a nonhuman approach named "objectivity."

Critical of such undue privileging of rationality, Lehman observes that "all researchers, implicitly and explicitly, choose sides in social conflict" (1992, p. 54) and that they "assume interests to advocate, perpetuate, and support" (p. 54) particular ideological positions. Stressing the ideological nature of being in the world, she observes that "Objectivity, as a basis for research, permits researchers to ignore the partisan interests that the research promotes" (1992, pp. 54–55). This point accords with Ormiston and Sassower's position that there are no issues of science and technology separate from their cultural and linguistic usage. Lehman cautions us to recognize that as long as one belongs to a culture—broadly defined as "a way of looking at the world"—one inevitably takes or is put in a position. Accepting "position" as ideology, there can be no ideology-free ways of being in the world. To be in the world is to be in a culture; it is to be in an ideology. In this case, then, our responsibility, as interpreters of phenomena, is to acknowledge these positions. Ritzer's shortcoming in his McDonaldization critique is the absence of ideology, he does not articulate the point that the prevalence of any system reflects the prevailing rhetoric (Billig, 1991) and that the prevailing rhetoric is linked to social power differentials. Simply stated, those with more money control the way things are examined and, therefore, the way things are understood (see Bagdikian, 1990).

And now, let me further elaborate on the linkage between language, culture, power, ideology, and domination with respect to the products of rationality.

ON CULTURE AS THE SITE FOR MEANINGFUL NEGOTIATION: MCDONALDIZATION AS SITE

Recognizing the ever-present competing ideologies and interests in society, Ormiston and Sassower stress that we cannot afford to seek to understand culture in isolation of its labyrinthine nature (its interconnections to the larger aspects of concrete human experiences such as ideology, power, and class relations). Arguing that every manner of discourse presents itself as the universal or the paradigm social configuration, they observe that

Each system is cast as an attempt to remake or redesign the world *counter* to what it interprets as the dominant model or narrative. This is to say, each and every interpretation presents itself as a replacement that overcomes the deficiencies and incompleteness of other interpretations. (1989, p. x)

In this sense, Ormiston and Sassower's conception of culture, as a contested arena, accords with Witten's perspective that culture is "a set of capacities for thought and behavior—patterns of interpretation and 'strategies of action' . . . available to organizational members" (1993, p. 99). This definition fits well, if we conceptualize society as a grand organization that is in an endless reinvention mode. McDonaldization can be conceptualized as the site on which social actors with varying ideologies negotiate the desirable social configuration (the endless reinvention); each participant assumes his or her position to best represent everyone. Competing social configurations not only represent the competing ideologies, they also illustrate the perspective nature in which social actors interpret the world. But the system that ultimately prevails, such as McDonaldization, is a proxy of the social actors who put it in place; it has discursive power; it is not necessarily universally good.

Ritzer's book fails to clarify the perspective nature in which human beings see the world and the fact that there are no universal *social* structures. Because of this drawback, Ritzer ends up framing the discussion in binary axiological terms of "good" versus "bad" rationality rather than simply using a discursive rationality. On one hand, he accepts some social configurations as "obvious" benefits, on the other hand, he rejects other social configurations as "obvious" drawbacks. In addition, Ritzer does not acknowledge his own ideology; he sees himself as the neutral referee telling the tale "as it is" rather than "as he sees it *through his cultural lens.*" As a result of these two drawbacks, Ritzer undermines his own project.

For example, regarding education, Ritzer argues that the rational system is efficient; he points out, using many examples, that students are able to reconstitute their priorities in accord with the freedom that mcdonaldized educational systems provide them (1996, p. 43). In order to take a-critique-of-ideology approach in the analysis, we need to acknowledge the fact that, since there are competing perspectives over resolution of any issue, social actors make choices that are guided by their individual, not universal, interest.

With respect to efficiency, Ritzer merely cites examples of the "McUniversities" (pp. 42–43), for example, the multiple-choice exam in which students simply fill the box, computer grading that eliminates teacher biases, publishers who provide ready-made tests, professors who select only the questions they desire for their tests, and so forth, without making the connection to ideology. It is important to contextualize the analysis in a broader perspective that recognizes the ideological nature of being in a culture, in this case, the culture of capitalism. That way, rather than drawing a bold conclusion that this is objective proof of "obvious" benefits or drawbacks, we can recognize the sense in which the various systems represent the ideological biases of the various social actors. For example, to acknowledge that some of these solutions may have arisen from "profit-seeking motives" rather than "education enhancement motives" helps us to appreciate the sense in which rational solutions need not be accepted as apolitical. Such broad contextualization is necessary for serious critical inquiry.

According to Billig, "people, in using language, are not merely saying things but they are in practice *doing* things" (1991, p. 14). In the same vein, people, in using McDonaldized systems, are not merely doing things but they are in practice *affirming* a particular way of doing things and, simultaneously, *negating* alternative ways of doing things. It is in participating in culture that individuals constitute their identities; culture is the mirror and the template that aids in meaning formation. Thus, McDonaldization is pervasive because, as a culture, it aids in meaning formation; once placed and fixed at the center by those who propose the various McDonaldized systems, everything else revolves from the periphery.

As earlier pointed out in the traffic light example, with this kind of matrix in place, social actors organize their activities in accordance with McDonaldized systems rather than the other way around. This is the sense in which

McDonaldization, as a culture, is legitimated through the everyday unquestioned usage of the systems. As Billig observes, "If individuals think themselves to be the agents of their own actions, then they are victims of an imagination, which itself has been shaped by ideology" (1991, p. 11). Ritzer's McDonaldization can be understood in this sense; people affirm the McDonaldized systems as they use them in their everyday lives. It is not that they get a chance to propose or argue alternative systems, they simply are participants. Our media systems perpetually announce romanticized versions of "improvements" that are not reflected upon; as a result, impressions are created that we are "objectively" better off with each new invention. The underside of rational systems is reported in unconnected ways such that the social actors do not necessarily understand the contradictions. I propose that because we act according to the way we interpret our circumstances, and because metaphors are the ways in which we see our circumstances, understanding the role of language in the decision-making process is a necessity (Schon, 1988).

THE METAPHORIC STRUCTURE OF MCDONALDIZED SYSTEMS AS THE STANDARDS FOR SOCIAL CONFIGURATION

According to metaphor theory (Black, 1962, 1977; Deetz, 1986; Deetz & Mumby, 1985; Ivie, 1987; MacCormac, 1985; Richards, 1936; Schon, 1988; wa Mwachofi, 1993, 1995), we come to understand that which we do not know by comparing it to that which we know. The experience of knowing that which is new is ideological in that the "knowing" process is *influenced* ("limited") by the guiding metaphor (that which we know already). MacCormac observes that "in choosing a metaphor to both define and organize the facts, *we limit the ways in which we think about a problem*" [italics added] (1985, p. 202). If we substitute the word "metaphor" with "technology" in MacCormac's quote, we have a parallel construction that informs us that "in choosing a technology to both define and organize the facts, *we limit the ways in which we think about a problem.*" A limit is an ideology in which acceptance of one way of doing things eclipses other equally legitimate alternative ways of doing things. Rationality is such an example.

Putting together both Witten's and Mickunas's perspectives on culture and MacCormac's perspective on metaphor provides an important link between culture, metaphor, and ideology. Whereas Hall has conceptualized ideology "[as the] work of *fixing* meaning through establishing, *by selection and combination*, a chain of equivalences" [italics added] (1985, p. 93), metaphors fix meaning by "limiting" the way we think about the social world. Hall has further observed that "ideologies are the *frameworks* [italics added] of thinking and calculation about the world—the 'ideas' which people use to figure out how the social world works, what their place is in it and what they *ought* to do" (1985, p. 99).

In this sense, in line with Ormiston and Sassower (1989), ideologies are competing frames (metaphors) about what people interpret or want to see as the dominant model or narrative. The notions of "fixing" meaning and "frameworks of calculation" accord with Witten's idea of culture as "patterns of interpretation and 'strategies of action'" (1993, p. 99) which implies intentions on the part of social actors who would like to have a social configuration that meets their own interests (Deetz & Mumby, 1985). McDonaldization reflects the concretization of rational systems, beyond the metaphor.

I argue that conceptualization is ideological because it is an experience that occurs within a cultural context. Thus, our world view of McDonaldization is not an objective "essence" that is "revealed" to us; rather, it is a "frame" (metaphor) that we "construct" or "accept" within governing cultural milieu that is presented to us in society through language (speech acts or metaphoric structuring). Thus, with regard to the "limiting" effects of metaphors, Mickunas explains the sense in which our cultures limit our scope of perspectives. He observes that, "differences (i.e., *diversity*, which constitutes the *particular structures*) are perceivable in relation to an identical or common background (i.e., *identity* which provides the *constant structure*)" (1973, p. 180).

In other words, we make choices or decisions, in our social world, by constantly referring back to our "dictionaries" (our dominant metaphors that become our everyday consciousness—a product of the experiences we have acquired over years of being in the world, interacting within our culture). In the same vein, McDonaldization represents the making of the dictionary. In this sense, the dictionary provides the basis for comparisons and confirmations of what we desire. We like McDonalds, not necessarily because it is better than alternatives, but because it is familiar. Mickunas's perspective provides a good rationale for comparative analyses—a way of getting out of one's cultural paradigm locks in order to acquire a "removed" position.

I propose that one way to get out of McDonaldization is to simply carry out a comparative analysis between cultures. We can see the sense in which different people in different parts of the world, by following different metaphorical structures, encounter different experiences as a result of their choices. The fact that a good number of people in the United States suffer from diseases that have to do with diet ("diseases of opulence") suggests the intricate link between diet and culture. Also, the high expectations that have resulted from the mechanized processes of doing things have also resulted in high stress where people are hurrying to fulfill these sky-is-the-limit expectations; the hurry, in turn, calls for further McDonaldization. While it may seem difficult to identify the origin of these paradoxes, comparative analyses can illuminate the confusion; we will find that societies organized around profit as an "end" in itself, operate very differently from those organized around "*human needs*" (Greenbaum, 1995; Yates, 1994).

Metaphors, ideologies, or culture inscribe the world for us into *politically* meaningful or convincing patterns (not necessarily supportive of everybody's interests). McDonaldization operates within the unquestioned paradigm of "speed" as the "normal" way of doing things. Despite stress, efficiency overrides all the consequences. Within our overwhelming belief and acceptance of computers in our modern business world, the metaphors we use do more than simply naming; to elaborate on this point, consider Greenbaum's observation that

Even the creation of terms like "computer illiterate" makes people believe that it is somehow their fault that they have been left out of the televised version of a high-tech society. Yet it is no more possible to be computer illiterate than it is to be telephone illiterate, for using computer applications, like using telephones, depends mainly on knowing the task that you are doing. Pushing the right buttons follows. (1995, p. 10)

In other words, the way we conceptualize our lives and identities is a function of the language-in-use. In this case, the way the computer is framed (the metaphoric structuration) "makes people believe that it is somehow their fault that they have been left out of the televised version of a high-tech society" (Greenbaum, 1995, p. 10). This is a good example of the matrix of computer at the center and human beings at the periphery. Those at the periphery have to dance to the tune of the center. In this sense, language is the guide through culture where culture is that "common sense view" of science. When the computer invades the workplace that it then changes, expectations increase. But, whereas one would expect that, due to computers cutting down on the amount of time to accomplish tasks, workers would work fewer hours for the same pay in order to have more family-time, instead the profit motive (ideology) leaves business owners taking out all the benefits of the computer rather than sharing them. Culturally, this selfishness is seen as normal; it is because culture has implications for both the way we will think and, consequently, the way we will act and vice versa. It illustrates the difference between doing things for people or profit.

Billig in his discussion of "social representation" observes that "Terms have passed from scientific and technical discourse into lay language, altering their meanings in their passage and, in their turn, affecting the nature of common sense" (1991, p. 62). Through metaphoric structuration, "science made common" is an instance of culturation in which science is not only a product of the culture, but also becomes the arbiter (a *significant* participant) in the shaping of the cultural process itself. In Greenbaum's example, the term "computer illiterate" illustrates the sense in which the proliferation of computers in society has resulted in the computer imperative reorganizing the social world; the human being has been "normalized" to the point that emphasis is placed on the "failures" of the person lacking the computer skills. While this emphasis represents simply one frame of thinking about the issue, once it is accepted, it becomes *the* standard, and using the phrase "computer illiterate" sounds normal because, through language, the frame has naturalized into culture. Language creates; it legitimizes.

Of course there can be alternative frames for thinking about the introduction of computers into society. For example, if emphasis is placed on the human being as the standard that determines what is worthy of knowing, then, instead of the frame "computer illiterate," the frame "ignored machine" could be the alternative. With the human being at the center and the computer at the periphery of the social configuration, the choice of "ignored machine" over "computer illiterate" becomes common sense. Of course the two frames are two equally legitimate competing rhetorical "positions" or "ideologies"; their acceptance depends on the social configuration. This is the sense in which technologies or rational (McDonaldized) systems become a "lifeworld" (Ihde, 1990) and, at the same time, determine the social configuration and dictate thought and talk about phenomena.

Once we unreflectively accept positions as proposed, if we simply think of language as innocent (language only "describes"), we will be unable to question the legitimacy of rhetorical positions on thought and talk about technologies, much less come up with alternatives. Rather than being innocent, language creates. Ritzer's main drawback is the failure to look into rationality as a language, a culture, and an ideology.

Language is not neutral; it more than describes, it prescribes, produces, and reproduces meanings (our everyday consciousness). Ormiston and Sassower's perspective is instructive here; they observe that

language is no longer conceived of simply as a tool or a set of tools by which we describe a particular state of affairs, "worldly" conditions, or, even, the theoretical and practical interplay of science and technology. Nor is language conceived of merely as a tool for prescribing the conditions of human activity. Based on the writings of Wittgenstein, J. L. Austin, Derrida, Foucault, and Lyotard, language is understood *in a more productive or performative sense: language creates the conditions, that is to say the labyrinth of fictions, that make its performance possible; it creates the culture in which it is performed.* [italics added] (1989, p. 17)

The more a frame (such as "computer illiterate") becomes part of culture, the more it escapes scrutiny; also, the less "visible" it becomes. In other words, paradoxically, it becomes more absent as it becomes more present. And ironically, the less visible it becomes the more power it gains because it escapes our scrutiny. In a sense, then, despite many positive attributes of culture, we are victims of culture because, as long as we do not reflect on it, we live with it by adapting to its imperatives. We can say that we live with a false sense of "knowing" since we act like we need not question that which is common sense.

It is worth noting that the implications of the phrase "computer illiterate" go far and beyond; they reorganize the cultural matrix. Taking a concrete case, for example, Greenbaum observes that "Labor Secretary Robert Reich has repeatedly pointed to the widening wage gap between educated and uneducated workers, and the need to stress training to help bridge this gap" (1995, p. 131). Well, the bad news is that with ever-changing technologies, workers are finding themselves to be in need of perpetual schooling (metaphorically framed as "retooling"!). But workers are finding that because of the "death of permanence" (Grassboff, 1972), as soon as they are finished mastering a particular computer configuration, a new one is on the market—their "new" skill is obsolete. Profit motives, not human needs, relentlessly compel corporations to adopt new technologies in order to stay competitive.

This is an example of the ideology of technology where mathematical relationships (projections of profit targets) override human relations. Again, in order to go beyond description, Ritzer's lament needs to be contextualized in ideology terms.

Greenbaum observes that "in keeping with the business philosophy behind

reengineering, risks are to be taken by individuals [workers], not the company"
(1995, p. 131). The technological imperative has meant that, rather than the
machine being fitted to the workers' comfort levels, it is the workers who have to
flex to meet the machine imperatives. In the same vein, we are always struggling
to fit the McDonaldized society.

CONCLUDING REMARKS

In a culture where the sky-is-the-limit for the individual pursuit of the ultimate
satisfaction, rationality will demand businesses to continue with the search for
cheaper alternatives to their current practices and for members of society to be
"commanded" to follow the rational systems. The latest use of ATM machines to
get cash is a good example of this "commanding" in which banks have decided to
impose a fee if a customer chooses to use services of a real human being. Again,
while the motivation is to cut labor cost in order to increase profits, it should not be
any surprise that once customers know the system, banks can then impose a
service fee for using the card (teach them to get comfortable with the card,
introduce a new culture, and then begin to cash in on the "service"). This is already
happening. Again, the defining point is the "profit motive" as opposed to "human
service motive." In this sense, according to mathematical logic, an argument could
be made that increases in McDonaldization are not a reflection of things "going
wrong," as Ritzer suggests; rather, as a sad irony, it is a manifestation of the self-
adjusting ("objective") mechanism of a "perfectly rationalized and efficient"
system; those McDonaldized are simply victims of a rational order. And the
rational order is only "rational" according to the shareholders (those who benefit);
for the simple fact that shareholders have the money to invest in the organization,
their sense of order is what prevails; customers and employees have to be
compelled to fit the shareholder's imperative. This is the sense by which, in
attempting to understand McDonaldization, the critique of "pure reason" from a
cultural and "a philosophy of language" perspective can serve as a critical
component because it illuminates not only rationality but the underlying
philosophy of power in society.

The transformation of "means" to "ends" exemplifies the ideological nature of
systems; for example, Grassboff's reference to "the death of permanence" (which
is about technology and social change) is akin to Howard's *The Death of Common
Sense* which is about "rules that replace thinking" (1994). Howard is writing about
the rule books that dictate the daily business of the U.S. government because those
rules have transformed into being an end in themselves. He addresses the meaning
of bureaucracy in the Taylorian sense; his main focus is the legal system that is on
an endless legislation mode, and where the very laws intended to balance
everyone's welfare impede those possibilities.

In a sense, McDonaldization can be understood as the "Trojan horse" that
helps some members of society; the horse blurs the presence of competing
interests. Through language, mass media proliferate in the social and political
arena, the site for negotiating meaning, where social contradictions are smoothed

out. Through rhetoric, the management (shareholders)/labor dichotomy is eliminated while the interests of the owners of capital are legitimated and privileged. McDonaldization is an ideology that primarily benefits the owners of capital and secondarily benefits the consumers and workers; those secondarily gaining are the ones harmed the most while those primarily benefiting are the harmed the least. These are the primary conflict-based issues that Ritzer has described but failed to adequately analyze—partially as a result of his assumption of objectivity which is due to his failure to acknowledge ideology, including his own.

REFERENCES

Aronowitz, S. (1988). *Science as power: Discourse and ideology in modern society.* Minneapolis, MN: University of Minnesota Press.

Bagdikian, B. (1990). *The media monopoly.* Boston: Beacon.

Billig, M. (1991). *Ideology and opinions.* Newbury Park: Sage.

Black, M. (1962). *Models and metaphors.* Ithaca, NY: Cornell University Press.

Black, M. (1977). More about metaphor. *Dialectica*, 33, 431–457.

Deetz, S. (1986). Metaphors and the discursive production and reproduction of organization. In L. Thayer (Ed.), *Organization communication: Emerging perspectives I* (pp. 168–182). Norwood, NJ: Ablex.

Deetz, S. (1992). *Democracy in an age of corporate colonization: Development in communication and the politics of everyday life.* New York: State University of New York.

Deetz, S., & Mumby, D. (1985). Metaphors, information, and power. *Information and Behavior*, 5, 369–386.

Grassboff, A. (1972). *Future Shock* [Motion Picture]. Del Mar, CA: McGraw-Hill Films.

Green, R. W. (Ed.). (1995). *Protestantism and capitalism: The Weber thesis and its critics.* Boston: D. C. Heath.

Greenbaum, J. (1995). *Windows on the workplace: Computers, jobs, and the organization of office work in the late twentieth century.* New York: Monthly Review.

Hall, S. (1989). Signification, representation, ideology: Althusser and the post-structuralist debates. *Critical Studies in Mass Communication*, 2, 91–114.

Hisao, O. (1976). *Max Weber on the spirit of capitalism.* Tokyo, Japan: East West.

Howard, P. (1994). *The death of common sense: How law is suffocating America.* New York: Random House.

Ihde, D. (1990). *Technology and the lifeworld: From garden to earth.* Bloomington & Indianapolis: Indiana University Press.

Ivie, R. L. (1987). Metaphor and the rhetorical invention of cold war idealists. *Communication Monograph*, 54, 165–182.

Lehman, C. R. (1992). *Accounting's changing role in social conflict.* New York & Princeton, NJ: Markus Wiener.

Leiss, W. (1990). *Under technology's thumb.* Montreal & Kingston: McGill-Queen's University Press.

MacCormac, E. R. (1985). *A cognitive theory of metaphor.* Cambridge, London: MIT Press.

Marcuse, H. (1962). *Eros and civilization: A philosophical inquiry into Freud.* New York: Vintage.

Mickunas, A. (1973, May-June). Civilizations as structures of consciousness. *Main*

Currents in Modern Thought 29(5), 179–185.

Ormiston, G. L., & Sassower, R. (1989). *Narrative experiments: The discursive authority of science and technology.* Minneapolis, MN: University of Minnesota Press.

Richards, I. A. (1936). *Philosophy of rhetoric.* London: Oxford University Press.

Ritzer, G. (1996). *The McDonaldization of society (Rev. ed.).* Thousand Oaks, CA and London: Pine Forge.

Schon, D. A. (1988). Generative metaphor: A perspective on problem-setting in social policy. In A. Ortony (Ed.), *Metaphor and thought* (pp. 254–283). Cambridge: Cambridge University Press.

wa Mwachofi, N. (1993). On blurring the distinction between capitalism and socialism: A critique of "scientificism" via a rhetorical approach. In R. L. Ensign & L. M. Patsouras (Eds.), *Challenging social injustice: Essays on socialism and the devaluation of human spirit* (pp. 137–155). Lewiston, NY: Edwin Mellen.

wa Mwachofi, N. (1995). Apprehending the power and ideological import of metaphor in de Klerk's rhetoric. *Howard Journal of Communication, 5,* 331–352.

wa Mwachofi, N. (in press). The Discursive Nature of Science and Technology: A Conflict-Based Inquiry on Rationality. In G. Barnett, (Ed.), *Organizational communication: Emerging perspectives,* Vol. 6. Norwood, NJ: Ablex.

Weber, M. (1958). *The protestant ethic and the spirit of capitalism.* New York: Charles Scribner's Sons.

Weber, M. (1969). *The sociology of religion.* Boston: Beacon Press.

Witten, M. (1993). Narrative and the culture of obedience at the workplace. In D. Mumby (Ed.), *Narrative and social control* (pp. 97–118). Newbury Park, CA: Sage.

Yates, M. (1994). *Longer hours, fewer jobs: Employment & unemployment in the United States.* New York: Monthly Review Press.

10

The Bunless Burger

Robin Wynyard

If people are what they eat, then McDonald's is the place to research both food and people. All through the time my children were growing I had been reluctantly bullied into the place. When this happened I never gave McDonald's a second look, as I was always fighting hard to get in as easily as possible and out as speedily as possible. With hindsight this was a mistaken and short-sighted attitude, and until a year or so ago I had all but forgotten my McDonald's experiences, as both my children were off my hands. During this fallow McDonald's-less time, if the organisation did crop up in conversation—as it did quite regularly in the media—as a *sophisticated,* or so I thought, parent, I made all the usual moans about junk food, despairing the part McDonald's played in the destruction of the environment, rain forest, and culture in general. I suppose that prior to any real thought on the subject, I had a view of McDonald's inexorably moving the twentieth century towards the millennium and Armageddon.

However, fate took a hand, and for some reason I cannot now remember, I visited my local McDonald's one Sunday lunch time, soon after it had been built. This visit was something of an eye-opener and reawakened the sociologist as opposed to the teacher. What I saw seemed to give a new paradigmatic view of society. It also seemed to give some purchase on the relationship between theory and practice, something I always struggled to get a grip on.

Prior to this visit, if I had been asked about the typical clientele of McDonald's, out would have come fairly stereotypical opinions: young, gullible, less intelligent, and generally having more money than sense. Imagine the feeling of bewilderment sitting there that Sunday lunch time, seeing a constant stream of different people of both sexes come through the doors and readily stand in line. There were old and young, there were singles and families, professionals and blue-collar workers, down-at-heel and unemployed. Added was a fair mix of ethnic diversity.

This visit was fortuitous; as a teacher of undergraduates, I was at breakdown point, puzzling how to put the finer points of postmodernity and postmodern thought over to my students. Fairly quickly I realised that McDonald's would be a new and exciting way of entering the murky world of Derrida, Lyotard, Baudrillard, and all the other theorists, architects, and artists who went to make up this thing called *postmodernity.*

Neologisms like *simulacrum, legitimation, differénce, hyper-reality, tropes* and so forth in this nascent study of McDonald's seemed, if not exactly crystal clear, at least more in focus and grounded in something young undergraduates could relate to.

Rather like Morris Zapp, the poststructuralist professor in David Lodge's campus novels, I eagerly set about deconstructing then reconstructing what was a growing McDonald's *phenomenon* from every angle possible. In the literature search that I hoped would uncover all that had been written about the McDonald's organisation, Ritzer's book (Ritzer, 1993) became one I was anxious to read. Obtaining it, I read it like a novel quickly from cover to cover. When finished, sad to say my initial hunger for explanations (not for burgers) had not been satiated, but on the contrary, intensified.

Certainly I owe a debt to Ritzer. I thought then as I still do, that he had engaged the McDonald's *phenomenon* head-on, doing a great service to awaken interest in the very modern fact of fast food. However, I was also aware of gaps and lacunae which cried out to be dealt with. Like Ritzer, fascinated by the world in which I find myself, I felt that he had at a theoretical level got it wrong. Theory is the way forward to further study and in linking related concepts, becomes the steppingstone for later explanations. No matter how insightful Ritzer's empirical observations are (and they often are), they never seem to click with theory. Rather than connect with other modern twentieth-century phenomena, they seemed to lead back to a simple (albeit interesting) discussion of McDonald's and fast-food outlets in general. Interesting though this is, it is not sociology; it does not contain any analysis and its lack of conceptual definition does not make it useful, except in a "round the houses" kind of discussion.

Academics in book reviews were far from unanimous in their view of Ritzer's work. "This is populist pseudoscience high on hyperbole and short on argument and analysis" (Gilling, 1996). If you think other than this after having read the book, then there are other reviews to choose from. "This volume is an enjoyable illustration of the scope and importance of Weber's sociology of rationalization and will be a valuable teaching aid in undergraduate theory programmes" (Turner, 1994). This statement focuses on the "heart of the matter," that is, the theorist Max Weber. Although the work of the German sociologist Weber is central to Ritzer's book, I share the thought of one of the contributors to this volume, when he wrote, "Ritzer comes at the subject from the point of view of a rather simplistic (but nevertheless persuasive) application of Max Weber's concepts of rationality and bureaucracy" (Wood, 1994). Thinking about Weber, I became more and more convinced that the Ritzer burger did not have a bun. The bun is, of course, crucial in the construction of a hamburger. Without it the various ingredients comprising the burger constitute a right mess. Like the human body without a skeleton the bunless burger would be a nonstarter. There is nothing wrong with buns on their own, and they can be of the highest quality. "You are really asking an awful lot from a bun . . . you are asking it to be toasted, to be sealed so that it doesn't make it soggy, and yet for it still to be springy . . . because quality is important to them, they would find a way, even if it meant flying the buns in from America" (Billen, 1993).

Following the hamburger analogy, I cannot now see Ritzer's book as anything other than a high-quality bunless burger. The bun *is* crucial to the Big Mac, necessary but not sufficient. A high-quality McDonald's bun might be fun to eat once in a while, but without the other Big Mac ingredients would soon lose its appeal and cease to give satisfaction. Both the bun and its contents are important and do not really make for a satisfactory either/or choice. Try to imagine the following scenario and work out which you prefer: You get home from work late and cannot be bothered to cook. A trip to your local "golden arches" seems a good idea. As you drive all the way there, you keep thinking about that Big Mac. The mayonnaise, cheese, cucumber, salad. Best of all is the thought of that big juicy burger dripping with goodness, contained within a luscious, white doughy bun. You pay your money, rush home, pull the Big Mac out of its little bag and bite. It tastes all wrong. You look inside the bun and find no contents. The second scenario follows the first up to the point where you put your hand inside the little carry-out bag, and yuck! You are up to your wrist in gooh. As you have guessed, the person at the counter has failed to give you a bun.

In both situations, you might find a little note in the bag apologising by saying, this is not supposed to happen. I am not suggesting that McDonald's staff make this kind of mistake, but they *could.* This seems an essential role of theory, that is, to take account of conceivable (if rare) occurrences.

McDonaldization as used by Ritzer certainly has a certain cachet; not only does it sound impressive, it is also a plausible story. It is common sense, isn't it; McDonald's *is* about efficiency, calculability, predictability and control (Ritzer 1993, p. 9). Oh yes! They are global. Even China has succumbed. On the face of it as Ritzer argues, his work seems to sit squarely within the formal sociology of Weber, the theorist on whom Ritzer exclusively relies. "To Weber formal rationality means that the search by people for the optimum means to a given end is shaped by rules, regulations, and social structures" (Ritzer, 1993, p. 19). This is developed by Ritzer to take account of the more empirically substantive world. In Weberian fashion, he develops analytical categories to which the McDonald's phenomena can measure up. "The fast-food restaurant is well defined by the four basic components of formal rationality—efficiency, predictability, quantification and control" (22). The massive expansion of McDonald's does need explanation, if only to understand the way people behave and the kind of world which they want to inhabit. In the United Kingdom to go from one restaurant employing 72 staff in 1974 to 650 restaurants employing 36,978 staff in 1995 is impressive, putting it mildly. This is certainly phenomenal growth but is it any form of rationality, let alone the way Weber used rationality?

McDonaldization gets applied quite easily to other important aspects of culture, for example, education. The word crops up quite often in non-fast-food circles. Again all credit to Ritzer. "Will we all be finally trapped in what Ritzer calls "the iron cage of McDonaldization? . . . The McDonald's burger is a standardised product: the same thing in Birmingham as Beijing. Perhaps education is going the same way" (Walter, 1995, p. 15).

Weber was a complex and a great interpreter of the society in which he lived. We must, however, also note when he lived and died. Modern society in 1920, although sharing some features in common with the world coming up to the millennium, is by no means identical to the world of the 1990s. Weber was highly selective with what he chose to flesh out in the more theoretical, formal side of his sociology. He had an interest in the growing technology of the century and how it related to capitalism. However, this interest only went as far as evidence showed capitalism to be a purely Western phenomenon. Whatever the rights and wrongs of his approach, it seems very hard today to even attempt justification of capitalism as a purely Western phenomena. So it might seem that Ritzer is a little too enthusiastic in his use of Weber to support the capitalistic rationality of his McDonaldization thesis. "It is worth remarking . . . that Weber is really very little interested in industrialism as such. . . . Despite this commentators have tried to make much of him as an industrial sociologist . . . but it is impossible to see Weber as a major analyst in this area" (MacRae, 1974, p. 77).

This is also the case with his book *The Protestant Ethic and the Spirit of Capitalism* (Weber, 1930), which has been applied—or misapplied as MacRae argues—to many of the expanding economies of the non-Western world (p. 13).

Weber, as sociologist, was concerned with the world that was rapidly changing around him in the early decades of the twentieth century, and he observed these changes at first hand.

Weber thought beyond the simple calculable rationality exemplified by the devolving division of labour into more and more minute tasks. I will argue later that calculability and rationality, however relevant as an analytical tool, were historically specific to the time he was writing. Weber was a good enough theorist to appreciate this fact, and as Holton and Turner point out, saw the ambiguities and potential for change. "Weber had two views of modernisation . . . one producing a world of stable calculations and another pointing in the direction of an incoherent and meaningless world of polytheistic values and nihilism" (1989, pp. 69, 88).

Ritzer, not wrongly or without interest, focuses on that part of Weber's work dealing with rationality and calculation, but in doing so ignores anything concerning *an incoherent and meaningless world of polytheistic values and nihilism*. With the growing wealth of the new white-collar class and its influence on culture, old traditional and religious loyalties were being replaced by newer, more secular ideologies (Ritzer, 1993, p. 100). This was a crucial ingredient in Weber's thought.

From the vast corpus of Weber's output Ritzer abstracts "bureaucracy" and "rationalisation." This is fair enough, but such concepts have to be seen in conjunction with Weber's other writings. The McDonaldization thesis gives us no linkages to the way Weber used "ideal types" in his formal sociology. There is no discussion along Weber's lines of how rationality might take different forms, depending on place, time, and culture.

Ritzer's major interest in Weber lies in what he had to say about the "iron cage of rationality." These references are made by Weber in *The Protestant Ethic*. Here Weber's major concern is capitalism and not the simple desire for wealth, which has infected most societies throughout history. The book contains the nub of his rationality argument, used by Ritzer to justify the McDonaldization thesis. In *The Protestant Ethic,* Weber is clearly aware of changes in the world going on around him. Material changes advancing rapidly in countries like the United States, Germany, and Great Britain had to be explained, as they were not happening at anywhere near the same speed in the rest of the world. Weber saw advantages to material and economic growth which when perceived by nations without, would see nonpossessing nations striving to catch up. There was also a downside, in the reduction of basic humanity which lay in the rigorous, systematic, and rational growth of profit. Ritzer notes this when he discusses the irrationality of rationalisation. The insights Ritzer gives concerning this are very good and pertinent to the situation in Britain today. In particular the British National Health Service, which in pursuit of rationality, increased efficiency, and profit, has simply led to a reduction in the quality of health care (Ritzer, 1993, p. 141).

Weber argues that technology, like everything else in culture, will be subsumed under this growing cloak of rationality. Not only would there be increased consumer demand, but such demand for growing consumer goods and services, ultimately leads to new production processes making these goods cheaper and more available. Following rationality through, the public becomes more and more dependent on the products of advanced economies. In fact it might be said that the economy is becoming supply-side led. This is where Weber introduces the notion of the iron cage of rationality. He seems to dismiss the idea that we are purveyors of our own free will, as the demand for external possessions cannot be cast off like a "light cloak" where "fate decreed that the cloak should become an iron cage" (Weber, 1930, p. 181).

With some justification Weber asserts that material goods have gained such a hold over men and women as has never been known before. Perhaps not unreasonably, Weber saw the grip-like march of material possessions and the hold they had over people as somewhat inexorable. Older historical aestheticism "has escaped from the cage," as "wealth stripped of its religious and ethical meaning, tends to become associated with purely mundane passion." Weber finally concludes: "No one knows who will live in this cage in the future, or whether at the end of this tremendous development entirely new prophets will arise" (1930, p. 182).

Weber as Ritzer's master chef is all well and good as far as the rationality of burger production and consumption goes, but new prophets have arisen. Maybe what is needed is no longer a master chef but more, if less intellectually agile, short-order chefs.

We might perceive a pessimism on Weber's part in the way society was going, but he cannot be accused of a closed door. Weber's view of any increasing rationality was based on what he knew concerning contemporary Prussian bureaucracy, and highly efficient, increasingly standardised industrial methods. Weber, as Ritzer shows, assumed a rational component in human behaviour. There is nothing new in the history of thought in this view. The philosopher Kant, on whom Weber drew quite heavily, had posited ethical rationality as an inevitable outcome of history. This presented the human race with calculation, free from traditional and emotional constraints (Kant, 1926, pp. 6, 7).

In the way that Kant tried to separate out the empirical from the rational part containing the questions of morality, Weber saw rationality as a value word and used it in a way that could be neither good nor bad. Rationality for Weber was not a call to battle, but simply part of his theoretical kitchenware, used to isolate and study certain world phenomena.

What is problematical in all of this is not Ritzer's observations about fast-food outlets like McDonald's—Ritzer does have a valid point of view—but the confusion created when he tries to mix the complexities of Weber's thought into shapeless dough intended for cerebral consumption. Ritzer uses many high-quality components in his burger mix, and there is much to follow through of substantive and empirical nature, but this is only part of the story. More is required.

Like Weber, Ritzer wants to tell a convincing story, one which is historical, abstract, and strong on narrative. Whereas Weber's story goes back to the thirteenth century and encompasses the civilisations of Europe, Asia and the Far East, the story of McDonaldization goes back only three-and-a-half decades, to the 1960s and Ray Kroc, founder of modern McDonald's.

Ritzer's argument is a simple, causal, historical, and evolutionary one. This has a great attraction—simplicity gives plausibility and readability. In itself it has a lot to recommend it, but if the story runs something like the following, then it is going to leave the critical eater unsatisfied: Someone once said "the purpose of bread is merely to convey the contents to the mouth." This was the origin of the sandwich. Containing at first simple contents, over time people began to demand more and more elaborate fillings. Different breads and doughs were developed to satisfy the burgeoning demand for a food which could be eaten at speed without mess. Mess and slowness were not welcome attributes for the newly employed, thousands of white-collar and clerical workers, programmed to desk and timetable. An economic genius of an entrepreneur called Kroc varies the standard theme. He replaces bread with buns, cold are replaced by hot fillings. The shape changes from square to round so that it can fit into the mouth more easily. He later brought along his stalwart friend, the clown Ronald McDonald, to initiate children into the new manna from heaven. Society sees the benefits of all of this and changes accordingly, but no one lives happily ever after.

At one level it makes a good story, but we get back to it not being Ritzer's contents which can and do get continually arranged in discussions with students, but more the lack of a suitable theory in the shape of a bun. Weber tries something similar on a much bigger scale, but even the great master chef's dough will not hold together; he needs other *commis* chefs to help him mix the incredible range of ingredients. Often the order of the ingredients is not what is important, but the right ones and the right amounts appropriate to how many buns you want to make always are. Regarding the storytelling aspect of Weber, one sociologist said: "The Greek science was much better than the medieval but in technology it was the other way round. Nevertheless, by and large the three processes are sufficiently linked to justify a concept which covers them all. 'Evolution' might do, but 'rationalisation' will not" (Andreski, 1984, p. 73).

In summary then, Ritzer's book *The McDonaldization of Society* provides an easy and entertaining read. It also contains a lot of topical relevance, which can be linked directly or indirectly to world problems. An example of this is the current concern over a perceived dissolution of community and its replacement by an uncaring code of the professional. Of course, something like the McDonald's phenomenon could be argued both ways. Firstly, one could argue that it helps destroy the idea of a meal where the family all sit down together. Or, conversely it can be argued the weekly treat at McDonald's takes the family out together. There would, it seems, be much of empirical interest surrounding questions like this. But, it has to be said that Ritzer has not written this kind of book, that is, one that gets students to think about possibilities. He, unfortunately, is fixated with a kind of end of rationality thesis, with Weber acting as the spiritual mover behind the narrative.

In any case, behind all of this is a general discourse concerning the decline of high culture replaced by mass culture, appealing to the lowest common denominator in people and society. Such debate has a long pedigree, featuring such big names as Matthew Arnold, Frank Leavis, and Raymond Williams. Engaging this kind of debate from the fast food/*cordon bleu* dichotomy would, in my view, give weight to the study of McDonald's as a pedagogic tool.

This might be nit-picking for, as I have already said, Ritzer has produced a very readable book. What is more serious to my mind are the rather naïve and simplistic assumptions underlying what passes as theory. To imply that we become what organisations like McDonald's make us, (Ritzer, 1993, pp. 100, 101) is crass and patently untrue. At the end of the day, no one is forced to eat a Big Mac, and by using McDonaldization as both analytical tool and also as self-fulfilling justification for what he says, Ritzer does Weber a disservice. Ritzer's doing so glosses over what Weber really was concerned to show, that is, the reasons people give to their actions. Like similar observations I have carried out in art galleries (Wynyard, 1986), the reasons why people visit institutions is often far from clear. So people do not necessarily go to art galleries to view the paintings on the wall, likewise it is far from clear that people go to McDonald's purely to eat. This last is not a profound statement and is well known by undergraduates; "We assumed that a fast food restaurant would function as a quick, convenient place to eat. Certainly it fulfilled these functions, but dining in [McDonald's] was particularly structured and convenience had multiple meanings for participants" (Chen & Weinert, 1994, p. 16).

McDonaldization is not the end of a systematic and relentless process of rationality that Ritzer claims it to be. In any case, what is it? Would those who could define rationality be able to give (a) a precise definition of the word and

(b) secure its vindication with the available evidence? What we have to remember is that Ritzer is not at the end of the day just talking about fast food. His argument is extended to all kinds of worldly phenomena: doctors, dentists, banks, supermarkets, and so on (Ritzer, 1993, p. 44). In any case, McDonaldization is an emotive word, far removed from value freedom as posited by Max Weber. In the hands of good teachers, Ritzer's ideas could provide the stimulus for a wider, more analytical exploration of modern society. This would, however, require a lot of input and exploration of the ideas of thinkers more in tune with such modern society. I do not dismiss Weber in a cavalier fashion, but in the wrong hands and out of context, he becomes too much of a blunt instrument.

At the end of the day, if there is a McDonaldization to understand, such understandings would concern the consumption and not merely the production of burgers. This would be more in tune with Weber's thought, but it is precisely what Ritzer fails to understand. Ritzer's use of Weber gets nowhere near telling us why a Muscovite would quite willingly invest a week's wages in the purchase of a Big Mac and fries. Ritzer still needs a bun. As one cultural interpreter put it: "yet we still expect to have bread on hand at every meal, as background, as completion, as dependable comforter and recompense for any stress and disappointment the rest of the meal might occasion" (Visser, 1993, p. 2).

What I share with Ritzer is a fascination with McDonald's. It is unique and undoubtedly does give pleasure to a lot of people. McDonald's continued rise says something about the late twentieth century. We would also both agree on the burger's ingredients like McDonald's attempted standardisation of the food process, efficiency in production, global spread, and so on. Where we disagree lies in the nature of explanations, or what I have called the bun.

It is not simply, that the whole of McDonaldization is staked on Weber as the explanatory master chef. Weber may have a part to play in mixing explanatory ingredients, but there is more than a hint of suspicion that either too much selection of Weber's work has taken place or the real thrust of Weber's explanatory thought has been overlooked. It is a complex play between subjectivity and objectivity Ritzer misses. McDonaldization is presented purely as an objective process, something thrust upon poor unsuspecting eaters. Even if we accept that the rationality behind McDonald's is an inexorable process, where is the Weberian attempt to get to grips with the nature of subjectivity and meaning? As Weber said: "we shall speak of social action when human action is meaningfully related to the behaviour of other persons" (Weber, 1968, p. 1375).

Situations can exist where it is some sort of crime not to eat the food you are involuntary given. As a child I was forced to eat awful school meals and made to sit at the dinner table, all afternoon if necessary, until they were eaten. This did not stop me from inventing devious strategies, like throwing soggy cabbage under the table, so implicating as many unsuspecting scholars as possible. Naughty I know! but, meaningful human behaviour all the same. It is this kind of humanity I find lacking in the McDonaldization thesis, but not in the work of Weber.

I strongly suspect that both Weber's narrative and Ritzer's sense of history are inappropriate. If McDonaldization exists, then it existed before fast food and the supposed extension to McDoctor's and McDentist's. A lot of other Mc's have been around a long time, including McPublisher's:

More than at any time since the invention of printing and the beginnings of the first commodified literary genre, the novel, printed matter in general was becoming just another "novelty" to be devoured or consumed as fast as fashions changed. Production might in extreme cases be systematized to the extent of New York's "literary factories" which produced a regular quota of "written-by-the-yard" novels commissioned out to a list of competent workers. (Bowlby, 1985, p. 8)

So, if not Weber, who else can we look to in order to help us slide the burger ingredients into a suitable bun? The trouble lies in employing Weber purely as the master chef. For the kind of meal Ritzer has in mind, a series of short-order chefs seem more appropriate. Love or loath them, the fact is that such interpreters of modern society like Jean-François Lyotard are here to stay. Ritzer acknowledges as much. But the author of McDonaldization has little time for what they say (p. 157).

If there is any problem in using Weber's theory, it lies in the fact that his sociology assumes an underlying societal pattern which can be discovered. This is a complex issue and beyond the scope of the present essay, but looking for such a pattern was probably a credible option in Weber's day. It is a human trait to want to find a pattern in life, for most things, in order to make sense of our individual existences. It seems to me that with phenomena like McDonald's, in spite of the McDonaldization argument currently under scrutiny, societal issues are more, not less, complicated. They cannot simply be brought under the formula proposed by Ritzer (Ritzer, 1993, p. 34). Attempting to look for a pattern is doomed to failure and will lead to colossal frustration on the part of the searcher.

This is the point in which to introduce three postmodern short-order chefs. There are more, but too many fingers in the dough will lead to unnecessary complications. It is simply the case that some postmodernist ideas are just too good to go to waste and can be thought of as possible stabilisers when it comes to fixing the dough. With this in mind I quickly want to look at very selected aspects of the work of three thinkers. Not that these can be used with any certainty, there never seems to be a beginning or end with postmodern thought. For, as has been said: "Postmodernism paradoxically manages to legitimize culture (high and low) even as it subverts it" (Jenks, 1993, p. 147). Our major problem is that there is not just one or even two cultures, that is high and low. There are many cultures in modern society competing for our attention, so much so, that the word needs modification. "There is a sense in which perhaps I should say consumer culture, because we can now watch 'Dallas,' or eat Big Macs and drink Coke anywhere, multiple consumer cultures is more accurate" (Lyon, 1994, p. 57).

The first of our mixers who might shed some illumination on the millions of burgers munched through every day of the week is Jean-François Lyotard. His thought is born of despair of "grand narratives." Put more simply, because modern society is hopelessly fragmented and indivisible, the sort of story or unfragmented narrative thinkers like Weber try to tell is simply not appropriate for modern times. That a fragmented society is here to stay is a result of the expansion of language games and not the clash of a limited range of ideologies. So, the iron cage of rationality can no more explain the Protestant ethic than can the action of a toothbrush going up and down explain clean teeth. Following Wittgenstein, we need to look more to language and the nature of language games. Language presupposes newer forms of knowledge and a movement away from simple narrative. Simple narrative is not redundant, but other competing story forms exist along side of it, as equally valid. It is rather like the move from Grimm's fairy tales to the cut-and-paste novels of William Burroughs. As Lyotard says: "These [*different*] languages are not employed haphazardly, however. Their use is subject to a condition we could call pragmatic: each must formulate its own rules and petition the addressee to accept them" (Lyotard, 1986, p. 42). Cutting his thought down to basic principles, in modern society there is no longer a unified and hierarchical knowledge, validated by bodies such as universities. There might no longer be knowledge at all; in fact Lyotard seems to prefer eclecticism.

Eclecticism is the degree zero of contemporary general culture: one listens to reggae, watches a western, eats McDonald's food for lunch and local cuisine for dinner, wears Paris perfume in Tokyo and "retro" clothes in Hong Kong; knowledge is a matter for TV games. It is easy to find a public for eclectic works. (Lyotard, 1986, p. 76)

Lyotard's help lies in the realm of epistemology, that is, there is not one form of knowledge or knowing. There is however a much used and older scientific form of knowledge which posits a simple relationship between signifier and signified. It is this earlier form that has paved the way for all of society's grand narratives. This is not to say that such narratives do not have worth, but they do exert an inordinate influence. An example of this might be the Utilitarian philosophers' view, that we pursue pleasure over pain. Such narratives lead to metanarratives, and the Protestant ethic, plus the rationality that goes with it, would according to Lyotard be an example of a metanarrative. I do not want to tar Weber with what he did not say. However, it is a short step from this to assumptions of the superiority of the free market in the Western world. Here we only know we are part of the chosen, when through thrift and hard work (plus skillful investment) we see our bank balances treble and quadruple. As Lyotard points out, grand narratives are notoriously unstable and can easily crash down around our heads.

The production of Big Macs, given what we know about the efficient and cost-effective way they are made, says something about the profits McDonald's makes. But what is good for economics does not make good philosophy. The kind of narrative leading to millions of fingers pointing to millions of brightly coloured and visually represented hamburgers in McDonald's restaurants around the globe is not the same as the thought process that enables me to say to myself, "I want a burger now!"

Knowledge of such things as Big Macs is not the kind of objective reality we presuppose. It is objective to us all right, but the need simply for food becomes distorted and subverted to our own individual desires. Lyotard seems to be suggesting that we do not deliberately choose the burgers because of what we know they look like, ergo, the profits to be made from capitalist production of a particular sort. Rather, the way production works, is that it tries to reproduce, in the simplest way possible, the best guess about our eating habits. This might be based on an empirical observation, for example, that more young than old people use McDonald's restaurants, but more likely a gut assumption that we like more or less of this or that on our burgers. The more accurately you conform to this and sort of get it right, the more money an organisation like McDonald's makes. But McDonald's beware, it does not go on forever, so there is no need for complacency. Each consumer is playing out his or her own mental language game, which can quite easily become disengaged from your production process.

The reason I eat my burgers in McDonald's as opposed to Wendy's is that I prefer round to square burgers. However, when I am in Athens, I always drink in the Wendy's not McDonald's, because I can get tea in the one and not in the other. The reason I eat *and* drink in McDonald's in the UK, is that they sell both tea and round burgers and as far as I know Wendy's does not operate in the United Kingdom. This might be silly and one could go on in this vein, but the point I hope it makes is, following Lyotard, knowledge is not a universal package. More importantly for the argument here, McDonaldization simply will not do, it is too simple.

The service Lyotard gives us is, firstly, I think that he sows enough epistemological doubt in our minds for us to be sceptical about the whole Ritzer argument. Yes, it reads well and at a superficial level convinces, but at the end of the day what do we know that we did not know before?

Secondly, McDonald's does not make money out of knowledge for knowledge's sake. The great burger kings are in the business of reinforcing what we know about burgers. We want that particular big round doughy bun, with all that lovely gooey stuff inside it, we just know that it is bigger and gooier than anyone else's.

The next short-order chef I would pull in to help mix the dough is Jean Baudrillard. If Lyotard contributes the flour to the bun mix, then Baudrillard's contribution is the yeast to make the dough rise. Baudrillard's world, of which McDonald's is a part, is very different from Weber's world where it was not.

McDonald's is not selling fast food, but a family adventure of eating out together, intergenerational bonding, and sharing love, as their advertising campaigns reiterate over and over in various ways. Ingesting a specific food item is only one part of this total experience. (Kellner, 1994, p. 100)

In Baudrillard's world, things get linked together for far from obvious reasons. Baudrillard's world is *postmodern* as opposed to *modern*. Postmodern thought like Baudrillard's is the subject of a fair degree of vagueness. Vagueness in knowing where it starts and stops and what in particular distinguishes it from other thought. There are, for example, no clues as to when *modern* stops and *postmodern* begins.

This is the stuff of much unresolved contemporary debate and also includes the idea that the postmodern is not a radical break from the modern, but more a complex and interesting extension of it.

We are left with that pure and random play of signifiers that we call postmodernism, which no longer provides monumental works of the modernist type but ceaselessly reshuffles the fragments of prexisting texts, the building blocks of older cultural and social production, in some new and heightened *bricolage*. (Jameson, 1991, p. 96)

We can be reasonably sure with Baudrillard's thought that the work of those like Marx and Weber belongs to the *modern* and not the *postmodern*. Along with this goes an appropriate and earlier epistemology.

For Baudrillard, modern societies are organised around the production and consumption of commodities, while postmodern societies are organised around simulation and the play of images and signs, denoting a situation in which codes, models and signs are the organising principles of a new social order. (Kellner, 1994, p. 8)

For Baudrillard we do not just go into McDonald's for food which has a calculable use and exchange value. Rather we purchase a whole new identity and way of life. "The product itself is not of primary interest, it must be sold by grafting onto it a set of meanings that have no inherent connection with the product" (Kellner, 1994, p. 77).

But Big Macs are part of a bigger scheme of things, linked inextricably in the purchaser's mind with other, not necessarily, related things. This is like Lyotard's eclecticism, where along with your burger goes Coca-Cola, Adidas training shoes, a Benson and Hedges baseball cap, and for all I know a Rolex (ersatz or real) wristwatch as well.

This presages a new classification system, not necessarily based on anything that has gone before. We are what we consume, but, and this is a major proviso, we do not all buy into the same identity in munching a Big Mac.

As Ritzer clearly points out in his book, McDonald's does attempt to standardise its product around the globe. This in itself, though, is not the point. The point is the illusory and not the real burger and what it does to the individual purchaser. This is what is important. Weber's world might have been real to him, but Baudrillard's world is hyperreal, eating Big Macs, listening to quadraphonic sound, surfing the net—lift one out of the banal and ordinary. The big plus is that you do not need to be wealthy to indulge yourself. This is what virtual reality is all about. Accumulation of signs today, according to Baudrillard, is just as important as the acquisition of objects. As much as I hate to say it, when I travel around the world McDonald's golden arches give me reassurance—of what I don't know!

Like Lyotard, Baudrillard will not give us an overarching theory and one would hesitate to use either in the way Ritzer uses Weber. Ritzer's use of Weber is not wrong, but perhaps he fails to notice that one's perception and reading of it alters with the era in which we live. It just might be, that the Protestant ethic by which he sets so great store, is not all about rationality. It might be akin to something more appropriately modern and psychologically deeper.

Following Max Weber's analysis of *The Protestant Ethic and the Spirit of Capitalism*, Baudrillard suggests that fear of death and desire to prove one's immortality, one's divine election fuelled the era of production and accumulation in industrial capitalism. (Kellner, 1989, p. 104)

That is, it might be something about our fragility of existence in the world and not a self-fulfilling justification.

If Big Macs were around in Weber's day, then they probably would be devoured for the nourishment they provided. Today, without a doubt there are more nutritious things to eat, and they get eaten for other more critical factors, such as the provision of fun and pleasure for our children or the exchange of conversation when we go out and sit down once again as a family. It lies not just in the doing, but what it signifies to others as well. Of course McDonald's agrees with this, and any suggestion that it is only about service times, cleanliness, standardised product, and value for money is disingenuous in the extreme.

One senses implicitly the connection of every consumer object with the discourse of objects; the food on your plate and the picture in the menu or behind the counter of the item you have chosen are inseparable at the moment of consumption—the object and the sign are fused together in a cultural "system" which is independent of immediate social conditions at any of its entry points. (Levin, 1996, p. 48)

McDonald's, for Baudrillard, is just an aspect of the expansion of consumption. It is a consumption, though, which has no firm footing in anything other than what passes for discourse in modern society. There are no fixed referents according to Baudrillard in such a society and words and images can be arranged in any way we like. The trope for Baudrillard's McDonald's is metonymy, where apart from any food connotations, we purchase a feast of other branded things that go with it from drink to clothing—a whole way of life. As Baudrillard puts it:

Consumption is a system which assures the regulation of signs and the integration of the group: it is simultaneously a morality (a system of ideological values) and a system of communication, a structure of exchange. (Poster, 1988, p. 46)

Going into McDonald's is like going into Disneyland, that is, we do not do it alone; we have bought into something much bigger, which we share like a coded secret with thousands of others. The message does not have to be spelt out—just being there is enough and says it all!

So Baudrillard and Lyotard take us away from the implicit message that for Ritzer links *McDonaldization* to the production process. I am not denying that modern technology has played a part in the production of bigger and better Big Macs. I simply want to reiterate the point I made earlier, that Ritzer's thesis will not help us explain why a Muscovite will willingly spend a week's salary on a Big

Mac and fries.

If Lyotard supplies the flour and Baudrillard the yeast, something else is still needed. Seasoning. The pinches of salt and flavouring to improve the taste are supplied by the final mixer in the form of Sharon Zukin. In a highly thought-provoking book, she makes us confront the modern world not only as it is, but also as it ought to be (Zukin, 1991).

The trouble with Ritzer's thesis is that it assumes that we, the punters, who buy Big Macs, are innocent dupes of the McDonald's production process. Now this will not do for Zukin, who puts forward the idea that we have more control over our cultural activity (including eating) than we think we have.

Zukin explores how what happens at an international level often belies what can be done at the local, more communal level. Her assumption is that market forces in the United States, have totally reshaped the *landscape*. The industrial infrastructure based on the scientific-based order of the nineteenth century has crashed, bringing in its wake a new order based not on production but on consumerism.

Like our other two other chefs, Zukin posits an epistemological break which she places sometime in the nineteenth century. The term landscape is used to paint a much broader canvas of societal change than that of English country gardens in the eighteenth century. As well as physical change in the way gardens looked, society today means change in cultural thought as well. I include within the latter what is socially acceptable to eat in large amounts "Since the nineteenth century shifting from one landscape to another has depended less on individual mobility than a broad-scale, varied reworking of the landscape itself" (Zukin, 1991, p. 18).

Landscaping, rather like Ritzer's McDonaldization, is imposed and can be bad for your health (Ritzer, 1993, p. 130). But apart from a superficial similarity, Zukin's thought is more akin to that of Baudrillard's. *Landscape* seems similar to his use of the term *simulacrum*, that is where perception of image has merged imperceptibly with *reality*. Like Baudrillard's, this is a world where the relationship between signifier and signified has totally broken down, thus propelling us into a world that is *hyperreal*. In this world signs and images as opposed to material objects jostle for our attention.

This sort of world as perceived by Zukin and Baudrillard involves a pragmatic conflation of signs. Signs have become international and breed incestuously. The McDonald's golden arches, like many other well-known images, is a supreme supplier of the very visual form of the modern world.

Familiarity is provided by institutional context rather than social interaction; the form of consuming is vital not the cultural activity of consumption. (Zukin, 1991, p. 197)

Arguments about whether we are now a consumption rather than a production society are complex and beyond the present scope of the article. But Zukin and Ritzer do seem to inhabit two different worlds, where phenomena like that of McDonald's is concerned. If we are now a society of consumers, then Zukin's arguments seem to be more pertinent in order to understand what is going on around us. The way we organise our consumption for ourselves and our family is just as important—possibly more so—in terms of the way we organise and feel comfortable in the world we have to live in. At this stage of Zukin's thought, there seems to be the argument, *if you can't beat it, join it.* This is unlike the McDonaldization that Ritzer espouses, which is thrust perniciously and perhaps unwillingly upon us. If Zukin were to use such a word, then it would be something we actively choose to go along with, that is, until we arrange the visual images in our perceptual range in some other better more convenient way.

I cannot say that the three mixers presented above will give any certain and overarching theory in the quest to understand how and why McDonald's has captured the heart and soul of most nations on earth. Societal predictability in any form is uncertain to say the least. We can assume that McDonald's will go on in our lifetime to conquer the remaining nations on earth. Adjustments are constantly being made, such as how to produce a satisfactory non-beef patty for India. If this process is rationalisation of an inexorable nondeviationary form envisaged by Ritzer then my article does him a disservice. If, as I strongly suspect, there are flaws in his stimulating argument, then the addition of a few chefs more can only add to the creation of a new, exciting dish. Unfortunately, it will be one which, initially tastier, will not have the endurance of a Big Mac.

REFERENCES

Andreski, S. (1984). *Max Weber's insights and errors.* London and Boston: Routledge and Kegan Paul.

Billen, A. (1993, April 25). The beefy world of Big Mac. *The Sunday Observer,* pp. 49–50.

Bowlby, R. (1985). *Just looking.* London: Methuen.

Chen, J. P., & Weinert, S. (1994, April). McDonald's: An ethnographic study of an urban fast food restaurant. Unpublished study presented at NWCA, Coeur d'Alene, ID.

Gane, M. (Ed.). *Baudrillard live.* London and New York: Routledge.

Gilling, A. (1996, August 16). Where there's mc there's brass. *Times Higher Education Supplement,* p. 24.

Holton, R., & Turner, B. (1989). *Max Weber on economy and society.* London and New York: Routledge.

Jameson, F. (1991). *Postmodernism: Or the cultural logic of late capitalism.* London and New York: Verso.

Jenks, C. (1993). *Culture.* London and New York: Routledge.

Kant, I. (1926). *Fundamental principles of the metaphysics of ethics.* London: Longmans Green.

Kellner, D. (1989). *From Marxism to postmodernism and beyond.* Cambridge, MA: Polity.

Kellner, D. (Ed.). (1994). *Baudrillard: A critical reader.* Oxford, UK, and Cambridge, MA: Blackwell.

Levin, C. (1996). *Jean Baudrillard a study in cultural metaphysics.* London and New York: Prentice-Hall.

Lyon, D. (1994). *Postmodernity.* Milton Keynes: Open University Press.

Lyotard, Jean-François. (1986). *The postmodern condition: A report on knowledge.* Manchester, England: Manchester University Press.

Lyotard, Jean-François. (1993a). *Political writings.* London: UCL Press.

Lyotard, Jean-François. (1993b). *Toward the post-modern.* NJ: Humanities Press.

MacRae, D. G. (1974). *Weber.* Glasgow, Scotland: Fontana.

Poster, M. (Ed.). (1988). *Jean Baudrillard: Selected writings.* Cambridge, MA: Polity.

Ritzer, G. (1993). *The McDonaldization of society.* Thousand Oaks, CA: Pine Forge.

Turner, B. (1994, June). The McDonaldization of society. *British Journal of Sociology,* June, 325–326.

Visser, M. (1993). *The rituals of dinner.* London: Penguin, 1993.

Walter, R. (1995, Spring). Short order for FE. *NATFHE Journal,* 15–16.

Weber, M. (1930). *The Protestant ethic and the spirit of capitalism.* London: Allen and Unwin.

Weber, M. (1968). *Economy and society* (Vol 3). New York: Bedminster.

Wood, R. (1994). Misunderstanding and misinterpreting mcdonaldization: A comment on Lyon, Taylor and Smith. *International Journal of Hospitality Management, 13*(4), 293–295.

Wynyard, R. (1986). Painting and technological society. *British Journal of Aesthetics, 26*(1), 57–61.

Zukin, S. (1991). *Landscapes of power.* Berkeley, CA: University of California Press.

11

Postmodern Hamburgers: Taking a Postmodern Attitude Toward McDonald's

Mark Alfino

When the famous postmodern theorist, Jean-François Lyotard, finally gets around to mentioning McDonald's in *The Postmodern Condition*, it is a brief passing reference in an essay included as an appendix to the main work. It is still a significant passage, coming as it does in an essay entitled, "What is Postmodernism?" and it gives us some hope for an authoritative *locus classicus* for understanding the relationship between the two cultural phenomena. Mention of the burger chain in the highly theoretical work of a French philosopher is remarkable for other reasons as well. Elite intellectuals tend not to acknowledge the existence of enterprises like McDonald's. The main essay, "The Postmodern Condition: A Report on Knowledge," focuses on a very theoretical problem, the change in the status of knowledge in industrialized countries, not something as mundane as cheap restaurant food.

In the passage in question, Lyotard is discussing "eclecticism" both as a postmodern aesthetic response to what he sees as a reactionary effort to limit experimentation in the arts and as the culmination of a contemporary culture which "capitalizes" on the "confusion which reigns in the 'taste' of the patrons." He writes:

Eclecticism is the degree zero of contemporary general culture: one listens to reggae, watches a western, eats McDonald's food for lunch and local cuisine for dinner, wears Paris perfume in Tokyo and "retro" clothes in Hong Kong; knowledge is a matter for TV games. (Lyotard, 1984b, p. 76)

Anyone looking for a simple answer from this master of postmodern theory will be disappointed. Does Lyotard like McDonald's? Does he go, if only for lunch? Is McDonald's complicit in the insidious leveling of taste, the attack on the *avant garde*, that Lyotard deplores? Or is the very hypothetical subject of this eclecticism just the sort of postmodern who *can* go to McDonald's precisely because doing so does not *mean* much, does not exclude local cuisine for dinner, for instance. Once the complex relationship between postmodernism and McDonald's is sorted out, we shall see that so much depends upon our understanding of the cultural codes invoked, willingly and not, in stepping through the golden arches.

Our subject is best approached by a strategic retreat and regrouping. What motivates an effort to think through the improbable relationship between McDonald's and postmodernism? The unlikelihood of the topic should be appreciated. First, postmodernism is often understood theoretically at an extremely high level of abstraction. It comes to street level in neighborhoods and cultural activities that McDonald's is slow to penetrate: in *avant garde* shops and galleries, but also in famous architecture and in theatrical events attended primarily by people who would not talk about hamburgers. If the *cognoscenti* of postmodernism do not condescend to discuss it, and the consumers of postmodern culture would prefer not to be seen in the drive-through, then what hope is there for a theory of the relationship between postmodernism and McDonald's?

The efficient cause for this effort is George Ritzer's *The McDonaldization of Society*, which, as reviewers have noted, has been serving thousands a McDonaldized version of Max Weber since 1993 (Nichols, 1994; Fairlie, 1993; Gilling, 1996). The real virtue of Ritzer's book is precisely that he applies a simplified version of Weber's thesis of "bureaucratic rationalization" to a concrete and common token of contemporary culture. For a first approximation to Weber's view, Ritzer works. But at several key places the introductory treatment needs more complexity and depth. One such place occurs in chapter 8, where one finds a brief mention of postmodernism. Here our question is first focused by Ritzer, though in a peculiar way: he asks, Is there such a thing as postmodernism (as a distinct break from modernism) and is McDonaldization an instance of it, or does McDonaldization remain thoroughly rooted in modernist contemporary capitalism? (Ritzer, 1993, p. 156).

So far then, we have two distinct dialogues to open: Weber's relationship to postmodernism and Ritzer's understanding of the postmodern in relation to McDonaldization. Complicating both of these dialogues is the difficulty of presenting, in a McNugget as it were, a serviceable definition of postmodernism. As noted above, there are at least two broad senses of postmodernism— postmodernism as a kind of theoretical critique and postmodernism as a form of popular culture. The two have less to do with one another than one might intuitively assume. For while the contemporary cultural critic cannot work without bringing the critical resources of postmodernism to bear on real instances of it (e.g., as a critic of postmodern culture, what do I say about this or that postmodern art?), the abstract theoretician, whether in literature, philosophy, or social theory, has the luxury of denying that there is such a thing as postmodern thought or denying that postmodern thought, if it does exist, has any potency or relevance to evaluating contemporary culture. A sufficiently ambitious theoretician can even deny that there is any such thing as postmodern culture, in spite of the fairly enormous catalog of artifacts that might be offered as examples. The two main strategies for this denial are reduction and deligitimation. Examples of postmodern culture could be analyzed to show that their "postmodern" features have roots at least as old as early modernism and reduce to it. Or, the examples could be challenged as debased and illegitimate examples of "culture." In the course of our work, we will encounter these strategies. Ritzer, for example, deploys the first directly, and alludes to others who practice the second strategy (p. 157). At present, the point is simply to identify them as complications to the discussion.

Each of these complications threatens to preoccupy us with a lengthy digression that would effectively preclude a defense of the following main theses: (1) There is a distinctively postmodern attitude toward contemporary commercial culture in general and McDonald's in particular; (2) From this perspective McDonald's is not the arch (deluxe) villain in a cultural drama of "bureaucratic rationalization;" however, (3) Postmodernism encourages us to accept a qualified version of many of Weber's main concerns about rationalization in general and McDonald's in particular, but it also gives us strategies for resisting them. In short, postmodernism gives us a different way of criticizing McDonald's while leaving open a way of snatching a burger now and then in good faith. In casting postmodernism as an "attitude," I want to finesse a choice between the theoretical and cultural understandings of the phenomenon. A serious theoretician of postmodernism is likely to wind up with something he or she might agree to call a "postmodern attitude," but so might a moderately thoughtful contemporary consumer of culture. The goal of this essay will not be to give a philosophical defense of such an attitude, but only to show that it involves a distinctive and credible way of reading contemporary culture. Since the main goal of this work is to arrive at an appraisal of the postmodern attitude toward McDonald's in relation to one of its main competitors, Weberian social theory, we will take as our starting point a descriptive account of the postmodern attitude.

ADOPTING A POSTMODERN ATTITUDE ... TOWARD MCDONALD'S

> I have been trying to demonstrate a 'post-modern' attitude. Maybe you would characterize this attitude as a mixture of world weariness and cleverness, an attempt to make you think that I'm half kidding, though you're not quite sure about what. (Apple, 1984, p. 137)

Adopting a postmodern attitude is one thing, a theoretical enterprise. Applying that attitude toward McDonald's is another, more practical, matter. Following Ritzer's strategy, however, we will use the familiarity of popular culture as a means of illustrating the theoretical issue. We will start with a characterization of an *individual* postmodern attitude and move toward an understanding of a postmodern attitude toward *institutions*, or what might be called a postmodern social consciousness. There is a fairly natural way of grouping postmodern philosophers and social theorists according to this distinction. Figures like Jacques Derrida initially focused their work on the "aesthetic" or "individualistic" problem of what it means to be a postmodern, especially one looking back at Western philosophical culture. The "subject," if there is one, of Derrida's early texts is the traditional disembodied consciousness of the philosopher trying to make sense of the strange old terrain of Western thought in light of several poststructuralist insights. By the early 1980s, he was being drawn, perhaps by critics, perhaps by his own intellectual agenda, toward discussions of social life—friendship, politics, the law, for instance. Meanwhile, there had always been another group of postmoderns, Lyotard, Foucault, and Baudrillard prominent among them, who more or less began their work as social theorists. A complete picture of a postmodern attitude toward McDonald's will require both the individual and the social standpoints.

The primary trope of postmodernism is radical ironism. Irony has many meanings. There is the "Socratic irony" of pretending ignorance for the purpose of drawing out another. In ironic speech or writing, one's words have a double (or multiple) effect. The ironist can create strategic ambiguities by undermining or qualifying his or her own literal sense by authorizing a second "reading." In the hands of a master, this second level of meaning does not merely cancel out the first, but also "raises" it up to a new interpretation. A former professor of mine once defined irony broadly as "the strategy of giving unexpected responses." Often the goal of this sort of irony is to call attention to an uncritical oversimplification of a problem or an overlooked dimension of a typical treatment of a problem. The ironist often generates additional levels of meaning by using, with subtle alteration, the rhetoric of another's language. The classic and best known example of this for English speakers remains Jonathan Swift's "A Modest Proposal." Postmodern ironism is also interested in showing that there are additional meanings (polysemy) latent in our rhetoric and that this polysemy can usefully be brought out to reveal uncritical assumptions. What makes postmodern irony distinctive is that it is directed toward the *basic linguistic practices of intellectual discourse* rather than just the content of a particular thinker's thought. By calling attention to the way a text laboriously invokes semiotic codes and then, with equal textual effort, conceals the constructed character of its message, postmodern ironism denaturalizes meanings. In the process of exposing the constructed character of a particular thinker's work, Derrida often exposes a more general instability in the way languages produce meaning. A good, accessible example of this would be Jacques Derrida's "The time of a thesis," in which he discusses, among other things, the irony of being asked to offer one of his books as a "thesis" for a Ph.D. in philosophy given his views about the tendency of language to undermine the stability of meaning required to have a "thesis." The postmodern ironist's own message is always undercut by an uneasy awareness of the instability and constructed character of meaning.

Behind the playful irony of the early Derrida's "aesthetic postmodernism," there has always been a serious, indeed troubled, awareness of a new problem facing intellectuals. To account for a postmodern attitude as more than a kind of radical irony, we need to say something about what that new problem is and how it affects what I have referred to as "the basic linguistic practices of intellectual discourse." Like so many intellectuals, and, indeed, several whole disciplines (including interpretive sociology), postmodernism grows up in the shadow of Immanuel Kant's *Critique of Pure Reason*. Kant argued that we could only establish the *certainty* of human knowledge by thinking of knowledge as necessarily conditioned by the ways we have of knowing it. He supposed that we have a relatively fixed "manifold" for sensation and that the categories through which our concepts are made intelligible to us are also universal and unchanging. Kant focused entire generations of intellectuals *away from* any effort to understand reality apart from the way it is received and toward an understanding of reality as it is conditioned by the mind. Kant attempted to demonstrate that the desire to know unconditioned reality was merely an irresistible but unfathomable hope of reason. Kantian thinking encouraged a wide range of tendencies in intellectual history, including a search for structures of subjectivity more diverse and less universal that his original twelve categories of the understanding. Interpretive sociology, structuralism, structural anthropology, phenomenology, poststructuralism, and postmodernism all stand in this lineage.

This textbook characterization of the Kantian influence does not quite get us to postmodernism, however, much less to more features of a "postmodern attitude," except in the general sense that postmoderns agree with other heirs of Kant that the place to look for new insights about reality is in our individual and social "constructs" of reality, rather than some final metaphysical resolution about what is fundamentally (i.e., mind-independently) real. Postmoderns begin to part company with their Kantian cousins in the way they have taken on a particular view about the role of language and symbol in thought.

Traditionally, philosophers have treated language as an extrinsic feature of thought, a tool for communicating thoughts known directly by the mind. One of the main goals of Lyotard's "The Postmodern Condition" is to document a reversal of the typical account of the relationship between knowledge and language. Instead of seeing language as the vehicle for communicating knowledge, Lyotard encourages us to see language as a medium within which an "agonistics" or contest of power is taking place. Knowledge, understood as a set of social practices, is one of the principle products of the contest. Adopting the language of the rhetorical theorist, Lyotard shows how language "places" individuals as speakers and positions audiences as "addressees." Consider for example, the familiar slogan: "You deserve a break today." The innocent, naïve, traditional gloss of this slogan might be that as advertising it seeks to tempt the consumer to succumb to a short-term desire to eat quickly and cheaply. (We will pass over the truly naïve reading, which takes the slogan at its word.) The postmodern reads a bit more into the slogan: The slogan is a judgment. The "speaker" of this slogan is positioning him or herself (really, itself) as judge, establishing a hierarchical relationship to the addressee, announcing and, perhaps, confirming their own sense of merit. At the same time, this "speech act" positions McDonald's as the "break," a treat that must be earned but nevertheless is merited. By inflating the rhetoric of the slogan, however, we can better see the absurdity of it. After all, McDonald's uses this as a broadcast message to millions of people every day of the week. The relationship it seeks to establish presupposes a communicative context (personal judgment) which the context of the enunciation of the message (impersonal broadcast) contradicts.

A reasonable skeptic might point out that it does not require this much intellectual machinery to arrive at the conclusion that advertising is often absurd or self-contradictory. But like the ironist of "A Modest Proposal," the "news" in this analysis is not so much the conclusion that advertising is absurd as it is a more careful demonstration of the "constructed" and "contrived" character of language and the way that language constructs sender, addressee, and message. Long before Foucault wrote about the history of mental illness in *Madness and Civilization*, historians of mental illness knew about the specific history that established modern therapeutic regimes for mental illness. The "news" that made Foucault's work a significant contribution to postmodern social theory is that by detailing the institutional practices that led to the construction of the modern conception of insanity, we learn something about the relationship between the emerging therapeutic professions and other social spheres such as economics and politics. A "naïve" or "straight" history of mental health might begin by assuming that there had always been something called "insanity" which human beings finally came to "know" through medicine. The ironic postmodern reading leaves this literal reading in place, but qualifies it by suggesting that the birth of the clinic had curious thematic connections to other historical developments which connections make it implausible to see it as the outcome of a simple direct relationship between knowers (future mental health professionals) and reality (the objective condition of being insane). However intuitively plausible the naïve reading remains, it is not "simply" true, but rather the outcome of a specific historical process, one which casts doubt on the simple truth of the outcome. Finally, in the process of showing how sociolinguistic practices constructed "illness," Foucault also shows how the same practices correlatively define "reason" and "reasonableness." Like the postmodern gloss on the advertising slogan, the postmodern "archeology" of a social institution shows how language both constructs our understandings and then conceals the constructed character of those understandings.

Before discussing further the contribution to our topic of the "sociological postmodernists" such as Foucault and Baudrillard, we should summarize the postmodern attitude of radical ironism as it relates to McDonald's. Like all ironists, the postmodern ironist has a kind of concerned detachment from the phenomena he or she considers. One can attend a baseball game, civic parade, even go to McDonald's as an ironist and feel somehow inoculated against its more offensive or disturbing aspects. Having achieved some ironic distance on the cultural meaning of the phenomena, the ironist tends to believe that he or she is not just another gullible or uncritical participant.

Unfortunately, this highly individualistic and detached attitude is not completely successful for the postmodernist. As important as the insights of irony are to the postmodern, the postmodern attitude is intrinsically connected to a commitment to the notion (articulated by Saussure) that meanings derive from placement within a system (of signifiers) and that there is ultimately no "outside" to this system. There is no detached consciousness that transcends the system of social signifiers and which can then turn to observe it unaffected. Whatever McDonald's means to a postmodern consciousness, that consciousness cannot regard itself unaffected by it, or by the larger social forces—capitalism, cultural imperialism, globalization of markets, consumerism, bureaucratization of desires and needs, and so on—from which it emerges. Indeed, as thinkers like Bourdieu make clear, a full self-critical analysis must take account of the social system from which a culturally elite academic (like Lyotard, Ritzer, or any of the contributors to this volume) might make a critique of McDonald's. Therefore, I suggest that postmodern ironism, while an important and inevitable part of the postmodern attitude toward McDonald's, is unstable. Self-critical postmoderns will oscillate between this detached, self-controlled ironism and a realization that they are themselves implicated in a cultural system of signifiers that derives its specific meaning from this ironic detachment. Like the aesthete whose complete rejection of McDonald's helps define his own aesthetic, the postmodern ironist finds in McDonald's not merely another occasion for practicing irony, but an uneasy reminder that the self-deconstructing slogans of the fast-food giant are as unstable as the ironist's own *bona fides*. Both may be products of a system of cultural signification for which the critic is no match.

In a sense, this is a message of much postmodern social theory. Foucault's critical practices, for example, presuppose a limited transcendence, a limited critical distance on the phenomena he analyzes. We can gain enough distance from our imbeddedness in our culture's social practices to generate the critique, but not enough to see those practices as merely one among many, not enough to make a completely independent choice of those practices by means of a scale of values which transcends them. The dynamic of social power which seems to underlie social history has just this ambiguous hold on us, according to Foucault. Consistency and rigor lead him to conclude that the power that shapes and reshapes our cultural practices has no name, no final theory. We can get enough distance on social life to do archaeology, but not enough to completely escape the effects of the forces whose social artifacts we study.   One   postmodern   social theorist in particular, Jean Baudrillard, gives us a useful springboard for further reflections on McDonald's and the postmodern attitude toward it. While Baudrillard's work is both highly theoretical and highly controversial, a simplified version of his views can be pressed into service here. Traditional Marxist social theory is focused on the dialectical unfolding of the system of production distinctive to capitalism. One of the crucial assumptions of such theory is that physical objects have a fundamental use value that is distorted and mystified by capitalism, which presents objects in a commodity form according to their exchange value in the system of capitalist production. The use value of an object is commonly understood to be its utility in satisfying the material conditions of living. Marxism makes the assumption, naturally enough, that what people are really up to in their economic relationships is the satisfaction of utilitarian needs. Of course, defenders of the liberal tradition share this assumption. Even traditional social theory views the social meanings that come to be associated with particular patterns of consumption as accretions upon a more basic use value. For both groups of theorists, a solid gold letter opener is first a tool for opening letters and only acquires its social meaning (connoting a refinement and conspicuous display of wealth) later.

This common-sense understanding of utility as the basis for understanding the meaning of objects in economic relationships would seem unassailable. Baudrillard's assault on this assumption makes both the ground for his notoriety, as well as his postmodernism. As he wrote in *The System of Objects:*

Consumption is not a passive mode of assimilation (*absorption*) and appropriation which we can oppose to an active mode of production, in order to bring to bear naïve concepts of action (and alienation). . . .

We must clearly state that material goods are not the objects of consumption: they are merely the objects of need and satisfaction. We have all at times purchased, possessed, enjoyed, and spent, and yet not "consumed." "Primitive" festivities, the prodigality of the feudal lord, or the luxury of the nineteenth-century bourgeois—these are not acts of consumption. (Baudrillard, 1988, p. 21)

Baudrillard is making at least two points here: First, there is no primitive meaning to objects that we might call their use value. The object of economic exchange is already inscribed within a social system of meaning. Second, instead of thinking about the basic meaning of objects of economic exchange in terms of either their use value or exchange value, Baudrillard encourages us to think of consumption as the experience and reproduction of "sign value." Consumption turns out, then, to be a kind of work, a kind of production. Consumption is first and foremost a process of signification through which we experience and reproduce a "social message" constituted by the position of the commodity in the social system. At a very theoretical level, Baudrillard makes his case by showing that both Marxist and classical liberal economic theories can be seen as instances of semiotic theory. The structure of the sign (specifically a Saussurean theory of the sign) underlies both major modernist theories of political economy.

Our goal is not so much to reconstruct Baudrillard's theoretical position as to see how it contributes to the postmodern attitude toward McDonald's. The "scandal" of Baudrillard's theory is that we have to begin by saying that a trip to McDonald's is not about eating. McDonald's is not selling hamburgers which first satisfy our hunger and happen also to have various social connotations. Rather, as a form of consumption, eating at McDonald's is about consuming (and reproducing) the message of McDonald's.

And what is that? Foremost, the patron experiences a peculiar kind of abundance. Every meal is a "value" meal. Every meal is a "complete" meal, affordable by almost anyone. Like a visitor to a third world country, the patron at McDonald's is supposed to feel that his or her money (and concomitantly his or her own feeling of wealth and value) is worth more. Advertising for McDonald's consistently presents a fantasy land of play and abundance. Second, as we have already noted, the McDonald's slogan implies a deserved reward.

More recently, as McDonald's has formalized its merchandising agreements with Disney Corporation, the fast-food visit is communicated as an experience of imagination and wonder. Here the message is directed at both parents and children. Visiting McDonald's is an opportunity to refresh your child's happy memory of *101 Dalmatians* or "classic masterpieces" like *The Hunchback of Notre Dame.*

One irony of this account is that most people do not talk about their experience of McDonald's this way at all. Rather, people talk about fast food in terms of utility, especially convenience. Going to McDonald's is the "cheap" alternative to other restaurants. It is hard to imagine that people consciously experience an elevation in their perception of their wealth at McDonald's, even though it is true that more people can afford more items on the fast-food menu than at other restaurants. But this discontinuity between the message, understood literally and strategically, and its perception or experience by the consumer, may be characteristic of hyperbolic mass media communication. John Caputo's essay in this volume, "The Rhetoric of McDonaldization: A Social Semiotic Perspective," also works from the premise that the patron of McDonald's is consuming a "message," and gives a more developed analysis of what that narrative message is.

A postmodern attitude toward McDonald's, understood now as a social phenomena, would include the awareness of the experience as thoroughly "semiotic" or "coded." Like the savvy marketer, the postmodern reads space, color, architecture, and every element of design as participating in a code with analyzable effects. Unlike the marketer, however, the postmodern wonders, again with only partial ironic detachment, what the implications of his or her involvement in the McDonald's "code" are. Even if postmoderns cannot say, definitively, what "undistorted" or "healthy" consumption activity is, they can wonder about the relative merits and demerits of various kinds of coded experience. Even as products of the larger social code that also produces McDonald's, the limited critical distance of postmodern analysis allows one to frame a critical value question about the fast-food code.

So far we have been discussing the postmodern attitude in very "structural" terms as the awareness and appreciation of a coded structure. But a key feature of postmodern theory is the view that semiotic structures are ultimately ungrounded and unstable. This presents both a complication to our current project, as well as an opportunity. Because semiotic codes are unstable, it is hard to say how effective the McDonald's message will be in the future. Like other failed economic formations, the fast-food restaurant may not be able to sell its message of value, moral desert, and utopic abundance forever. Postmoderns do not believe in some future state in which distorted or destructive codes will finally be decoded by a liberated social consciousness, but they can take some, perhaps perverse, pleasure in seeing the effectiveness of a dominating and apparently harmful code unravel. Some of this unraveling occurs simply because of the rhetorical effects of repetition. In other cases the grip of the message weakens because of extrinsic variables. Economic change, a general elevation of workplace standards, or decline in local economies may take the "shine" off our cultural image of fast-food labor. The need for McDonald's to supplement its product by increasingly complex prizes, games, and giveaways might be interpreted as evidence of the weakening of the underlying message of the chain.

One of the legacies of Saussurean linguistic theory, once radicalized by postmodernism, is that it encourages us to see the semiotic value of the message as a pure function of its place in a system. As other values change, every value changes. If the postmodern attitude often comes across as a mixture of world weariness and ungrounded concern, the cause may be attributed to a conviction that systems of signs are always undergoing directed and undirected changes. Indeed, the fastest way to hasten the self-destruction (or deconstruction) of a social code is to take that attitude toward it that brings out its constructed character. This suggests a strategy of "parodic engagement"—to let one's self become engaged with the cultural message of McDonald's while taking a parody of its social meanings as one's self-understanding of the experience.

Postmodernism encourages a peculiar kind of ambivalence: on the one hand, there is little doubt about the power of the sign in the message of the international restaurant chain. McDonald's has become adept at inserting itself into dozens of cultures that share no culinary tradition with it or its original culture, the United States. (But then, this is not surprising to a postmodern since the success of the enterprise does not depend upon the food.) McDonald's exports a cultural message that is clearly appealing to billions of human beings. On the other hand, the postmodern faith in the instability of semiosis, in the impossibility of signification of the Same, suggests that the intentions of the smartest marketers at McDonald's may ultimately be subverted by individual and global cultural change. As one of the essays in this collection indicates, the rationalization process may give rise, in late-twentieth-century capitalism, to a process of mass customization. Another contributor to this volume, Steven Miles, suggests that rationalization may be put to some beneficial use by relatively self-aware youth. Further, a look at the history of McDonald's suggests that the message of McDonald's has changed over the past thirty years. While McDonald's efforts to become "green" are a sham by most accounts, this fact is also becoming more widely known. As fast-food chains become drawn into other social policy discussions, such as the minimum wage, people come to learn about the discrepancy between the image and the reality of work at McDonald's.

Ultimately, a postmodern attitude mixes the best of two tendencies: critical awareness of the insidious character of rationalized bureaucracy and a healthy skepticism about the permanence and sustainability of the rationalized message. This leaves postmodern burger eaters with more than a detached ironic attitude. Like other social critics the postmodern also looks for simple contradictions between the corporation's claims about the value of its enterprise and the actual realities of its business practice. Beyond this, however, postmodern social criticism looks toward the acceleration of the processes by which dominant cultural messages lose their efficacy. As Lyotard suggests at the end of *The Postmodern Condition*, postmodernism gives rise to a new kind of agonistics in which the social critic attends more closely to the "narrative of legitimation" at work (in this case) in the fast-food consumption message (Lyotard, 1984a). The strength of this narrative depends less upon a background theory of political economy (as Marxian or liberal criticism does) than upon a background theory of semiosis. The postmodern critic focuses us on ways of neutralizing the hyperbole of McDonald's by thinking about the peculiarities of its own narrative structure. Again, parody can be an effective tool for such rethinking. As the fast-food industry seeks more ties with media conglomerates to promote its message, they, ironically, commit themselves to even more hyperbolic claims about the special meaning of the fast-food meal. The plausibility of "low rhetoric" of a simple, local restaurant that offers only demonstrably better food is enhanced.

If it seems hopelessly naïve to be sanguine about the self-defeating rhetoric of ever larger corporate media communications, and to be championing narrative possibilities of parody, the small local sole proprietorship or nonprofit cooperative, perhaps some argumentation will help. To the extent that traditional market variables like economies of scale, vertical integration, and market share predict the success and dominance of an organization, it is true that corporate entities like McDonald's will likely continue to flourish. For example, in the area of mass media, these traditional considerations are still powerful. However, even Baudrillard's theories of mass communication fail famously to take account of emerging, individualized forms of mass communication which phenomena like the Internet and World Wide Web are making possible. While no panacea, a "postmodern capitalism," in which democratization of the semiotic process comes to displace monopolization of the means of production as a key to successful enterprise, may disrupt the traditional story of the "iron cage" which ends with Weber's famous and oft-quoted prediction of "specialists without spirit, sensualists without heart." At a minimum, Weberians must recognize the rationalization process at work in other spheres of cultural life that compete with or work against the message of McDonald's.

How does this postmodern attitude toward McDonald's affect our understanding of Ritzer's and (implicitly Weber's) analysis? First, we cannot linger very long over the question of whether there is such a thing as postmodernism or postmodern critical theory, as Ritzer does. There is simply no denying that critical theory has a rich array of analytic tools, some of which follow the familiar presuppositions of modernism and others which do not. Likewise, few dispute today that there is such a thing as postmodern culture. Our own account confirms the view that the postmodern attitude is decided different from its modernist predecessors, not only for its peculiar brand of irony, but for its reformulation of both Marxist and classical liberal political theory, as in the work of Jean Baudrillard. But as we mentioned very early in this essay, Ritzer adverts to a second strategy for neutralizing postmodernism. After trying to reduce it to the tendencies in modernism that it, of course, grew out of, Ritzer refers to two of the many critics who doubt the very possibility, the very coherence of postmodern critical theory. Before turning directly to a discussion of the relationship between postmodernism and Weber, we should address these critics.

POSTMODERNISM, MCDONALD'S, AND WEBER

Postmodernism is ripe for refutation at least in part because its adherents are committed to violating more conventions of intellectual discourse than preceding intellectual revolutionaries. There is some truth, then, to John O'Neill's criticism that postmoderns, Foucault and Lyotard in particular, "abandon the subject of politics and history to the history and politics of subjectivity and minoritarianism" (O'Neill,' 1995, p. 4). Like other commentators, he has noticed that these authors do not treat the self as the subject of a grand historical narrative. A second postmodern theme, "that knowledge is no longer power because power is now knowledge," (O'Neill, 1995, p. 3) is a premise in an even more basic, and widely made, critical argument: Since postmoderns treat knowledge as the outcome of power, they lose any critical purchase on rational criteria from which the legitimacy of specific power formations can be judged. In short, the postmodern has forgotten *for whom* we theorize in the human sciences, and that the goal of such theorizing is, at least in some social and political theory, to evaluate the legitimacy of specific power formations.

It should not be too hard to see how these criticisms apply to the postmodern attitude toward McDonald's. Our hypothetical postmodern burger eater "worries" about this or that feature of McDonald's, is "concerned" about various messages his kids get through their Happy Meals, but does he have a grounded theory of human development or political economy against which to judge the enterprise? Not really. The closest we came to such a background theory was the social semiotic perspective that came out of postmodern linguistic theory. Postmoderns are entitled to *feel* all the moral concern they want, but without a normative theory (and a prior commitment to some metaphysic of morals) they have no *rational* basis for adjudicating Ronald McDonald's crimes against humanity.

I think this criticism is *almost* completely well founded, but it leaves out the possibility that a form of theoretical reflection might take place in *lieu* of traditional moral theory that would nonetheless permit some kinds of moral judgments. The articulation of such a theory is complicated because two lines of argument must be joined: metaethical argument about the possibility of a nontraditional form of moral theory and an ethical theory that hews to postmodern thematics. Fortunately, there is an excellent example of such an effort in Todd May's *The Moral Theory of Poststructuralism.* In this recent, short work, May argues that postmodern theorists have opened themselves up to a criticism to which they could have responded, but failed to. Postmodernists do have distinctive moral intuitions that could contribute to moral theory, but they are unduly reticent because of a narrow conception of what a moral theory must be. May formulates the main intuition of postmodern ethical thinking as a principle of antirepresentationalism, which states: "People ought not, other things being equal, to engage in practices whose effect, among others, is the representation or commendation of certain intentional lives as either intrinsically superior or intrinsically inferior to others" (May, 1996, p. 48). May's work is careful, technical, and somewhat analytic, so it would not be practical to reconstruct it extensively here. But this much can be said to follow from a simple reading of the principle: It formalizes that tendency in postmodernism to make critical judgments while avoiding the globalizing tendency of some traditional moral thinking. May shows how social criticism can proceed with respect to particular means of achieving particular social ends without taking the next step toward promoting a way of being as intrinsically superior. In a very simple practical application of this intuition, it may turn out that we can argue against McDonald's message for specific practical reasons without having a global moral theory or essential analysis of the "goodness" or "badness" of McDonald's as a whole. The decision to go or not go to McDonald's may be founded on purely local, hypothetical reasoning about one's immediate goals.

Weber scholars will notice in both the critics cited above and in May's view an curious echo to what has come to be called Weber's "ethical decisionism." Describing the limits of social science in "Science as a Vocation," Weber writes:

In practice, you can take this or that position when concerned with a problem of value—for simplicity's sake, please think of social phenomena as examples. *If* you take such and such a stand, then, according to scientific experience, you have to use such and such a *means* in order to carry out your conviction practically . . . the ultimately possible attitudes toward life are irreconcilable, and hence their struggle can never be brought to a final conclusion. Thus it is necessary to make a decisive choice." (Weber, 1958, pp. 151–152)

Because Weber thought of social science as approximating the objectivity of science, he drew a careful limit to the role of norms and values in social theory, treating ethical commitment as lying with the private individual sphere, outside the methodology of science.

This creates an odd point of connection between Weber and postmodernism as concerns the practical attitude one might take toward value judgments as a consequence of one's social theorizing. For very different reasons, both Weber and Foucault, for instance, abstain from trying to ground normative judgments about the phenomena they study. John O'Neill points out how plausible it is to think of Weber and Foucault together as "archaeologists" of the power man exerts over himself. Both are "resolutely separated from any transcendental rationality."   In the same passage, O'Neill cites this methodological claim by Foucault which complements Weber's "decisionism":

One isn't assessing things in terms of an absolute against which they could be evaluated as constituting more or less perfect forms of rationality, but rather explaining how forms of rationality inscribe themselves in practices or systems or practices, and what role they play within them. (Foucault cited in O'Neill, 1995, p. 44)

Neither thinker treats the results of his or her inquiry as inherently normative. While both are aware of the obvious *desire* of the theorist for a politics, neither (though Foucault more resolutely) violate their principled conviction that social theory simply does not authorize such conclusions. Where Weber scholars have tried to press their hero into service as some kind of liberal, they make themselves vulnerable to refutation, as in Richard Wolin's review of a recent biography of Weber by John Diggins (Wolin, 1996).

Of course this point of similarity should not make us confuse Weber with postmodernism. Weber holds to a kind of positivism about knowledge and to the possibility of social theory following a version, albeit different in complex ways, of the objectivity of the natural sciences. While Weber endorsed the fact-value distinction in its traditional form—as the denial that values can be inferred from facts or vice versa—postmoderns try to undercut the distinction by seeing both as products of a social construction, an interaction with reality that cannot be captured in thought prior to its occurrence. Yet, like Weber, postmoderns believe that important decisions depend upon the convictions one forms from studying social life. As Susan Hekman puts it, "For Weber the meaninglessness of the world constitutes a personal challenge. It is the individual's responsibility to endow the world with meaning through his or her moral choices" (Hekman, 1994, p. 283). Ironically, then, each party comes to "ethical decisionism" with different motives and different goals, yet each affirm the importance of the moral response. Hekman's quotation could easily be rewritten for a postmodern thinker as well.

If it seems unsatisfying, then, that our postmodern attitude does not evolve a global story of McDonald's with a decisively happy or unhappy ending, it may not be because no value is ever at stake in such discussion (nihilism) or because it depends upon your perspective (relativism). Rather, it may be that the postmodern regards the moral consequences of his attitudes as intensely important, yet somehow not representable in theory, and this because of a theoretical commitment to "antirepresentationalism," as discussed above. What one settles for by way of public reasons is a kind of instrumentalism. Numerous competing hypothetical values must be weighed while scrupulously avoiding the deception that some underlying theory of human nature or society will finally order the priority of each competing claim or authorize an essential normative judgment about McDonald's, or, indeed, more putatively global phenomena just as bureaucratic rationalization.

I have tried to represent postmodernism as a kind of iconoclasm. Our postmodern-at-McDonald's sees the iron cage of rationalization, as well as the countermeasures of popular and local culture. He sees his children's "irrational" preferences for Happy Meals, alongside their ennui as the toy that comes with it quickly finds its way deep into the car seat or to the back of the toy shelf. Alongside McDonald's well-orchestrated media campaign, there is the simple competition of sports, books, and picnics. We cannot ignore the fact that for many people there is nothing simple about the alternatives to McDonaldization—no simple alternative to that kind of employment or that kind of convenience, or that kind of pleasure. But neither can we oversimplify the effects of rationalization by supposing that the individual's attitude and approach to the experience is irrelevant. As Freud might have said, sometimes a Big Mac is just a burger.

REFERENCES

Apple, M. (1984). Postmodernism. In *Free agents* (pp. 135–139). New York: Harper & Row.

Baudrillard, J. (1988). The system of objects. In M. Poster (Ed.), *Jean Baudrillard: Selected writings* (pp. 10–28). Stanford, CA: Stanford University Press.

Derrida, J. (1983). The time of a thesis: Punctuations. In A. Montefiore (Ed.), *Philosophy in France today* (pp. 34–50). Cambridge, England: Cambridge University Press.

Fairlie, S. (1993). Stop the mcworld, I want to get off! *The Ecologist, 23*(2), 73–74.

Gilling, A. (1996, August). Where there's mc there's brass. *The Times Higher*, 16.

Hekman, S. (1994). Max Weber and post-positivist social theory. In A. Horowitz, & T. Maley (Eds.), *The barbarism of reason: Max Weber and the twilight of enlightenment* (pp. 267–286). Toronto, Canada: University of Toronto Press.

Lyotard, J. F. (1984a). The postmodern condition. In *The postmodern condition: A report on knowledge* (pp. 1–67). Minneapolis, MN: University of Minnesota Press.

Lyotard, J. F. (1984b). What is postmodernism? In *The postmodern condition: A report on knowledge* (pp. 71–82). Minneapolis, MN: University of Minnesota Press.

May, T. (1996). *The moral theory of poststructuralism*. University Park, PA: Pennsylania State University.

Nichols, T. (1994). [Review of *The McDonaldization of society*]. *Sociology, 23*(2), 322–324.

O'Neill, J. (1995). *The poverty of postmodernism*. London: Routledge.

Ritzer, G. (1993). *The McDonaldization of society.* Thousand Oaks, CA: Pine Forge.

Weber, M. (1958). Science as a vocation. In H. H. Gerth, & C. W. Mills (Eds.), *From Max Weber: Essays in society* (pp. 129–156). New York: Galaxy.

Wolin, R. (1996). Liberalism as a vocation [Review of *Max Weber: Politics and the spirit of tragedy*]. *The New Republic*, 34–41.

Index

Contributors

MARK ALFINO is an associate professor of philosophy at Gonzaga University in Spokane, Washington. He received his Ph.D. in philosophy from The University of Texas at Austin in 1989. His teaching and research interests include philosophy of language, contemporary philosophy, and applied ethics. He is a regular columnist for the *Journal of Information Ethics* and has written on professional ethics, business ethics, and postmodernism.

JOHN S. CAPUTO is professor and chair of Communication Arts at Gonzaga University in Spokane, Washington. He holds B.A. and M.A. degrees from California State University, Long Beach, and M.A. and Ph.D. degrees in Language and Communication from the Claremont Graduate School. Dr. Caputo has published three books and numerous articles. He has also been honored as a visiting scholar-in-residence at the University of Kent at Canterbury, England.

PHILIP D. HOLLEY received his doctorate in sociology from Iowa State University in 1982. He is professor of sociology and criminal justice at Southwestern Oklahoma State University. In addition to teaching, he has served as an expert witness in civil and criminal cases, most recently in a lesbian mother-child custody case. His recent research has focused on incarcerated women, "speak outs" in prison, prison "boot camps," and lesbianism.

THOMAS M. JEANNOT is an associate professor of philosophy at Gonzaga University. He received his Ph.D. from St. Louis University in 1992. His research interests include Marxism, critical theory, and classical American philosophy. His articles have appeared in *The New Scholasticism, Transactions of the Charles S. Peirce Society, International Philosophical Quarterly,* and *International Journal of Social Economics.* He is currently working on a book about John Dewey and Karl Marx.

DOUGLAS KELLNER is Professor of Philosophy of the University of Texas at Austin and George Kneller Chair in the Philosophy of Education at UCLA. He is author of many books on social theory, politics, history, and culture, including *Camera Politica: The Politics and Ideology of Contemporary Hollywood Film,* co-authored with Michael Ryan; *Critical Theory, Marxism, and Modernity; Jean Baudrillard: From Marxism to Postmodernism and Beyond; Postmodern Theory: Critical Interrogations,* co-authored with Steven Best; *Television and the Crisis of Democracy; The Persian Gulf TV War; Media Culture;* and *The Postmodern Turn* (with Steven Best). He is currently working on the impact of new information and entertainment technologies on society and culture.

PHIL LYON has a B.S. in sociology from the University of London, an M.A. from the University of Essex, and a Ph.D. from the University of Wales. His main interest is ageism and the impact of aging on labor product markets. Currently he is head of the School of Management and Consumer Studies at Dundee University.

STEVEN MILES is a lecturer in sociology at the University of Plymouth, England. In 1996 he received his doctorate from the Behavioural Sciences Department at the University of Huddersfield, England. He has published several articles on the subject of youth consumption and the construction of identities in journals such as *Culture and Psychology* and *Youth and Policy.* His first book, *Consumerism as a Way of Life,* will shortly be published by Sage, and he will be a guest editor of a review edition of *Urban Studies* on "Urban Consumption" in May 1998.

MARTIN PARKER works in the Centre for Social Theory and Technology and Department of Management at the University of Keele, North Staffordshire. He holds degrees in Anthropology and Sociology from the Universities of Sussex, London, and Staffordshire. He previously taught sociology at Staffordshire University in Stoke-on-Trent. His research and writing is mainly concerned with social and organizational theory, but he dabbles in cultural studies when he feels he has something interesting to say.

JANE A. RINEHART is an associate professor of sociology and women's studies at Gonzaga University in Spokane, Washington. She received her Ph.D. from New York University and is the author of several articles and co-editor of *Taking Parts: Ingredients of Leadership, Participation, and Empowerment.*

SHEENA SMITH lectures in Operations at the School of Management and Consumer Studies, University of Dundee, Scotland. After graduating from the Norwich Hotel School, she pursued careers in both the retail and hospitality industry. Her M.B.A. dissertation focused on internationalization strategies. Current research interests include customization and consumer-buying behavior.

STEPHEN TAYLOR holds M.B.A., D.M.S., and Dip.M. degrees and lectures in strategic management at the University of Dundee, Scotland, United Kingdom. He is currently completing a Ph.D. in strategic management at the University of St. Andrews. His work has been published in a number of academic journals. His main research interests are the performance determinants of new ventures and in the field of services marketing.

NGURE WA MWACHOFI is an associate professor of communication at Florida Gulf Coast University. He has an interdisciplinary background in political science, developmental economics, international affairs, and African history and holds a Ph.D. in communication from Ohio University. He has authored several journal articles, and his research interests revolve around culture, ideology, and power and domination as they relate to the politics of meaning.

ROY C. WOOD is professor of hospitality management at The Scottish Hotel School, University of Strathclyde, Glasgow, Scotland, United Kingdom. He has published widely in the field of human resource management in the hospitality industry, including four books and numerous papers, and has also published extensively on food and social consumption. A sociologist by training, he is currently researching and writing a book on the sociology of hospitality.

DAVID E. WRIGHT, Jr. is an assistant professor of Sociology and Criminal Justice at Southwestern Oklahoma State University. His degrees are from Texas A&M University. His writings include research on theory, crime rates, alternative sentencing, and minorities.

ROBIN WYNYARD holds B.S., M.A., and Ph.D. degrees in sociology. Before taking very early retirement, he worked for several British universities, including those of Greenwich, London, and South Bank. His research and writing is in the area of cultural transmission theory and the sociology of art and literature. Now working in a part-time capacity as an educational consultant, he regularly visits Pakistan and the United States.

ISBN 0-275-95819-1

90000>

EAN

9 780275 958190

HARDCOVER BAR CODE